On White-Collar Crime

On White-Collar Crime

Gilbert Geis
University of California, Irvine

LexingtonBooks
D.C. Heath and Company
Lexington, Massachusetts
Toronto

Library of Congress Cataloging in Publication Data

Geis, Gilbert.
   On white-collar crime.

   Collection of 12 papers written from 1950 to 1982. Includes
bibliographical references and index.   1. White collar crimes—United
States—Addresses, essays, lectures.   I. Title.
HV6635.G34 1982   364.1′68   81-47278
ISBN 0-669-04568-3   AACR2

Published simultaneously in Canada

Printed in the United States of America

International Standard Book Number: 0-669-04568-3

Library of Congress Catalog Card Number: 81-47278

For Ralph and Margaret Thomlinson

Contents

Preface and Acknowledgments

What common themes and what motifs may reasonably be said to run through and possibly unite the twelve chapters, written over a span of more than thirty years, that form the contents of this book? What strengths and what shortcomings do the chapters manifest when they are regarded as a unit of work? What do they tell us about the past and the future of the study of white-collar crime?

First, I believe that the subject of white-collar crime is a preeminently significant and much-neglected area of research and writing in the behavioral sciences and law. The issues often are highly complex, involving organizations and persons who possess enormous power. White-collar crime deals with intricate forms of rule making and rule breaking and with basic questions of the justice and efficacy of a wide range of control mechanisms and sanctions. The corporation is regarded as a person under law, and the implications of this definitional—and artificial—status are very far-ranging indeed. Are there other ways of viewing the corporation and would it be decent and useful to alter jurisprudence in a manner that changes the status of the corporation? This issue alone might preoccupy a scholar's lifetime of work.

The following chapters set forth some of the concerns and dimensions of inquiry into the subject of white-collar crime, and provide a background that raises some issues and contains some suggestions for the direction that ought to be taken for the investigation and control of white-collar crime.

Second, the study of white-collar crime offers a challenge to criminologists who are concerned with matters of power and its exercise, fundamental issues in social existence. Scrutiny of white-collar crime takes scholars and laymen away from dreary and dreadful consideration of street offenses and police stations. These matters obviously are of great importance but, for the scholar, work on them tends to be limited and limiting. That is, if I am correct in my assumption that the roots of street offenses lie almost exclusively in the nature of the social order in which the offenses occur, then the efforts of a criminology that focuses only on traditional crime and criminals is by definition highly truncated and far removed from any likely resolution. With white-collar crime we move much closer to the guts of the social system, and to the extent that we can refashion the exercise of power we have some hope of truly molding a better or, at least, a different kind of world.

So—in many ways—the following chapters on white-collar crime represent at heart a call to arms, an invitation to enter the fray, to rebut and to extend the materials and the arguments inherent or explicit in them. Of course, the chapters in this book are only a portion of what, at last, is becoming a burgeoning line of inquiry. One of the values of these chapters may be that they document changes—as well as regularities—not only in my own thinking but also in the sophistication of the field of study. There is, I think, a progression from the earlier to the later pieces, though that movement assuredly is at times erratic. That the tone of some of the chapters becomes tougher with the passage of time is in part, I'm certain, because of a frustration with the torturously slow manner in which change seems to have occurred and in part because of a certain growth in self-assertion. It would be interesting in this regard to determine how college professors alter their message as their time in the classroom passes. Are they more cavalier and more prone to unqualified assertions as they get older and learn that students rarely will challenge even the most outrageous opinions? Or do age and wisdom and self-doubt increase with time, as reflected by classroom lectures? Perhaps it is one way with some persons, and another with others.

The question of the proper definition of the term *white-collar crime* can be found to run through some of the earliest to the latest of the chapters set down in this book. At the very first, I pressed for a redefinition of white-collar crime so that only corporate offenses would be included in the category. That plea went unheeded—it was met with a wave of indifference—and I had to abandon it for want of a second. Some years later, Marshall Clinard and Richard Quinney in *Criminal Behavior Systems* came forward with a more acceptable scheme, using white-collar crime as the overriding designation and having as subordinate units occupational offenses and corporate violations. My initial polemical plunge into the definitional waters gave way in time to a rather casual attitude about the matter, writing it off as a semantic labyrinth that trapped the unwary and the pedantic. And as I became more militant in some of my writings about the subject of white-collar crime, I altered the early cry to abandon the term because of its scientific impurity and came to support the position that the designation had propagandistic strengths and therefore ought not to be jettisoned.

The chapters presented in this book seem to move from more factual to somewhat more theoretical domains. I remember during the year that I spent at the Harvard Law School a discussion between Harold Berman and Dean Erwin Griswold in regard to the scholarly focus of a younger faculty member. Berman noted that the man was heavily involved in complicated jurisprudential theory: Griswold airily dismissed this as inappropriate work. People ought to do substantive work when they are young, Griswold insisted, and then, in their later life, they might suitably be fit for theoretical speculation in regard to facts that they and others had uncovered and organized. I'm not at all certain of the correctness of such a position—presumably one ought to do what one does best and/or what one prefers to do when one wants to do it. But it does seem to me that the chapters from the later years attempt to bring together the factual material and to derive some policy and theoretical formulations from them. In this sense, it is as though many of the matters had lain dormant in my subconscious for years and finally emerged in more mature scientific form.

I have no doubt that the field of white-collar crime is going to move in other directions in addition to those that are represented by the chapters here collected. I hope that some of these chapters will provide springboards and challenges to undergird that movement. After I had given a lecture at Sheffield University a few years ago, Ian Taylor, one of the keener minds among the radical criminologists, suggested kindly, with no condescension, that I could take pleasure from the fact that my work on white-collar crime, while not Marxist, had at least provided some substance for the nourishment of Marxist thought in criminology. Marxist thought may come to prevail in criminology, though I rather doubt that it will unless it undergoes considerable modification to align its postulates with what we know about rules of human behavior and, particularly, about the exercise of power. But whatever fashion of criminological inquiry carries the day, I am almost certain that the material and the issues of white-collar crime will come to form a basic element in that system.

At the moment, it is arguable whether the term *white-collar crime* itself will survive or whether it will become an anachronistic item to be footnoted in passing in tomes about economic or otherwise-designated kinds of offenses. The ferment in the field of study is extraordinary and heady, despite some current slowdown in today's political climate. Superb lawyers, such as Christopher Stone, are struggling to determine whether the criminal law itself is not archaic as an instrument to deal with the offenses of powerful institutions. Sociologists are concentrating on organizational analysis in an attempt to make sense out of corporate offenses. In Europe, where the study of white-collar crime remains almost exclusively the work of lawyers, there are some nascent attempts to incorporate social-science methods into such work, and some sophisticated efforts to measure the importance of variant legal arrangements on the form and quantity of violations. The antitrust laws, for instance, are dramatically different in the United Kingdom and some European countries from those in the United States, and scholars are beginning to assess the importance of such variations. When economists finally discover that white-collar crime is preeminently an area that dovetails with many of their disciplinary skills and interests, we will see even more significant advances in the body of knowledge available for further analysis and integration.

The twelve chapters that follow are offered as a contribution to the history of the study of white-collar crime and as a springboard for progress in the study of the subject. Besides, I believe that they have intrinsic merit and interest for any reader concerned with the relationship of powerful institutions to the law in our time.

Acknowledgments

Lastly, I want to express some obligations. The dedication indicates my thoroughgoing appreciation for the friendship and help of Ralph and Margaret Thomlinson, both with this book and through the years. I also want to thank John S. Reynard Jr. and Paul Jesilow for their support, and Margaret Zusky, Susan J.S. Lasser, and Marjorie A. Glazer of Lexington Books for theirs. No words of any intensity or grace would be able to express adequately my appreciation to my wife, Robley, for everything she means to me and for all we have shared.

I'd like in conclusion to redeem a pledge to some of the kids that they will be duly acknowledged. Thanks go to Ellen Geis and Steve Temko and to their daughter, Janet; to Jeanie and Tim Oliver, and their soon-to-be-born child; to Joe and Kay Huston and Emily and Patrick; to Chris and Ted Huston and Megan and Kelly; and to Ann and Adrian Fernandes, and Eric, Aaron, and Molly.

Introduction:
On Getting into
White-Collar Crime

The writing of this introduction has caused me a great deal more travail than I had ever anticipated. Perhaps this is because, after three decades of more or less impersonal academic work, it is unnerving to try to write about myself.

At the same time, the need to put together this introduction has forced me to confront a number of uneasy questions about myself in relation to my work, and particularly that work on white-collar crime. I can understand much better now why some novelists become infuriated when others probe their psyche or request from them personal interpretations of their published materials. Let my material speak for itself, the novelists insist: read it, critique it on its own self-standing merits and deficiencies. Keep me out of it; my writing means only what it says itself.

This posture is, of course, disingenuous, though it is one that I've been tempted to adopt here. For one thing, I fear appearing pretentious or presumptuous, or taking either myself or this book too seriously. On the other hand, if I don't maintain that what is involved is ponderously important, no one else is apt to do so. " 'Dumas is a charming fellow,' it was the general view, 'but he is not serious-minded,' " André Maurois writes in his biography of the novelist, adding: "In France, if a man does not carry his head like the Blessed Sacrament, he may be regarded as an amusing character, but he is not respected. Bores enjoy priority."

By and large, the same may be said about American behaviorial science, particularly in regard to its theorists.

As I perceive it (and I may have fooled myself totally, of course), my basic philosophy of academic work—perhaps of life—is that you try to do the best you can but never allow yourself to be beguiled into believing you are either right or righteous. Persons are obligated to make moral choices, arrived at on the basis of the best information and reasoning they can command. It is a dangerous delusion, however, to believe that one necessarily is doing good. A short-term achievement, indeed, may well spell long-term disaster.

Such an attitude, with its rabbinical ambivalences, has severe disadvantages. Tom Wicker, in a biting biographical study of John Kennedy, found Kennedy as a national leader sorely inadequate because he could regard neither himself nor his policies somberly or seriously enough.

It was with this consideration in mind that I reread the twelve chapters included in the present book. I was pleased to see how little the chapters reflect any uncertainty about their conclusions. There is a harsh and punitive stance toward persons who abuse positions of trust and power. Of course, I do not know for certain that tough policies are likely to be the most effective means to achieve the kinds of social justice that I favor. I've always preached that aggression begets aggression—at least, it legitimates and highlights potentialities that otherwise may have remained dormant. But I remain convinced at this stage that the policies toward white-collar offenders advocated in the chapters that follow are desirable, whatever adjustments must later be made in dealing with white-collar crime to achieve stipulated goals under the conditions that then may prevail.

I would have preferred to write an introduction such as William Foote Whyte's marvelous preface to *Street-Corner Society* (revised edition) that sets forth the strategies and qualms and quirks of the work or one such as the graceful introduction Robert Lynd put before his report on Middle-town, with haunting reflections of life in an Indiana town. But my materials on white-collar crime are not the stuff out of which anecdotal field-note essays can be fashioned. By and large, they represent the product of a process of reading and thinking and writing, done under rather solitary conditions. So I have chosen in the remainder of this introduction to try to offer some information about how I came to the study of white-collar crime and how a few of the earlier articles came to be written.

For reasons that I would just as soon not understand totally, at the beginning of 1938, shortly before my thirteenth birthday, I started to keep a list of books that I read. I still do. At some point during the Second World War, I entered the list into a green notebook that I had commandeered from naval supplies, not the first nor assuredly the last bit of white-collar crime in which I have engaged. In 1945, I was transferred from the fleet to attend school, first at Colgate University, thereafter at the College of the Holy Cross. Earlier, in 1941-1942, I had gone to New York University, where I was a much better track sprinter than a scholar, though not much of a sprinter. Later, in 1949, I would get a master's degree in sociology at Brigham Young University. All told, it was an ecumenical education, with these schools in turn having student bodies that were predominantly Protestant, Catholic, Jewish, and Mormon. For me, alas, the major conclusion that I came to was that at least three of the four religions had to be wrong when they differed meaningfully on points of doctrine. Nor was I without suspicion at times that all four might well be misled.

I know for certain that I first read Edwin H. Sutherland's *White Collar Crime* during the fall of 1952, shortly after I began what were to be five uneasy years in the Department of Sociology at the University of Oklahoma, most of them at the now-deceased rank of instructor. I had attended the University of Stockholm for eight months, after graduating from Colgate in January 1947. Then, after Brigham Young and two years in the doctoral program at the University of Wisconsin, I had gone to Norway to write my dissertation. The Ph.D. work dealt with the operation of the municipally owned motion picture theaters in Oslo and with reactions of Norwegians to American films.

Svend Riemer was my Ph.D. advisor at Wisconsin and, after he left for a position at the University of California at Los Angeles, Hans Gerth replaced him in that role. My wife and I saw a lot of Riemer socially in California during later years, when he was fighting a terrible battle with multiple sclerosis, but he was a remote man, and I never was comfortable with him. At rare times, he would let out a flash of intimacy, though always put in oblique terms, and then would withdraw. His first wife had died in Sweden during childbirth, after Riemer had left her to come to the United States. From then on, he implied, he had spent his life guilt-ridden, standing outside of existence, sardonically looking on. During my oral examination in Scandinavian area studies, my minor field at Wisconsin, Riemer put about half-a-dozen questions in a row to me. For none did I have the faintest idea of the correct answer. It was utterly humiliating. Afterwards, Riemer invited me to his home for a drink. He was in an unusually good mood: "I really showed them how inadequate their curriculum is," he told me.

Gerth was, if anything, stranger than Riemer, but both these émigrés shared a surprising trait. Stumbling in spoken English at times, they could be dazzling with the written word of others, marvelous editors, probably because they had learned the foreign language formally. Gerth was very kind to me and, in typical fashion, dominated the two-hour oral examination on my dissertation by delivering an hour-and-a-half monologue that was at best tangentially related to my topic. Finally, the department chairman, Thomas McCormick, interrupted gently: "That's very interesting, Professor Gerth," he said. "Now, young man, why don't you tell us what your hypothesis was." By then, I had forgotten my hypothesis, presuming I ever knew it, and only the help of Einar Haugen, a preeminent Scandinavian linguist, extricated me. Haugen and Gerth were the only two who had read the dissertation. McCormick had a severe eye ailment, and Orville Brim had erred by being visible in the hallway minutes before the exam and had been dragooned into participation.

Later, McCormick took me aside and, rather uncharacteristically, put his arm around my shoulder. "I like you," he said. "Any time you need a job, I'll be glad to write a letter for you. What I like about you is that you know what it is that you don't know." I've always taken that as a high compliment.

The University of Oklahoma department needed someone to teach criminology and race relations. I had not ever had a course in criminology, but my thesis at B.Y.U. was on Latter-Day Saint (Mormon) attitudes to blacks. I was an English and journalism major as an undergraduate and had taken only Marriage and the Family in sociology—and then only because it was supposed to be racy stuff.

The University of Oklahoma paid me $3,000 when I arrived in 1952 and, with normal increments, I was making $3,500 when I left five years later. No one will ever convince me that $3,000 in those days is anywhere near equivalent to beginning academic salaries today.

For most of the five years, I taught twelve hours a week plus a three-hour course one night at the Federal Reformatory at El Reno, an assignment that involved a 112-mile round trip in an ancient car on remote country roads. Each summer I went into deeper exile. During the first two, I worked at East Central State College in Ada, Oklahoma, a town whose major grace, at least that I could discover, was that it had a Class D professional baseball team. Another summer, I taught sixteen hours a week at Adams State College in Alamosa, Colorado. The teaching chores in Colorado were completed by one in the afternoon, however, and there were few facilities for academic research, so I settled in and wrote a mystery novel—with a campus setting, of course. The book wasn't particularly good, but it sold many more copies than anything I've done in the academic marketplace.

Paul Reynolds, the New York agent who handled the paperback mystery, came to lecture at Oklahoma once and, rather wide-eyed, wanted to know if the kind of stuff that I had written about "really" went on in such bucolic surroundings. He assured me that I could make a decent living, an achievement that so far had quite escaped me, if I kept writing more of the same. But I rather surprised myself by easily concluding that I very much preferred doing scholarly work. It is much less lonesome than writing fiction—you have a core of intellectual compadres. Besides, you learn something while you engage in research, and you are free to try to understand anything that challenges or bothers you within your field.

It soon became apparent at Oklahoma that I had to choose between criminology and race relations for a research focus. I had worked with Bill Bittle, a brilliant anthropologist at the university, on a study of migration by blacks from Oklahoma to the Gold Coast in 1914, which Wayne State University Press published as *The Longest Way Home.* We chose the topic—Bill is a specialist in Athapaskan languages—because we wanted to collaborate and this area seemed to be a mutual ground of interest. When I visited the University of Minnesota a few years after the book was published, Arnold Rose told me that it was he who had recommended that Wayne State bring it out. "The manuscript was dog-eared, so I knew it had been around. But I liked it very much." So did Bill and I: it remains one of the better things I've done, though it sold fewer than one thousand copies.

This project was about as far as I ventured into research in race relations. It was the field of criminology that truly captured my interest. In part, this may have been because of a run of luck with undergraduate students at Oklahoma who did term papers that were so good I was able to work with them to achieve jointly authored publications.

Though the choice was made during the years at the University of Oklahoma, the seeds of my interest in crime, and particularly in white-collar crime, seem to have been firmly planted in my youth. I was an only child, and was brought up by my mother (she had been divorced when I was five) and my grandmother. My grandmother, who died when I was thirteen, had come to the United States from Poland as a young girl. She supported our family during the Depression by making bootleg liquor in the basement of our two-family house in Brooklyn, liquor that she marketed through the Dutch Schultz gang. My uncle, who lived with us, was arrested as a young man by prohibition agents who raided the house. Later, it took a good deal of explaining (and perhaps some money) to have the arrest expunged so that he could be admitted to the practice of law.

My grandmother was addicted to dime crime magazines. She devoured them, those rag paper periodicals with ominous looking orientals on the cover about to plunge crooked daggers into the heaving bosoms of struggling young women. I'd have the assignment of carting several dozen or more of these magazines from the Bronx (we lost the Brooklyn house during the Depression) across the bridge to a Manhattan store where I could trade them two-for-one. My grandmother would make a slight mark on a specified inside page of those she already had read so that I would not return with them.

My bachelor-lawyer uncle was almost totally uncommunicative about his work or his personal life, except for occasional reassurances to us that we need have no doubt that the judicial and municipal establishments of New York City (Mayor LaGuardia excepted) were unredeemably corrupt. He thought this matter so self-evident that he found it unnecessary to do more than pronounce the judgment, rarely bothering to document it. Years later, when I casually expressed the same belief—extending it to U.S. politics in general—to a seminar group at All Souls' College in Oxford, I was taken aback by the English students' uniform disbelief, and their accusation that I was displaying typical American overstatement and cynicism. The truth may lie somewhere between the perceptions of those students and mine, but I remained convinced that I was a good deal nearer to it than they were.

Politics at home were unswervingly Democratic and, besides LaGuardia, our heroes were Franklin Roosevelt, Joe Louis, and Jack Benny. My mother worked in the heart of the corporate world, as secretary to the president of the Ruberoid Company, its offices located high up in the building at 500 Fifth Avenue, across the street from the New York Public Library. During the war, in order to circumvent the wage freeze, they made her secretary of the corporation, a startling status for a woman who spent most of her childhood living behind her parents' butcher shop on the Lower East Side of New York and hating it. Her salary was never particularly good though, and her relationship to her boss was much like that of the servants in "Upstairs, Downstairs." She regaled us at supper with endless stories of his eccentricities. The business itself, rarely, if ever, seemed to be of much interest to her. When my mother's boss died and GAF absorbed Ruberoid, she went back, miserably, to the secretarial pool. She quit when she was about seventy, and died ten years later.

My own early working life offers only a few possible clues to my interest in and attitudes about white-collar crime. I was nastily cheated when an employment agency got me a job in my fifteenth summer in a company that duplicated wallet-sized photographs sent in by customers. The agency took a full week's salary—$15.50 for five-and-a-half-days work—for placing me. The company fired me after a month, and I learned from friends that I had made there that this was a typical stratagem to keep labor costs down by splitting the placement fee between the agency and the firm.

In the summer of 1941, I had my closest contact with white-collar crime, though it made only a slight impression. I was hired as an office boy at McKesson-Robbins. The company had just gone through one of the most sensational fraud episodes in the annals of corporate crime. Two former convicts, using assumed names, had gained control of McKesson-Robbins, and thereafter had stolen millions of dollars by fraudulent transactions. My job involved a few trips a day downtown to deliver papers, a goodly number of personal errands for the executives and their secretaries, and some hectic mailroom activity at the beginning and the end of each day. Otherwise, I was free to wander about, and I spent some time in the storage room where boxes full of the records of the conspiracy were kept, reading through them, though I had trouble understanding much of what I found there.

By this time, though, I suspect my political and ideological conceptions had been well fashioned, and the McKesson-Robbins documents only fortified beliefs toward which my high-school training had pointed me. I was in the first graduating class (1941) of the now-famed Bronx High School of Science. At Science, it was taken for granted that all students were politically liberal, and many, including faculty (as well-publicized investigations would later show), were very far left. The teachers were stunningly good and dedicated; the students, by my recollection, were awesomely bright. Quite a number of their parents were well known. Lewis Mumford's son was on the swimming team that I covered for the school newspaper; and Isaac don Levine, a biographer of Trotsky, had a child in our graduating class.

For the school newspaper, I once wrote about some varsity athletes goofing off and then added the phrase that they were standing around "like WPA workers leaning on their shovels." The WPA (Works Progress Administration) was, of course, the make-work program for the unemployed. Sidney Hirsch, the paper's faculty advisor, cut the offensive words from my story and tongue-lashed me: "These people deserve sympathy, not sarcasm."

It may offer a sense of the kind of place that the Bronx High School of Science was if I note that during our sophomore year the required reading in English was Dalton Trumbo's *Johnny Got His Gun,* a searing then-comtemporary antiwar novel. My friends at other schools at the time remained deep into *Mill on the Floss.*

It was this heritage that I brought to the study of white-collar crime. That work began with the first chapter in this book, which deals with the propaganda of the National Association of Manufacturers (NAM) that was flooding the schools. The chapter started as a term paper at Brigham Young. I think that I took up the subject because I was outraged at the election to the U.S. Senate by Utah citizens of Wallace Bennett, a former head of the NAM, and I was determined to air the troglodyte views of their representative.

I had selected Brigham Young for graduate work after a long session in the New York Public Library with college catalogues: it was the only tuition-free school I located. B.Y.U. proved, I think, an excellent choice for me: the sociology faculty was good, and its members held in check what must at times have been their bemusement, if not annoyance, at my views, and they provided me very reassuring personal and academic support. By Utah standards, I was a rather fiery dissident, living the oddly fractionated life of a graduate student, a sports reporter for the *Provo Herald,* and a coprovocateur with a small organized band of locals and outlanders who vehemently and regularly protested publicly against anything we came across that distressed us: rent-control gouging, racial injustice, gerrymandering. We were no true threat to anyone, though we occasionally served to goad into action a city administration that had no objection to acting decently if it wasn't too much trouble.

The NAM article was finished at Wisconsin, where I took advantage of the in-house NAM publications held by the John Commons Library in Sterling Hall. I learned at this time that one's targets often print their most incriminating material in their own newsletters, bragging to what they believe to be a wholly partisan audience. Morris Rubin, editor of *The Progressive,* accepted the article on a mail submission; later, in his office in downtown Madison, he showed me how to toughen it up a little. (The term *crowd* in the first sentence of the article is Rubin's insertion.)

The work that I thereafter did on the heavy electrical equipment antitrust case, while I was teaching in California after leaving Oklahoma in 1957, surely has to be regarded as the cornerstone of whatever reputation I came to have in regard to the study of white-collar crime. I don't know what turned my attention to the case, though it arose at a time—never since truly repeated—when I could focus relatively uninterruptedly on a single thing. I was unknown enough professionally not to be responding to writing requests and was not involved in the trivia of academic management. Nor were there grants available to bedazzle: you had to finance your own work, so you chose a subject that you could personally handle.

I know that I got involved in following the antitrust case relatively early: I still have the original *New York Times* clipping on the sentencing of the defendants. It was about this time too that I had conquered the intricacies of legal bibliography so that I felt comfortable with the juridical aspects of the case and antitrust law: fortunately, I lived very close to the superb Los Angeles County Law Library and had taken to writing for law journals.

I had an outlet for the antitrust material before I began to write, a reader being put together by Marshall Clinard and Richard Quinney, which provided a deadline. I despise deadlines, but find them almost essential for getting things done. Then I read everything I could locate about the case. I subscribed to the *Sharon* (Pa.) *Herald* and to the Schenectady (N.Y.) newspaper to try to get some information about local views from the sites where major operations of General Electric and Westinghouse were located. The 1961 U.S. Senate hearings on the case were a godsend: criminologists make too little use of such materials for white-collar crime study, just as they underutilize preliminary hearing and trial transcripts for the investigation of more traditional kinds of law breaking. In the antitrust Congressional hearings, Senator Estes Kefauver's acerbic questioning of witnesses made plowing through the thousands of pages of testimony particularly fascinating.

The major aim of the antitrust article, beyond an interpretative description of events and attitudes, was to align the details of the case with postulations that Sutherland had advanced, to refine and refurbish some of those ideas. During the summer school recess, I rewrote and rewrote that article, something I rarely do.

The antitrust manuscript, I recall, was last proofread by me in a desert motel in 1964, after I had started a driving trek east from California for a year's fellowship at the Harvard Law School. I kissed it goodbye—don't ask why: I literally kiss all my manuscripts goodbye and wish them a fair journey—and dropped it in the slot at the post office in Barstow.

During the following fifteen years, I remained virtually alone among sociologists in writing about white-collar crime. I've tried in several of the chapters that follow to account for the absence of scholarly focus on white-collar crime during this period. Certainly, in those years, the work was lonesome, and I know that my own efforts suffered from the absence of a cumulative literature. Though the topic was dear to me, I wandered away from it for long stretches, largely because there was no colleagueship, no advance in the line of inquiry by additive or critical response, and, in truth little of the kinds of reward that sometimes accompany good work in an important area. I believe, though, that my edited book of readings on *White-Collar Crime,* published by Atherton in 1968, and containing virtually all the relevant scholarly social-science material then extant, served an important function in keeping a spark of interest in the subject alive.

The temporal pattern of the original publication of the chapters in this book indicates something about the pace and timing of my own work. After the antitrust piece in 1967 and the reader on white-collar crime in 1968, only three chapters included in the book were written in the next fourteen years. Seven others have appeared within the past two years. That many of these later chapters are coauthored signifies in some measure the appearance of a coterie of scholars who are interested as a matter of career choice in establishing themselves in work on white-collar crime, work that demands an acquaintanceship with a very considerable array of knowledge located in quite diverse intellectual realms.

For me, the collaborations have been extremely invigorating. I have published with about seventy different persons, though I had early on decided that I would do my white-collar crime studies all by myself. I made an exception in an article written with Herb Edelhertz, because we had worked together earlier on other subjects. Then the resolution broke down completely when Bob Meier joined the University of California, Irvine, faculty, and it became obvious that he could teach me a good deal and that we worked well together. It would be difficult to overstate how fruitful and amiable I found the joint enterprises that we conducted, and that appear in this book. Similarly, John Braithwaite, with whom I wrote the last chapter in the book, was the kind of coworker that aging scholars dream of locating. He presented some ideas for a joint piece, we yelled jovially at each other about them, and then he refined the product and we got a manuscript out. Both Bob and John clearly were the major contributors on the chapters we did together, as the authorship order indicates.

Two other collaborations are with graduate students. I had decided that it was high time that I moved forcefully into a substantive area of white-collar crime—I had no great preference but felt the strong need for a factual base for further theorizing. I chose occupational health because there had been something of a furor about it locally, and there were clear indications about where I might start gathering material. I passed the topic off onto Tom Clay, who is now working on it for his Ph.D. dissertation. For the chapter that appears here, we contributed about evenly to the work. The biographical piece on Sutherland was largely my work, though Colin Goff helped greatly with the research and discussion of ideas. Since then, Colin has gone far beyond where we got together and is in the process of completing what I am certain will be a fine full-length study of Sutherland's background and work.

The chapters that follow have in some instances been cut to eliminate repetition, but there has been no tampering with content. Footnote style has been standardized, and some footnotes—particularly in the law-review chapters—have been eliminated.

1 The NAM in the Schools

It is more than twenty years now since the Federal Trade Commission first focused an embarrassingly bright spotlight on the "educational" activities of the private utility crowd. On the initiative of the late Senator Thomas J. Walsh of Montana, the Commission conducted a painstaking, three-year, 26-volume investigation of propaganda activities by the power industry. The hearings exposed, in the judgment of one scholar, "a record of misleading, biased, pseudofactual private utility information disguised as impartial facts."

Samuel Insull was the originator of the utility propaganda machinery. In 1919 he directed the organization of the Illinois Committee on Public Utility Information. Within two years, the Committee distributed more than five million pieces of literature. By 1924, Matthew S. Sloan, president of the Brooklyn Edison Company, decided that the work of the expanding public information committees was "the most important in the whole broad scope of the activities of the electric utilities." "Don't be afraid of expense," M.H. Ayleworth, managing director of the National Electric Light Association, told the public relations section. "The public pays the expense."

The original utility propaganda machine—emasculated by the FTC investigation, the spread of publicly owned power systems, and the revelations of Insull's financial manipulations—has long since become comparatively mute, except in its own special field of private versus public ownership of power resources.

But the private utilities have not been without a vibrant mouthpiece in the larger fields of politics and economics. Their goals, like those of other industries, today determine the propaganda activities of the powerful National Association of Manufacturers (NAM).

January marked the fifty-fifth year of the NAM's existence. It was at Cincinnati in 1895 that the organization adopted a program which stands for "the protection of industrial interests in the United States" and "the dissemination of information among the public with respect to individual liberty and ownership of property."

From *The Progressive*, 14 (March 1950), 10-12. Reprinted by persmission of *The Progressive*, 409 East Main Street, Madison, Wisconsin 53703. Copyright © 1950, The Progressive Inc.

Today, it is estimated that a million dollars are spent daily by the Association to make the American people believe that what is good for business is good for them.

Propaganda has been defined by Professor Leonard Doob of Cornell University as "the attempt to affect the personalities and to control the behavior of individuals toward ends considered unscientific or of doubtful value in a society at a particular time."

In this light it is interesting to examine some of the propaganda that the NAM has issued through the years. It will illustrate a characteristic often associated with long-term manipulation of public opinion—the operation of a short memory.

It was during the late '20s that the NAM did battle with the child labor measure which was up for consideration as the Twentieth Amendment to the Constitution. The manufacturers, in typical fashion, issued a booklet.

An impartial survey, the NAM reported, had shown that schools were wasting the money of business enterprises and other loyal taxpayers by requiring children to attend school when the factories could provide a much more practical education than that offered by the school system.

The NAM asked that "physically able children over 14 who are unable or unwilling to go further than the sixth grade and who in the judgment of their parents would be better employed at work should not be prevented by any state law." They noted that it is "cruel" to force a child to finish eighth grade when this same child could be doing productive labor under factory supervision.

The report sharply criticized the educational system:

"Why can't you come into the factories, work with us in the construction of curricula and define the conditions of a progressive training *which entitles employers to use the labor of children* and carry forward with a creative ideal of accomplishment in place of the ideals of idleness which you are installing today?" it asked.

John Dewey, among others, pointed out the weakness of the manufacturers' arguments when he asked: "Because some children are backward, shall they be deprived of all benefits of medical attention and supervision and care of the public school and turned over to the tender mercies of factory owners?"

The italics in the preceding NAM statement are mine—because the statement contrasts so sharply with another which appears in a booklet recently distributed by the Association. The booklet is titled "The Public Be Served" and it discusses the NAM's pioneering traditions through the years. With typical forthrightness, it boasts that:

"No one has realized more than the employee members of the NAM that men aren't machines. Today, it has a complete industrial relations program, but even in the early days *it put its full weight behind state legislation to wipe out the blight of child labor in the factories*."

In addition to its concern for the school-shackled youth of the nation, the NAM is also on record as opposing a reduction in the working week for children below 48 hours. This was justified on the ground that children tend to get into trouble if allowed too much leisure time beyond the bounds of factory supervision.

In 1932 the NAM had its say on this subject:

"It has been claimed that in addition to providing for a 48-hour-weekly limitation, we should further provide for an 8-hour-day limitation. We are not prepared to do so."

The reason was altruistic:

"We feel that such a suggestion for a legal limitation would be opposed by a majority of our directors and members, not because of any desire to work children long hours, but because of a belief that the recognition of a uniform eight-hour basis for a group of workers will be used as a 'peg' with which to pry free enactment of legislation stipulating a legal eight-hour day for all workers."

When social security legislation was introduced, the NAM offered a substitute proposal:

No government plan would work, it insisted, but "it is the moral responsibility of the private employer to encourage, assist, and inspire his employees with the importance and necessity of ways and means for making provisions for the contingencies of life."

It was in 1928, despite its boast that it had realized that "men aren't machines," that the NAM employed a staff of statisticians to make and chart researches designed to illustrate the advantages of factory work—especially for children.

There is a well-known academic saying that "statistics don't lie, but statisticians may." These are the three rather startling conclusions that were reached by the Association's committee:

1. Industrial employment does not cause physical or mental slowing up.
2. Increased schooling does not increase earning capacity for the large majority.
3. Employment in industry does not cause either moral delinquency or physical degeneration.

The LaFollette Civil Liberties Committee, investigating the activities of the NAM between 1933 and 1938, found that it "had blanketed the country with a propaganda which in technique has relied upon indirection of meaning, and in presentation, upon secrecy and deception."

The NAM today continues its war for the preservation of industrial laissez faire. It warns that government legislation aimed at improving industrial conditions for the workers will lead only to the eventual destruction of the American nation.

We hear overtones of another warning which foretold the dire consequences of passage of an eight-hour-day law affecting companies handling government contracts.

In 1904, the NAM predicted:

"The movement is unreasonable and most ill-timed, and no greater calamity could befall the industrial interests of the country than its success. It would drive out of business every manufacturer doing both government work and commerical work, and no manufacturer would risk disaster to his entire establishment by undertaking a government contract."

This bill, the NAM warned, would destroy the American shipbuilding industry. It was "arbitrary, needless, destructive, and dangerous."

A key to the tremendous propaganda flow from the NAM was provided by an Association leader in 1943 when he explained the effect of the inundation of the public by NAM literature.

"People in a mass . . . tend to think in blurs," he said. "They are moved primarily by simple, emotional ideas. The NIIC [National Industrial Information Committee—a branch of the NAM] will capitalize upon this fact with an aggressive program designed to inspire a crusade which will sweep free enterprise into public favor."

To move people in a mass by "simple, emotional ideas," the NAM during the first nine months of 1949 issued a total of 1,927,907 booklets, sponsored 46 network and 47 local radio programs, and conducted 98 workshops.

In addition, NAM movies were shown 15,939 times from January through September to an audience estimated at some two million persons. Thirty-nine recordings were distributed to almost eight thousand independent stations; 151,133 industrial press service clipsheets were mailed; 883,852 publications went to "community leaders"; 42 articles were prepared; and 20,000 copies of "Industry's Views" were distributed.

Holcombe Parke summarized the Association's movie campaign when he resigned as the NAM vice president in charge of public relations February 6:

"Although $30 million was spent in 1948 for industrial films, and their use is growing each day, the surface has hardly been scratched. The amazing results which have been obtained by companies that have used films . . . indicate that industrial films, well-conceived and well-produced, can accomplish almost any communications task with which industry is faced."

A major target of the NAM propaganda barrage is the youth of the country. *A Catalogue of Teaching Aids*, "for planning classroom work," went out to principals and heads of social science departments in more than twenty-five thousand public, parochial, and private schools in late October 1949. By mid-January of this year, this mailing had brought requests for more than three million pieces of free NAM literature.

A typical letter from a teacher to *Trends*, the NAM's magazine for "industry-education" cooperation which goes to seventy thousand educators and clergymen, shows the value of this type of propaganda.

"I find your material useful in my contemporary society class and very timely in my economics class," the teacher wrote.

NAM officials have claimed that their booklets are read by two out of every three American high school students; that many students are taught the history of the American labor movement from a NAM booklet; and that this material has become required reading for many students.

A recent addition to the NAM's youth drive is the College Speaking Program which calls for "leading industrialists to carry the message of American enterprise before student assemblies at institutions of higher learning across the nation." The Association estimates that some thirty thousand college and university students and fifteen hundred faculty members "have been impressed with the benefits of the individual enterprise system" during the College Speaking Program's first five months in operation.

The numerous propaganda activities of the NAM, it can be seen, range over a wide area. No better criteria by which to evaluate them can be found than that provided by a NAM official during the Association's 1926 convention who key-noted:

"Every activity of this Association . . . must, in the last analysis, be judged by this one standard—does it contribute to the immediate or ultimate profit of the Association members?"

2 Toward a Delineation of White-Collar Offenses

General Motors does not have an inferiority complex, United States Steel does not suffer from an unresolved Oedipus problem, and the Duponts do not desire to return to the womb, Edwin H. Sutherland noted sarcastically when he summarized the implications of his research into white-collar offenses.[1] It was a clever piece of invective, designed to decimate the position of clinical theorists in criminology. "The assumption that an offender may have some such pathological distortion of the intellect or the emotions seems to me absurd," Sutherland wrote, "and if it is absurd regarding the crimes of businessmen, it is equally absurd regarding the crimes of persons in the lower economic classes."[2] Having dealt with the presumptive opposition, correctly if not altogether logically,[3] Sutherland put forward his own hypothesis which, "for reasons of economy, simplicity, and logic" was to be used to explain both white-collar criminality and lower class criminality. It was, of course, the theory of differential association: "Criminality is learned . . . in direct or indirect association with those who already practice the behavior . . . "[4] Since criminality is so learned, Sutherland maintained, it can be and is learned at all social levels in a society. Thus, for Sutherland, white-collar crime was as readily accounted for as the more traditional forms of criminal behavior.

The thesis of this paper is that Sutherland was led by his theoretical preconceptions into a number of intellectual traps which rendered the concept of white-collar crime, as it presently stands, of dubious utility for the study of criminal behavior. Having at hand a theoretical framework which could embrace virtually the entire range of human conduct, Sutherland felt no need to differentiate carefully among an extraordinarily wide range of offenses—criminal, ethical, and moral—engaged in by persons who were "respected" and "socially accepted and approved."[5] All would fit neatly into his interpretative scheme for white-collar crime in the same manner that professional crime, aggressive behavior following encephalitis, and a host of other highly divergent forms of behavior earlier had been "explained" by differential association.[6]

It is important to realize that no one, of course, had ever maintained that General Motors, or its management personnel, all suffered from an inferiority complex, any more than any serious scholar would have taken the

From *Sociological Inquiry*, 32 (Spring 1962), 160-171. Reprinted with permission.

position that all criminals, either lower or upper class, are driven by an unrequited yearning to return to the womb. Sutherland was obviously flailing a theoretical nonesuch. It was, in fact, Sutherland himself who, in one vital respect, came nearest to the theories he was belaboring, with his insistence that *all* criminals could, and should, be analyzed in terms of a single theoretical interpretation.

It was this commitment that inevitably tended to blur action distinctions for Sutherland. As Merton has noted, "the decision to encompass a great variety of behaviors under one heading naturally leads us to assume that it is what these behaviors have in common that is most relevant, and this assumption leads us to look for an all-encompassing set of propositions which will account for the entire range of behavior. This is not too remote," Merton points out, "from the assumption of a John Brown or a Benjamin Rush that there must be *a* theory of disease, rather than distinct theories of disease—of tuberculosis and of arthritis, of typhoid and syphilis—theories which are diverse rather than single."[7]

The present need in regard to the concept of white-collar criminality appears to be to separate out those types of activity which reasonably can be said to fall within the range of criminal statutes and then to gather together into less ubiquitous groupings those forms of behavior which analytically resemble one another both in their manifestation and in terms of the ingredients which appear to enter into their origin. This need is a common one for the field of criminology.[8]

Crimes of Corporations

One of the tightest definitions that Sutherland gave to white-collar crime was that it applied to criminal acts of corporations and individuals acting in their corporate capacity. This was not the only meaning accorded the concept for, as Tappan shows,[9] Sutherland altered his definition radically on different occasions, not as a matter of growth and refinement, but rather because, as we have seen, it was not important, given his theoretical approach, for him to be precise. Faced with the range of definitions, and granting the desirability of making a choice, it would appear most promising to concentrate on the corporation crimes that Sutherland discusses in *White Collar Crime*, his major work in this area. This book is largely a recital of decisions rendered against the leading corporations in the United States for restraint of trade, infringement of patents, misrepresentation in advertising, unfair labor practices, and similar acts. In the book, Sutherland stressed that the term white-collar crime "principally refers to business managers and executives."[10] Then, within two pages of this pronouncement, Sutherland illustrated white-collar crime by examples of thefts by employees in chain stores, overcharges by garage mechanics and watch-repair men, and fee-splitting by doctors. This testifies to the inconstancy of his formulation and/or to the dearth of illustrative material. If the concept of white-collar crime is brought back and restricted to corporate offenses and highly cognate acts, however, it will have definitional integrity, fulfill the criteria of causal homogeneity, and provide a delimited area for significant criminological research.[11]

The major difficulty in *White Collar Crime* as criminological research lies in Sutherland's striking inability to differentiate between the corporations themselves and their executive management personnel. When, in order to illustrate the possible development of white-collar offenses, Sutherland reproduced case-history documents of such non-corporate types as graduate students who work part-time as shoe salesmen, he was forced to grant that "the documents would not demonstrate the genesis of illegal practices by the managers of large industries" and to justify the inclusion of this peripheral case-study material on the ground that "unfortunately, similar documents, even of a scattered nature, are not available for the managers of large industries. No first-hand research from this point of view has ever been reported."[12] It is, then, this lack of relevant personal material which forced Sutherland to "humanize" the corporations themselves and which seduced him into taking literally the personifications and reifications that he himself created, and to treat them as he might treat their individual components.

Corporations are, of course, legal entities which can be and are subjected to criminal processes. There is today little restriction on the range of crimes for which a corporation may be held responsible, though it cannot, for obvious reasons, be imprisoned.[13] For the purpose of criminological analysis, however, corporations cannot be considered persons, except by recourse to the same type of extrapolatory fiction that once brought about the punishment of inanimate objects. Sutherland attempted to resolve this obvious dilemma by maintaining, not without some acerbity, that the crimes of corporations are precisely the crimes of their executives and managers. "The customary plea of the executives of the corporation is that they were ignorant of and not responsible for the action of the special department," Sutherland wrote. "This plea is akin to the alibi of the ordinary criminal and need not be taken seriously."[14]

Sutherland offered no proof for his categoric assertion. The empirical evidence, as we shall see, would seem to indicate that he was at best only partially correct. It should be stressed that the courts are willing to hold corporate officers personally responsible for blatant acts of administrative omission,[15] and to convict such officers when evidence indicates that they knowingly participated in violations of criminal statutes designed to control business operations. However, the courts are understandably reluctant to impose penalties for acts not supported by some reasonably probative evidence of individual culpability.[16]

Sutherland's anthropomorphic attitude toward corporations also on occasion led him into analogs which are as unnecessarily inflammatory as they are inaccurate and misleading. Thus, despite his repeated disclaimers that he was not interested in muckraking but only in criminal theory, Sutherland was impelled several times to compare corporations *per se* to habitual and professional criminals. Both, he pointed out, are about forty-five years old (corporations presumably do not get the benefit of nonage principals) and both have violated the law more than four times during their lifetime.[17] As Emerson notes, Sutherland's approach was at times not far different from saying that the state of Rhode Island is criminalistic because a resident of Providence has violated the criminal law. Emerson also pointed out that the seventy corporations which Sutherland treated as single individuals were actually gigantic, rambling enterprises, often with hundreds of thousands of employees, and subject to hundreds of statutes and thousands of administrative regulations.[18] It is such diversionary tactics which left Sutherland open to charges that he was a "moralist"[19] and that the concept of white-collar crime was a "propagandist weapon, which under the meretricious guise of science is to be used for the establishment of a new order."[20] Neither of these strictures, of course, is germane to the theoretical integrity of Sutherland's position. However, such attacks have understandably tended to distract from the essential elements of Sutherland's position and to hinder its re-examination and the absorption of its more viable portions into the main body of criminological theory.

General Electric and Antitrust Crime

By restricting white-collar crime to the corporate setting, as is done in the main body of Sutherland's book and suggested in its introductory section, the concept can shed considerable light on a form of offenses accorded little attention by criminologists either before or after Sutherland's work. The recent involvement of manufacturers of heavy electric equipment in violations of the Sherman Antitrust Act provides a valuable lode of material. This case fills in some informational and personal document gaps whose existence Sutherland felt so keenly. Furthermore, this case allows closer scrutiny of a significant form of criminal activity, of the *individuals* who engage in such activity, and suggests fertile fields for further criminological cultivation.

The Sherman Antitrust Act is obviously a criminal statute.[21] It states that "every person who shall make any contract or engage in any combination or conspiracy declared [by the Act] to be illegal shall be guilty of a misdemeanor" and shall be punished by a fine or imprisonment.[22] The Act, passed in 1890, did not create a novel form of liability, but was based upon long-standing common law principles of tort, crimes, and contracts.[23] By restricting white-collar analyses to it and cognate statutes, criminologists would respond to Tappan's legitimate observation that under present conditions "one seeks in vain for criteria to determine this white-collar criminality . . . for purposes of empirical research or objective description."[24] Here, among the violators of corporate criminal statutes, we do not have gathered together en masse "the shrewd businessman, the inefficient workman, the immoral politician, and the unethical doctor or lawyer" all of whom have been "condemned as criminals by the stroke of the pen" rather than by means of stringent legal procedure.[25] Instead, we have a discernible group of violators whose values and attitudes would seem to be reasonably similar and whose behavior, in regard to the criminal statutes involved, would be relatively homogeneous.

It has sometimes been alleged that the concept of white-collar crime is an inept designation because the individuals to whom it refers do not conceive of themselves as criminals. Ernest W. Burgess put forward this argument with the observation that a "criminal is a person who regards himself as a criminal and is so regarded by society."[26] George Vold has insisted, in the same vein, that "there is a basic incongruity involved in the proposition that a community's leaders and more responsible elements are also its criminals."[27] A reading of the testimony in the General Electric cases, however, clearly shows how inappropriate such objections can be for this type of offense, except in the most basic sense that they represent attacks on the use of that ill-defined term *criminal* to categorize a person.[28]

How did the men indicted and sentenced in the antitrust cases regard themselves? "There goes my whole life," a General Electric vice president said. "Who's going to want to hire a jail bird? What am I going to tell my family?"[29] A management official in the same company told the Senate subcommittee investigating fixed prices: "I went to great lengths to conceal my activities so that I wouldn't get caught."[30] The president of a smaller firm stated emphatically that "No one attending the gatherings was so stupid that he didn't know [they] were in violation of the law."[31] Again and again witnesses testified that their convictions had an effect upon their families and their position in the community.

By concentrating upon individual corporate offenders and their behavior rather than upon amorphous corporate entities, several of Sutherland's explanations of white-collar criminality find support. However, some of his interpretative comments seem to show telling flaws. There is evidence, for example, to support Sutherland's stress on intimate personal relations as an initiating factor into price-fixing (or into "stabilizing prices" as the officers almost invariably labeled it). A General Electric man noted: "I had no other alternative but to believe that this was the way that business was conducted and this was my job to try to do the best I could to make a profit and build up the sales for our company."[32] A second man, like many others, explained: "I found it this way when I was introduced to competitive discussions, and just drifted into it . . . "[33] On the other hand, a number of persons expressed, and their fellow workers attributed to them, strong repugnance toward meeting with competitors, but they did so because they believed that they had been ordered to engage in such practices. As one noted: "I thought the pressure was such that I would attend."[34]

In addition, there were large segments of the management corps in the same companies which never engaged in price-fixing discussions. Those production and sales divisions which did not fall prone to erratic price swings, the threat of cutthroat competition, and low prices saw no need to collaborate with rivals to set prices and to distribute among themselves a pre-arranged portion of the available market. It was, therefore, not only personal associations which were important in determining participation in the price-fixing schemes, but also the economic structure against which such participation occurred. Several times, as the market swung to a more favorable position, price discussions came to an end, with a "leprosy policy" prevailing in regard to competitors. Then the economic pendulum again swung and the talks were resumed.

It is intricate, interwoven items such as these which probably led Sutherland to place near the conclusion of *White Collar Crime* a statement, which he elsewhere appears to contradict, that "supplements" to the hypotheses of social disorganization and differential association were needed to explain "adequately" the phenomena of white-collar crime.[35] A supplement such as Glaser's "differential identification"[36] would seem, for instance, to offer a more promising avenue toward understanding the individual in the General Electric management bloc who categorically refused to go along with price-fixing discussions once he had signed, as all other personnel had signed—they hypocritically, he devoutly—the company edict forbidding such discussions. "[H]e was so religious," his colleagues explained, "that since he had signed this slip of paper saying that he would observe the policy . . . he would not talk with competitors . . . even when they came to his home."[37] The immediate superior of this man decided that he was not "broad enough to hold down the job." He was transferred, and eventually retired. Another employee wrote a letter to the chairman of the General Electric board of directors, protesting that price-fixing was occurring in his division. Analysis of this individual's behavior, however, is complicated by the fact that he was apparently emotionally disturbed, and that he soon thereafter suffered a mental breakdown.[38] But these are the kinds of data that bear upon criminal offenses within the corporate world. These items must be gathered together into an interpretative scheme by criminologists and other social analysts. It will not do merely to concentrate upon the gross record of decisions rendered against the corporate entities.

It is noteworthy that Sutherland's fundamental tenet that corporate violations represent interchangeably the criminal activities of corporate officers appears unwarranted when the anti-trust case material is examined. The law declares that directors and officers shall be guilty if they *authorize, order,* or *do* any of the acts constituting violations;[39] it requires, therefore, as Sutherland does not, that these persons commit some positive act. Few persons reading the hearings of the Senate subcommittee would likely doubt the innocence of some corporate officials who, on the face of the matter, might have been presumed to have been aware of and condoned the price-fixing offenses. The obvious lack of knowledge of one Westinghouse manager, in whose division price-fixing meetings were occurring, led a Senator to declare that he was nothing more than "a corporate eunuch."[40] The witness explained it more simply: He was an engineer, interested in the mechanics of plant operation, and took no cognizance of sales matters.[41] In the same vein, the president and inside counsel of General Electric promulgated directives against price-fixing on several occasions. At least at the highest levels of the corporate hierarchy it does not seem unreasonable to conclude that these directives were meant to be taken literally.[42] If true, such data illustrates the danger of assuming that a criminal record can be built up against individuals by a superficial tabulation of decisions against their corporations. Such an approach falls far short of providing essential data on the internal dynamics of the offenses and its use would seem to constitute a serious shortcoming in Sutherland's study of white-collar corporate crime.

An Overview

It has not been the object of this paper to attempt to offer theoretical interpretations of corporate criminality, but rather to point the way toward a more restricted and meaningful definition of the concept of white-collar crime. As it now exists, the concept can fairly be said to stand convicted of Vold's charge that it is "ambiguous, uncertain, and controversial"[43] and Allen's allegation that it is "among the least perceptive and satisfactory of [Sutherland's] many valuable contributions."[44]

It is noteworthy that Sutherland, by virtue of his position in American sociology, the attractiveness of his terminology, and the illustrations he used to support it, broadened the horizons of criminological research well beyond their traditional limits. This contribution should not be undervalued. Donald Cressey, in his introduction to the re-issue of *White Collar Crime,* observes that "the lasting merit of this book . . . is its demonstration that a pattern of crime can be found to exist outside both the focus of popular preoccupation with crime and the focus of scientific investigation of crime and criminality."[45] Donald Newman suggests that Sutherland's contribution may "possibly [be] the most significant recent development in criminology."[46]

It has been this expansion of the interest of criminologists, largely through the impetus of Sutherland's work, that has led to an array of important studies. Among the better-known works are Clinard's investigation of wartime price ceiling and related offenses,[47] Cressey's study of embezzlers,[48] Hartung's examination of violations in the wholesale meat industry,[49] and Aubert's research into the behavior of lawyers.[50] Such studies, though intrinsically worthwhile, should not, however, indiscrimately be included within the framework of white-collar crime. Efforts need to be made to determine their generic nature and, perhaps, to coin descriptive designations for those which prove to be criminologically kindred. Otherwise, in the manner described above by Merton, the search for wide-sweeping causal linkage will lead to a continued emasculation of significant theory. In addition, partly because of its loose definitional framework, the term *white-collar crime* has been taken up by popular writers, who have employed it to lend academic legitimacy to diatribes against a wide range of violators of an even wider range of moral codes, legal statutes, administrative regulations, and even less clearly defined standards.[51]

It would seem desirable that studies of embezzlers, for instance, should be evaluated on their own merits (as Cressey generally did) rather than as investigations into a type of behavior similar to the crimes of corporate officials. Sutherland himself pointed out that "the ordinary case of embezzlement is a crime by a single individual in a subordinate position against a strong corporation,"[52] and Daniel Bell, after declaring that Sutherland's *White Collar Crime* is "misleadingly entitled," goes on to remark that bank embezzlers, as a group, are not upper-class offenders, but middle-class individuals.[53] Embezzlers, to carry the point somewhat further, usually work alone, while anti-trust violators must work in compact with other individuals. The embezzler benefits himself directly, and harms his employer. On the other hand, the anti-trust violator, though he undoubtedly operates in terms of personal advantage, can rationalize his offense as contributing to the fiscal health of his employer. These may not be crucial variations, but it would seem desirable to examine offenses such as embezzling, tax evasion, corporate violations, and fee-splitting as distinct forms of crime which may be related to each other in some ways and to other offenses in different ways. It would also appear reasonable to concentrate initially on the elements of the criminal act itself for purposes of grouping rather than upon the social characteristics of the perpetrators of the acts, and to group behavior in terms of the latter item only for the most compelling pragmatic or interpretative reasons. The crimes of medical doctors, for instance, would appear to be susceptible to differentiation on more meaningful terms than the professional status of their perpetrators. The offenses of fee-splitting and abortion, both committed by doctors, seem about as related in most essential respects as the offenses of infanticide and adultery, both of which are committed by mothers.

It has been the aim of this paper, then, to suggest that the concept of white-collar crime be restricted to corporate violations of a reasonably homogenous nature and to cognate criminal acts. The concept should be tied to the legal codes which state and define such offenses. Attention should be concentrated on the behavior of individuals within the corporate structure rather than upon the artificial construct of "corporate crime." The absence of relevant data in this area will undoubtedly continue to hamstring criminologists. Perhaps some day we may look for the Kinsey of the corporate world; in the interim, field studies into the illegal behavior of corporate officers would seem to offer an attractive form of criminological inquiry.

It is suggested, finally, that unless the concept of white-collar crime is restricted, in line with the above or similar ideas, it will continue to remain prey to the legitimate criticisms of numerous scholars, some of whom have been quoted here, and it will continue to be so broad and indefinite as to fall into inevitable desuetude. Considering the potential value as well as the historical importance of this concept in the field of criminology, such a development would be unfortunate.

Notes

1. Edwin H. Sutherland, "Crimes of Corporations," in eds. Albert Cohen, Alfred Lindesmith, and Karl Schuessler, *The Sutherland Papers* (Bloomington: Indiana University Press, 1956), p. 96.

2. *Ibid.*

3. That upper-class criminals do not have pathological disturbances does not, of course, serve to disprove the proposition that lower-class criminals may have such disturbances. It is not an illogical proposition, just an unlikely one. Sutherland does not overcome it, even with his questionable insistence that all criminals share similar explanatory concepts, since he does not demonstrate the absence of such disturbances in the individuals committing the corporate offenses.

4. Edwin H. Sutherland, "White-Collar Criminality," *American Sociological Review,* 5 (February, 1940), p. 10. Reprinted with permission. The theory of differential association is elaborated in Edwin H. Sutherland and Donald R. Cressey, *Principles of Criminology,* 6th edition (Philadelphia: Lippincott, 1960), pp. 74-80. Recent statements have concen-

trated on refining and shoring up the theory. See Donald R. Cressey, "Epidemiology and Individual Conduct: A Case from Criminology," *Pacific Sociological Review,* 3 (Fall, 1960), pp. 47-58; and Daniel Glaser, "The Differential-Association Theory of Crime," in ed. Arnold M. Rose, *Human Behavior and Social Processes* (Boston: Houghton Mifflin, 1962), pp. 425-442. For a review of differential association's seeming merits and demerits see Herbert A. Bloch and Gilbert Geis, *Man, Crime, and Society* (New York: Random House, 1962), ch. 5.

5. Sutherland, "White-Collar Criminality," p. 4, fn. 2.

6. Sutherland and Cressey, *Principles of Criminology.*

7. In eds. Helen L. Witmer and Ruth Kotinsky, *New Perspectives for Research on Juvenile Delinquency,* Children's Bureau Publication No. 356, 1956, p. 27.

8. On this point, see Gilbert Geis, "Sociology of Crime," in Joseph S. Roucek, *The Sociology of Crime* (New York: Philosophical Library, 1960), pp. 7-33.

9. Paul W. Tappan, "Who is the Criminal?" *American Sociological Review,* 12 (February, 1947), p. 98.

10. Edwin H. Sutherland, *White Collar Crime* (New York: Dryden Press, 1949), p. 9, fn. 7.

11. This is not meant to indicate that valuable studies cannot be made of crimes related to things such as the practice of medicine or the sale of used cars. Nor is it meant to indicate that worthwhile results cannot be had from examinations of the criminal behavior of indivduals similarly situated in the class and occupational structure in order to learn how their position influences their adherence to criminal codes. It is meant to indicate that these studies cannot be grouped together as white-collar crime unless we wish to retain the present definitional anarchy.

12. Sutherland, *White Collar Crime,* p. 240.

13. See Glanville Williams, *Criminal Law—the General Part,* 2nd edition (London: Stevens, 1961), ch. 22; R.S. Welsh, "The Criminal Liability of Corporations," *Law Quarterly Review,* 62 (October, 1946), pp. 345-365; Orville C. Snyder, *Criminal Justice* (New York: Prentice-Hall, 1953), pp. 728-736.

14. Sutherland, *White Collar Crime,* p. 54.

15. Note, for instance, after the disastrous 1942 fire, the conviction for manslaughter of the owner of the Cocoanut Grove, Inc. for "intentional failure to take such care in disregard of the harmful possible consequences . . . " despite the fact that he was in the hospital at the time of the fire and claimed corporate, not personal, responsibility. Commonwealth v. Welansky, 316 Mass. 383, 55 N.E. 2d 902 (1944).

16. Acts of omission pose difficult problems both for criminologists and students of criminal jurisprudence, but it would seem desirable that

some substantial doctrine of fault be attached to acts carrying criminal penalties. Note, in accord with this idea, Hall's emphasis on "some 'causal' relationship between the legally forbidden harms and the voluntary misconduct." Jerome Hall, *Principles of Criminal Law* (Indianapolis: Bobbs Merrill, 1947), p. 11.

17. Sutherland, *White Collar Crime,* pp. 25, 217-221.

18. Thomas I. Emerson, Book Review, *Yale Law Journal,* 59 (February, 1950), pp. 581-585.

19. Howard Jones, *Crime and the Penal System* (London: University Tutorial Press, 1956), pp. 6-8.

20. Robert Caldwell, Book Review, *Journal of Criminal Law, Criminology, and Police Science,* 50 (September-October, 1959), p. 282.

21. "The act . . . creates an offense, a crime, describing what the crime is." United States v. Patterson, 201 F. 697, 714 (Dist. Ct. Ohio 1912); "The Sherman act is primarily a criminal statute." United States v. Swift, 188 F. 92, 96 (Dist. Ct. Ill. 1911). Note the important observation that "The [Sherman] Act . . . prohibits conduct rather than status . . . This is obvious from the fact that the statute carries criminal as well as civil sanctions." United States v. E.I. du Pont de Nemours, 118 F. Supp. 41 (1953). In the first Supreme Court decision since 1798 on whether a statute was penal, Chief Justice Warren in 1958 suggested that "the inquiry must be directed to substance" and that "a statute that prescribes the consequences that will befall one who fails to abide by these regulatory provisions is a penal law . . . Even a clear legislative classification of a statute as non-penal would not alter the fundamental nature of a plainly penal statute," Warren wrote. Trop v. Dulles, 356 U.S. 86 (1958). It is a bit of judicial common sense, important to bear in mind when laying out the boundaries of the criminological realm.

22. U.S.C.A. section 7 (1951). The best and most comprehensive interpretation of American anti-trust law is A.D. Neale, *Antitrust Laws of the United States* (Cambridge, Eng.: Cambridge University Press, 1960).

23. Eugene V. Rostow, *Planning for Freedom: The Public Law of American Capitalism* (New Haven: Yale University Press, 1959), p. 276.

24. Tappan, "Who is Criminal?" p. 98.

25. Robert G. Caldwell, *Criminology* (New York: Ronald Press, 1956), p. 70.

26. Ernest W. Burgess, Comment, *American Journal of Sociology, 56* (July, 1950), p. 34.

27. George B. Vold, *Theoretical Criminology* (New York: Oxford University Press, 1958), p. 253.

28. When does a person become or stop being a criminal? Are misdemeanants criminals? Is everybody a criminal? The term is so vague and invidious as to be self-defeating for analytical purposes. "Criminals," it

would seem, should be designated in terms of the offenses they have committed (for example, murderers, rapists, anti-trust offenders), and grouped together (for example, professional criminals, sex offenders, white-collar criminals) and then sub-divided only after a careful delineation of the types of acts and actors being denominated.

29. Quoted in Richard Austin Smith, "The Incredible Electrical Conspiracy," *Fortune,* 63 (April, 1961), p. 133. Reprinted with permission.

30. U.S. Senate, Subcommittee on Antitrust and Monopoly, Committee of the Judiciary, 87th Cong., 2nd Sess., 1961, "Administered Prices," *Hearings,* pt. 27, p. 16683.

31. Quoted by Senator Kefauver, *Hearings,* pt. 27, p. 16511.

32. *Hearings,* pt. 27, p. 16633.

33. *Ibid.,* p. 16668.

34. *Ibid.,* p. 16867.

35. Sutherland, *White Collar Crime,* p. 264.

36. Daniel Glaser, "Criminological Theories and Behavioral Images," *American Journal of Sociology,* 61 (March, 1956), pp. 433-444.

37. *Hearings,* pt. 27, p. 16736; Smith, "Electrical Conspiracy," p. 136.

38. *Hearings,* pt. 28, pp. 17274-17278.

39. U.S.C.A. section 24 (1951).

40. *Hearings,* pt. 27, p. 16571.

41. *Ibid.,* pp. 16539-16577.

42. See ibid., pt. 28, pp. 17201-18290 (testimony of Robert Paxton), pt. 28, pp. 17669-17772 (testimony of Ralph J. Cordiner).

43. Vold, *Theoretical Criminology,* p. 253.

44. Francis Allen, "Criminal Justice, Legal Values, and the Rehabilitative Ideal," *Journal of Criminal Law, Criminology, and Police Science,* 50 (September-October, 1959), p. 228.

45. Donald R. Cressey, Foreword, *White Collar Crime* (New York: Holt, Rinehart, and Winston, 1961), p. xii.

46. Donald J. Newman, "White-Collar Crime," *Law and Contemporary Problems,* 23 (Autumn, 1958), p. 735. Newman notes that studies of white-collar offenses have almost exclusively to-date concentrated on *crimes,* not *criminals,* in contrast to research into more traditional types of offenses. Ibid., p. 742.

47. Marshall B. Clinard, *The Black Market* (New York: Rinehart, 1952).

48. Donald R. Cressey, *Other People's Money* (Glencoe, Ill.: The Free Press, 1953).

49. Frank E. Hartung, "White-Collar Offenses in the Wholesale Meat Industry in Detroit," *American Journal of Sociology,* 56 (July, 1950), pp. 25-32.

50. Vilhelm Aubert, "White Collar Crime and Social Structure,"

American Journal of Sociology, 58 (November, 1952), pp. 263-271.

51. See, for instance, Frank Gibney, *The Operators* (New York: Harpers, 1960), and Normal Jaspan and Hillel Black, *The Thief in the White Collar* (New York: Lippincott, 1960).

52. Sutherland, *White Collar Crime*, p. 231.

53. Daniel Bell, *The End of Ideology* (Glencoe, Ill.: The Free Press, 1960), p. 382, fn. 42.

3 The Heavy Electrical Equipment Antitrust Cases of 1961

An inadvertent bit of humor by a defense attorney provided one of the major criminological motifs for "the most serious violations of the antitrust laws since the time of their passage at the turn of the century."[1] The defendants, including several vice presidents of the General Electric Corporation and the Westinghouse Electric Corporation—the two largest companies in the heavy electrical equipment industry—stood somberly in a federal courtroom in Philadelphia on February 6, 1961. They were aptly described by a newspaper reporter as "middle-class men in Ivy League suits—typical businessmen in appearance, men who would never be taken for lawbreakers." Several were deacons or vestrymen of their churches. One was president of his local chamber of commerce; another, a hospital board member; another, chief fund raiser for the Community Chest; another a bank director; another, director of the taxpayer's association; another, organizer of the local Little League.

The attorney for a General Electric executive attacked the government's demand for a jail sentence for his client, calling it "cold-blooded." The lawyer insisted that government prosecutors did not understand what it would do to his client, "this fine man," to be put "behind bars" with "common criminals who have been convicted of embezzlement and other serious crimes."[2]

The difficulty of defense counsel in considering antitrust violations "serious crimes," crimes at least equivalent to embezzling, indicates in part why the 1961 prosecutions provide such fascinating material for criminological study. Edwin H. Sutherland, who originated the term *white-collar crime* to categorize offenders such as antitrust violators, had lamented that his pioneering work was handicapped by the absence of adequate case histories of corporate offenders. "No first-hand research from this point of view has ever been reported,"[3] Sutherland noted, and, lacking such data, he proceeded to employ prosaic stories of derelictions by rather unimportant persons in small enterprises upon which to build an interpretative and theoretical structure for white-collar crime.

To explain corporate offenses and offenders, Sutherland had to rely primarily upon the criminal biographies of various large companies, as these were disclosed in the annals of trial courts and administrative agen-

From Marshall Clinard and Richard Quinney (eds.), *Criminal Behavior Systems*, pp. 139-150. Copyright © 1967 by Holt, Rinehart and Winston. Reprinted by permission of Holt, Rinehart and Winston, CBS College Publishing.

cies. In the absence of information about human offenders, the legal fiction of corporate humanity, a kind of economic anthropomorphism, found its way into criminological literature. Factual gaps were filled by shrewd guesses, definitional and semantic strategies, and a good deal of extrapolation. It was as if an attempt were being made to explain murder by reference only to the listed rap sheet offenses of a murderer and the life stories and identification data of several lesser offenders.[4]

Sutherland was writing, of course, before the antitrust violations in the heavy electrical equipment industry became part of the public record. Though much of the data regarding them is tantalizingly incomplete and unresponsive to fine points of criminological concern, the antitrust offenses nonetheless represent extraordinary case studies of white-collar crime, that designation which, according to Sutherland, applies to behavior by "a person of high socioeconomic status who violates the laws designed to regulate his occupational activities"[5] and "principally refers to business managers and executives."[6] In particular, the antitrust cases provide the researcher with a mass of raw data against which to test and to refine earlier hunches and hypotheses regarding white-collar crime.

Facts of the Antitrust Violations

The most notable characteristic of the 1961 antitrust conspiracy was its willful and blatant nature. These were not complex acts only doubtfully in violation of a highly complicated statute. They were flagrant, criminal offenses, patently in contradiction to the letter and the spirit of the Sherman Antitrust Act of 1890, which forbade price-fixing arrangements as restraints upon free trade.[7]

The details of the conspiracy must be drawn together from diverse second-hand sources, because grand jury hearings upon which the criminal indictments were based were not made public. The decision to keep the records closed was reached on the ground that the traditional secrecy of grand jury proceedings took precedence over public interest in obtaining information about the conspiracy and over the interest of different purchasers in acquiring background data upon which to base civil suits against the offending corporations for allegedly fraudulent sales.[8]

The federal government had initiated the grand jury probes in mid-1959, apparently after receiving complaints from officials of the Tennessee Valley Authority concerning identical bids they were getting from manufacturers of higly technical electrical equipment, even though the bids were submitted in sealed envelopes.[9] Four grand juries were ultimately convened and subpoenaed 196 persons, some of whom obviously revealed the intimate details of the price-fixing procedures. A package of twenty indictments was handed down, involving forty-five individual defendants and twenty-nine corporations. Almost all of the corporate defendants pleaded guilty; the company officials tended to enter pleas of *nolo contendere* (no contest) which, in this case, might reasonably be taken to indicate that they did not see much likelihood of escaping conviction.

The pleas negated the necessity for a public trial and for public knowledge of the precise machinations involved in the offenses. At the sentencing hearing, fines amounting to $1,924,000 were levied against the defendants, $1,787,000 falling upon the corporations and $137,000 upon different individuals. The major fines were set against General Electric ($437,500) and Westinghouse ($372,500). Much more eye-catching were the jail terms of thirty days imposed upon seven defendants, four of whom were vice presidents; two, division managers; and one, a sales manager.

The defendants sentenced to jail were handled essentially the same as other offenders with similar dispositions. They were handcuffed in pairs in the back seat of an automobile on their way to the Montgomery County Jail in Norristown, Pennsylvania, fingerprinted on entry, and dressed in the standard blue denim uniforms. During their stay, they were described as "model prisoners," and several were transferred to the prison farm. The remainder, working an eight-hour day for thirty cents, earned recognition from the warden as "the most intelligent prisoners" he had had during the year on a project concerned with organizing prison records. None of the seven men had visitors during the Wednesday and Saturday periods reserved for visiting; all indicated a desire not to be seen by their families or friends.

Good behavior earned the men a five-day reduction in their sentence. Toward the end of the year, the remaining defendants, who had been placed on probation, were released from that status, despite the strong protests of government officials. The judge, the same man who had imposed the original sentences, explained his action by noting that he "didn't think that this was the type of offense that probation lent itself readily to or was designed for." Supervision was seen as meaningless for men with such clean past records and such little likelihood of recidivism, particularly since the probation office was already "clogged to the gunwales"[10] with cases.

The major economic consequences to the corporations arose from civil suits for treble damages filed against them as provided in the antitrust laws. The original fines were, of course, negligible: For General Electric, a half-million dollar loss was no more unsettling than a three dollar parking fine would be to a man with an income of $175,000 a year. Throughout the early stages of negotiations over the damage suits, General Electric maintained that it would resist such actions on grounds which are noteworthy as an indication of the source and the content of the rationale that underlay the self-justification of individual participants in the price-fixing conspiracy:

> We believe that the purchasers of electrical apparatus have received fair value by any reasonable standard. The prices which they have paid during the past years were appropriate to value received and reasonable as compared with the general trends of prices in the economy, the price trends for materials, salaries, and wages. The foresight of the electrical utilities and the design and manufacturing skills of companies such as General Electric have kept electricity one of today's greatest bargains.[11]

By 1962, General Electric was granting that settlements totaling between $45 and $50 million would have to be arranged to satisfy claimants. Municipalities and other purchasers of heavy electrical equipment were taking the period of lowest prices, when they assumed the price-rigging was least effective, using these prices as "legitimate," and calculating higher payments as products of the price conspiracy. The initial General Electric estimate soon proved untenable. A mid-1964 calculation showed that 90 per cent of some eighteen hundred claims had been settled for a total of $160 million, but General Electric could derive some solace from the fact that most of these payments would be tax-deductible.

Techniques of the Conspiracy

The modus operandi for the antitrust violators shows clearly the awareness of the participants that their behavior was such that it had better be carried on as secretly as possible. Some comparison might be made between the antitrust offenses and other forms of fraud occurring in lower economic classes. It was one of Sutherland's most telling contentions that neither the method by which a crime is committed nor the manner in which it is handled by public agencies alters the essential criminal nature of the act and the criminal status of the perpetrator.[12] Selling faucet water on a street corner to a blind man who is led to believe that the product is specially prepared to relieve his ailment is seen as no different from selling a fifty million dollar turbine to a city which is laboring under the misapprehension that it is purchasing the product at the best price possible from closed competitive bidding. The same may be said in regard to methods of treatment. Tuberculosis, for example, remains tuberculosis and its victim a tubercular whether the condition is treated in a sanitarium or whether it is ignored, overlooked, or even condoned by public authorities. So too with crime. As Miss Stein might have said: A crime is a crime is a crime.

Like most reasonably adept and optimistic criminals, the antitrust violators had hoped to escape apprehension. "I didn't expect to get caught and I went to great lengths to conceal my activities so that I wouldn't get caught," one of them said.[13] Another went into some detail concerning the techniques of concealment:

It was considered discreet to not be too obvious and to minimize telephone calls, to use plain envelopes if mailing material to each other, not to be seen together on traveling, and so forth . . . not leave wastepaper, of which there was a lot, strewn around a room when leaving.

The plans themselves, while there were some slight variations over time and in terms of different participants, were essentially similar. The offenders hid behind a camouflage of fictitious names and conspiratorial codes. The attendance roster for the meetings was known as the "Christmas card list" and the gatherings, interestingly enough, as "choir practice."[14] The offenders used public telephones for much of their communication, and they either met at trade association conventions, where their relationship would appear reasonable, or at sites selected for their anonymity. It is quite noteworthy, in this respect, that while some of the men filed false travel claims, so as to mislead their superiors regarding the city they had visited, they never asked for expense money to places more distant than those they had actually gone to—on the theory, apparently, that whatever else was occurring, it would not do to cheat the company.

At the meetings, negotiations centered about the establishment of a "reasonable" division of the market for the various products. Generally, participating companies were allocated essentially that part of the market which they had previously garnered. If Company A, for instance, had under competitive conditions secured 20 percent of the available business, then agreement might be reached that it would be given the opportunity to submit the lowest bid on 20 percent of the new contracts. A low price would be established, and the remainder of the companies would bid at approximately equivalent, though higher, levels. It sometimes happened, however, that because of things such as company reputation or available servicing arrangements, the final contract was awarded to a firm which had not submitted the lowest bid. For this, among other reasons, debate among the conspirators was often acrimonious about the proper division of spoils, about alleged failures to observe previous agreements, and about other intramural matters. Sometimes, depending upon the contract, the conspirators would draw lots to determine who would submit the lowest bid; at other times, the appropriate arrangement would be determined under a rotating system that was conspiratorially referred to as the "phase of the moon."

Explanations of the Conspiracy

Attempts to understand the reasons for and the general significance of the price-fixing conspiracy have been numerous. They include re-examination of the antitrust laws,[15] as well as denunciations of the corporate ethos and the general pattern of American life and American values.[16] A not inconsiderable number of the defendants took the line that their behavior, while technically criminal, had really served a worthwhile purpose by "stabilizing prices" (a much-favored phrase of the conspirators). This altruistic interpretation almost invariably was combined with an attempted distinction among illegal, criminal, and immoral acts, with the offender expressing the view that what he had done might have been designated by the statutes as criminal, but either he was unaware of such a designation or he thought it unreasonable that acts with admirable consequences should be considered criminal. The testimony of a Westinghouse executive during hearings by the Senate Subcommittee on Antitrust and Monopoly clearly illustrates this point of view:

> *Committee attorney:* Did you know that these meetings with competitors were illegal?
> *Witness:* Illegal? Yes, but not criminal. I didn't find that out until I read the indictment. . . . I assumed that criminal action meant damaging someone, and we did not do that. . . . I thought that we were more or less working on a survival basis in order to try to make enough to keep our plant and our employees.

This theme was repeated in essentially similar language by a number of witnesses. "It is against the law," an official of the Ingersoll-Rand Corporation granted, but he added: "I do not know that it is against public welfare because I am not certain that the consumer was actually injured by this operation." A Carrier Corporation executive testified that he was "reasonably in doubt" that the price-fixing meetings violated the antitrust law. "Certainly, we were in a gray area. I think the degree of violation, if you can speak of it that way, is what was in doubt." Some of these views are gathered together in a statement by a former sales manager of the I-T-E Circuit Breaker Company:

> One faces a decision, I guess, at such times, about how far to go with company instructions, and since the spirit of such meetings only appeared to be correcting a horrible price level situation, that there was not an attempt to actually damage customers, charge excessive prices, there was no personal gain in it for me, the company did not seem actually to be defrauding, corporate statements can evidence the fact that there have been poor profits during all these years. . . . So I guess morally it did not seem quite so bad as might be inferred by the definition of the activity itself.

For the most part, personal explanations for the acts were sought in the structure of corporate pressures rather than in the avarice or lack of law-abiding character of the men involved. The defendants almost invariably testified that they came new to a job, found price fixing an established way of life, and simply entered into it as they did into other aspects of their job. This explanatory scheme fit into a pattern that Senator Philip A. Hart of Michigan, during the subcommittee hearings, labeled "imbued fraud."[17]

There was considerable agreement concerning the manner in which the men initially became involved in price fixing. "My first actual experience was back in the 1930s," a General Electric official said. "I was taken there by my boss . . . to sit down and price a job." An Ingersoll-Rand executive said, "[My superior] took me to a meeting to introduce me to some of our competitors . . . and at that meeting pricing of condensers was discussed with the competitors." Essentially the same comment is repeated by witness after witness. A General Electric officer said, "Every direct supervisor that I had directed me to meet with competition. . . . It had become so common and gone on for so many years that I think we lost sight of the fact that it was illegal." Price fixing, whether or not recognized as illegal by the offenders, was clearly an integral part of their jobs. "Meeting with competitors was just one of the many facets of responsibility that was delegated to me," one witness testified.

What might have happened to the men if, for reasons of conscience or perhaps through a fear of the possible consequences, they had objected to the "duty" to participate in price-fixing schemes? This point was raised only by the General Electric employees, perhaps because they alone had some actual evidence upon which to base their speculations. In 1946, General Electric had first issued a directive, number 20.5, which spelled out the company's policy against price fixing in terms stronger than those found in the antitrust laws. A considerable number of the executives believed, in the words of one, that the directive was only for "public consumption," and not to be taken seriously. One man, however, refused to engage in price fixing after he had initialed the document forbidding it. A witness explained to the Senate subcommittee what followed:

> [My superior] told me, "This fellow is a fine fellow, he is capable in every respect except he was not broad enough for his job, that he was so religious that he thought, in spite of what his superiors said, he thought having signed that, that he should not do any of this and he is getting us in trouble with competition."

The man who succeeded the troublesome official, one of the defendants in the Philadelphia hearing, said that he had been told that he "would be expected to do otherwise" and that this "was why I was offered that promotion to Philadelphia because this man would not do it." At the same time, however, the General Electric witnesses specified clearly that it was not their job with the company that would be in jeopardy if they failed to price fix, but rather the particular assignment they had. "If I didn't do it, I felt that somebody else would," said one, with an obvious note of self-justification. "I would be removed and somebody else would do it."

Westinghouse and General Electric differed considerably in their reactions to the exposure of the offenses, with Westinghouse electing to retain in its employ persons involved in the conspiracy, and General Electric deciding to dismiss the employees who had been before the court. The reasoning of the companies throws light both on the case and on the relationship between antitrust offenses and the more traditionally viewed forms of criminal behavior.

Westinghouse put forward four justifications for its retention decision. First, it declared, the men involved had not sought personal aggrandizement—"While their actions cannot in any way be condoned, these men did not act for personal gain, but in the belief, misguided though it may have been, that they were furthering the company's interest"; second, "the punishment incurred by them already was harsh" and "no further penalties would serve any useful purpose"; third, "each of these individuals is in every sense a reputable citizen, a respected and valuable member of the community and of high moral character"; and fourth, there was virtually no likelihood that the individuals would repeat their offense.[18]

General Electric's punitive line toward its employees was justified on the ground that the men had violated not only federal law but also a basic company policy and that they therefore deserved severe punishment. The company's action met with something less than whole-hearted acclaim; rather, it was often interpreted as an attempt to scapegoat particular individuals for what was essentially the responsibility of the corporate enterprise and its top executives. "I do not understand the holier-than-thou attitude in GE when your directions came from very high at the top," Senator Kefauver said during his committee's hearings; while Senator John A. Carroll of Colorado expressed his view through a leading question: "Do you think you were thrown to the wolves to ease the public relations situation . . . that has developed since these indictments?" he asked a discharged General Electric employee. The witness thought that he had.

Perhaps most striking is the fact that though many offenders quite clearly stressed the likely consequences for them if they failed to conform to price-fixing expectations, not one hinted at the benefits he might expect, the personal and professional rewards, from participation in the criminal conspiracy. It remained for the sentencing judge and two top General Electric executives to deliver the harshest denunciations of the personal motives and qualities of the conspirators to be put forth during the case.

The statement of Judge J. Cullen Ganey, read prior to imposing sentence, received widespread attention. In it, he sharply criticized the corporations as the major culprits, but he also pictured the defendants in a light other than they chose to shed upon themselves:

> They were torn between conscience and an approved corporate policy, with the rewarding objective of promotion, comfortable security, and large

salaries. They were the organization, or company, man; the conformist who goes along with his superiors and finds balm for his conscience in additional comforts and security of his place in the corporate set-up.[19]

The repeated emphasis on "comfort" and "security" constitutes the basic element of Ganey's view of the motivations of the offenders. Stress on passive acquiescence occurs in remarks by two General Electric executives viewing the derelictions of their subordinates. Robert Paxton, the retired company president, called antitrust agreements "monkey business" and denounced in vitriolic terms one of his former superiors who, when Paxton first joined General Electric, had put him to work attempting to secure a bid on a contract that had already been prearranged by a price-fixing agreement. Ralph Cordiner, the president and board chairman of General Electric, thought that the antitrust offenses were motivated by drives for easily acquired power. Cordiner's statement is noteworthy for its dismissal of the explanations of the offenders as "rationalizations":

> One reason for the offenses was a desire to be "Mr. Transformer" or "Mr. Switchgear"[20] . . . and to have influence over a larger segment of the industry. . . . The second was that it was an indolent, lazy way to do business. When you get all through with the rationalizations, you have to come back to one or the other of these conclusions.

There were other explanations as well. One truculent offender, the sixty-eight-year-old president of a smaller company who had been spared a jail sentence only because of his age and the illness of his wife, categorically denied the illegality of his behavior. "We did not fix prices," he said. "I can't agree with you. I am telling you that all we did was recover costs." Some persons blamed the system of decentralization in the larger companies, which, they said, placed a heavy burden to produce profit on each of the relatively autonomous divisions, particularly when bonuses—"incentive compensation"—were at stake; others maintained that the "dog-eat-dog" business conditions in the heavy electrical equipment industry were responsible for the violations. Perhaps the simplest explanation came from a General Electric executive. "I think," he said, "the boys could resist everything but temptation."

Portrait of an Offender

The highest-paid executive to be given a jail sentence was a General Electric vice president, earning $135,000 a year—about $2,600 every week. The details of his career and his participation in the conspiracy provide additional insight into the operations of white-collar crime and white-collar criminals.

The General Electric vice president was one of the disproportionate number of Southerners involved in the antitrust violations. He had been born in Atlanta and was forty-six years old at the time he was sentenced to jail. He had graduated with a degree in electrical engineering from Georgia Tech and received an honorary doctorate degree from Siena College in 1958; he was married and the father of three children. He had served in the Navy during World War II, rising to the rank of lieutenant commander; he was a director of the Schenectady Boy's Club, on the board of trustees of Miss Hall's School, and, not without some irony, he was a member of Governor Rockefeller's Temporary State Committee on Economic Expansion.

Almost immediately after his sentencing, he issued a statement to the press, noting that he was to serve a jail term "for conduct which has been interpreted as being in conflict with the complex antitrust laws." He commented that "General Electric, Schenectady, and its people have undergone many ordeals together and we have not only survived them, but have come out stronger, more vigorous, more alive than ever. We shall again." Then he voiced his appreciation for "the letters and calls from people all over the country, the community, the shops, and the offices . . . expressing confidence and support."[21]

The vice president was neither so sentimental about his company nor so certain about the complexity of the antitrust regulations when he appeared before the Kefauver committee five months later. "I don't get mad, Senator," he said at one point, referring to his behavior during a meeting with competitors; but he took another line when he attempted to explain why he was no longer associated with General Electric:

> When I got out of being a guest of the government for thirty days, I had found out that we were not to be paid while we were there [A matter of some $11,000 for the jail term], and I got, frankly, madder than hell.

Previously, he had been mentioned as a possible president of General Electric, described by the then president, as "an exceptionally eager and promising individual." Employed by the company shortly after graduation from college, he had risen dramatically through the managerial ranks, and passed that point, described by a higher executive, "where the man, if his work has been sufficiently promising, has an opportunity to step across the barrier out of his function into the field of general management." In 1946, he had his first contact with price fixing, being introduced to competitors by his superior and told that he "should be the one to contact them as far as power transformers were concerned in the future."

The meetings that he attended ran a rather erratic course, with numerous squabbles between the participants. Continual efforts had to be made to keep knowledge of the meetings from "the manufacturing people, the engineers, and especially the lawyers," but this was achieved, the witness tried to convince the Kefauver committee, because commercial transactions remained unquestioned by managerial personnel so long as they showed a reasonable profit. The price-fixing meetings continued from 1946 until 1949. At that time, a federal investigation of licensing and cross-patent activities in the transformer industry sent the conspirators scurrying. "The iron curtain was completely down" for a year, and sales people at General Electric were forbidden to attend gatherings of the National Electical Manufacturers' Association, where they had traditionally connived with competitors.

Meetings resumed, however, when the witness' superior, described by him as "a great communicator, a great philosopher, and, frankly, a great believer in stabilities of prices," decided that "the market was getting in chaotic condition" and that they "had better go out and see what could be done about it." He was told to keep knowledge of the meetings from Robert Paxton, "an Adam Smith advocate" and then the plant works manager, because Paxton "don't understand these things."

Promoted to general manager in 1954, the witness was called to New York by the president of General Electric and told specifically, possibly in part because he had a reputation of being "a bad boy," to comply with the company policy and with the antitrust laws and to see that his subordinates did so too. This instruction lasted as long as it took him to get from New York back to Massachusetts, where his superior there told him, "Now, keep on doing the way that you have been doing but just . . . be sensible about it and use your head on the subject." The price-fixing meetings therefore continued unabated, particularly as market conditions were aggravated by overproduction which had taken place during the Korean War. In the late 1950s, foreign competition entered the picture, and lower bids from abroad often forced the American firms to give up on particular price-fixing attempts.

In 1957, the witness was promoted to vice president, and again brought to New York for a lecture from the company president on the evils of price fixing. This time, his "air cover gone"—he now had to report directly to top management—he decided to abandon altogether his involvement in price fixing. He returned to his plant and issued stringent orders to his subordinates that they were no longer to attend meetings with competitors. Not surprisingly, since he himself had rarely obeyed such injunctions, neither did the sales persons in his division.

The witness was interrogated closely about his moral feelings regarding criminal behavior. He fumbled most of the questions, avoiding answering them directly, but ultimately coming to the point of saying that the consequences visited upon him represented the major reason for a re-evaluation of his actions. He would not behave in the same manner again because of what "I have been through and what I have done to my family." He was also vexed with the treatment he had received from the newspapers: "They have never laid off a second. They have used some terms which I don't think are necessarily—they don't use the term *price fixing*. It is always *price rigging* or trying to make it as sensational as possible."[22] The taint of a jail sentence, he said, had the effect of making people "start looking at the moral values a little bit." Senator Hart drew the following conclusions from the witness's comments:

> *Hart:* This was what I was wondering about, whether absent the introduction of this element of fear, there would have been any re-examination of the moral implications.
>
> *Witness:* I wonder, Senator. That is a pretty tough one to answer.
>
> *Hart:* If I understand you correctly, you have already answered it. . . . After the fear, there came the moral re-evaluation.

All things said, the former General Electric vice president viewed his situation philosophically. Regarding his resignation from the company, it was "the way the ball has bounced." He hoped that he would have "the opportunity to continue in American industry and do a job," and he wished some of the other men who had been dismissed a lot of good luck. "I want to leave the company with no bitterness and to go out and see if I can't start a new venture along the right lines." Eight days later, he accepted a job as assistant to the president in charge of product research in a large corporation located outside of Philadelphia. Slightly more than a month after that, he was named president of the company, at a salary reported to be somewhat less than the $74,000 yearly received by his predecessor.

A Summing-Up

The antitrust violations in the heavy electrical industry permit a re-evaluation of many of the earlier speculations about white-collar crime. The price-fixing behavior, flagrant in nature, was clearly in violation of the criminal provisions of the Sherman Antitrust Act of 1890 which had been aimed at furthering "industrial liberty." Rather, the price-fixing arrangements represented attempts at "corporate socialism," and in the words of Senator Kefauver to a subcommittee witness:

> It makes a complete mockery not only of how we have always lived and what we have believed in and have laws to protect, but what you were doing was to make a complete mockery of the carefully worded laws of the

government of the United States, ordinances of the cities, rules of the REA's [Rural Electrification Administration], with reference to sealed secret bids in order to get competition.

The facts of the antitrust conspiracy would seem clearly to resolve in the affirmative any debate concerning the criminal nature and the relevance for criminological study of such forms of white-collar behavior,[23] though warnings regarding an indefinite and unwarranted extension of the designation *crime* to all acts abhorrent to academic criminologists must remain in force. Many of Sutherland's ideas concerning the behavior of corporate offenders also receive substantiation. His stress on learning and associational patterns as important elements in the genesis of the violations receives strong support;[24] so too does his emphasis on national trade conventions as the sites of corporate criminal conspiracies.[25]

Others of Sutherland's views appear to require overhaul. His belief, for example, that "those who are responsible for the system of criminal justice are afraid to antagonize businessmen"[26] seems less than totally true in terms of the electrical industry prosecutions. Sutherland's thesis that "the customary pleas of the executives of the corporation . . . that they were ignorant of and not responsible for the action of the special department . . . is akin to the alibi of the ordinary criminal and need not be taken seriously"[27] also seems to be a rather injudicious blanket condemnation. The accuracy of the statement for the antitrust conspiracy must remain moot, but it would seem important that traditional safeguards concerning guilty knowledge as a basic ingredient in criminal responsibility be accorded great respect. Nor, in terms of antitrust data, does Sutherland appear altogether correct in his view that "the public agencies of communication, which continually define ordinary violations of the criminal code in a very critical manner, do not make similar definitions of white-collar crime."[28]

Various analytical schemes and theoretical statements in criminology and related fields provide some insight into elements of the price-fixing conspiracy. Galbraith's caustic observation regarding the traditional academic view of corporate price-fixing arrangements represents a worthwhile point of departure:

> Restraints on competition and the free movement of prices, the principal source of uncertainty to business firms, have been principally deplored by university professors on lifelong appointments. Such security of tenure is deemed essential for fruitful and unremitting thought.[29]

It seems apparent, looking at the antitrust offenses in this light, that the attractiveness of a secure market arrangement represented a major ingredient drawing corporate officers to the price-fixing violations. The elimination of competition meant the avoidance of uncertainty, the formalization and predictability of outcome, the minimization of risks. It is, of course, this incentive which accounts for much of human activity, be it deviant or "normal," and this tendency that Weber found pronounced in bureaucracies in their move from vital but erratic beginnings to more staid and more comfortable middle and old age.[30]

For the conspirators there had necessarily to be a conjunction of factors before they could participate in the violations. First, of course, they had to perceive that there would be gains accruing from their behavior. Such gains might be personal and professional, in terms of corporate advancement toward prestige and power; they might be vocational, in terms of a more expedient and secure method of carrying out assigned tasks. The offenders also apparently had to be able to neutralize or rationalize their behavior in a manner keeping with their image of themselves as law-abiding, decent, and respectable persons.[31] The ebb and flow of the price-fixing conspiracy also clearly indicates the relationship, often overlooked in explanations of criminal behavior, between extrinsic conditions and illegal acts. When the market behaved in a manner the executives thought satisfactory or when enforcement agencies seemed particularly threatening, the conspiracy desisted. When market conditions deteriorated, while corporate pressures for achieving attractive profit-and-loss statements remained constant, and enforcement activity abated, the price-fixing agreements flourished.

More than anything else, however, a plunge into the elaborate documentation of the antitrust cases of 1961 and an attempt to relate them to other segments of criminological work point up the considerable need for more and better monographic field studies of law violators and of systems of criminal behavior, followed by attempts to establish theoretical guidelines and to review and refine current interpretative viewpoints. There have probably been no more than a dozen, if that many, full-length studies of types of criminal (not delinquent) behavior in the past decade. The need for such work seems overriding, and the 1961 antitrust cases represent but one of a number of instances, whether in the field of white-collar crime, organized crime, sex offenses, personal or property crimes, or similar areas of concern, where we are still faced with a less than adequate supply of basic and comparative material upon which to base valid and useful theoretical statements.

Notes

1. Judge J. Cullen Ganey, in *Application of the State of California,* 195 F. Supp. 39 (E.D. Pa. 1961).

2. *New York Times* (February 7, 1961).

3. Edwin H. Sutherland, *White Collar Crime* (New York: Dryden

Press, 1949), p. 240. Note: "Private enterprise remains extraordinarily private. . . . We know more about the motives, habits, and most intimate arcana of primitive peoples in New Guinea . . . than we do of the denizens of executive suites in Unilever House, Citroen, or General Electric (at least until a recent Congressional investigation)." Roy Lewis and Rosemary Steward, *The Managers* (New York: New American Library, 1961), pp. 111-112.

4. For an elaboration of this point, see Gilbert Geis, "Toward a Delineation of White-Collar Offenses," *Sociological Inquiry* 32 (Spring, 1962), 160-171.

5. Edwin H. Sutherland in Vernon C. Branham and Samuel B. Kutash, *Encyclopedia of Criminology* (New York: Philosophical Library, 1949), p. 511.

6. Sutherland, *White Collar Crime,* p. 9, fn. 7.

7. *United States Statutes,* 26 (1890), p. 209; *United States Code,* 15 (1958), 1, 2. See also William L. Letwin, "Congress and the Sherman Antitrust Law, 1887-1890," *University of Chicago Law Review* 23 (Winter, 1956), pp. 221-258; and Paul E. Hadlick, *Criminal Prosecutions under the Sherman Anti-Trust Act* (Washington, D.C.: Ransdell, 1939).

8. Note, "Release of the Grand Jury Minutes in the National Deposition Program of the Electrical Equipment Cases," *University of Pennsylvania Law Review* 112 (June, 1964), pp. 1133-1145.

9. John Herling, *The Great Price Conspiracy* (Washington, D.C.: Robert B. Luce, 1962), pp. 1-12; John G. Fuller, *The Gentleman Conspirators* (New York: Grove Press, 1962), pp. 7-11. See also Myron W. Watkins, "Electrical Equipment Antitrust Cases—Their Implications for Government and Business," *University of Chicago Law Review* 29 (August, 1961), pp. 97-110.

10. Telephone interview with Judge Ganey, Philadelphia, August 31, 1964; *New York Times* (December 20, 1961).

11. *New York Times* (February 7, 1961). Reprinted with permission.

12. Edwin H. Sutherland, "White-Collar Criminality," *American Sociological Review,* 5 (February, 1940), pp. 1-12.

13. U.S. Senate, Subcommittee on Antitrust and Monopoly, Committee on the Judiciary, 87th Cong., 2d Sess. 1961, "Administered Prices," *Hearings,* pts. 27 and 28. Unless otherwise indicated, subsequent data and quotations are taken from these documents. Space considerations dictate omission of citation to precise pages.

14. The quotation is from an excellent article by Richard Austin Smith, "The Incredible Electrical Conspiracy," *Fortune* 63 (April, 1961), pp. 132-137, and 63 (May, 1961), pp. 161-164ff. Reprinted with permission.

15. See Leland Hazard, "Are Big Businessmen Crooks?" *Atlantic* 208 (November, 1961), pp. 57-61.

16. See Anthony Lewis, *New York Times* (February 12, 1961).

17. *Hearings,* pt. 27, p. 16773. Analysis of the relationship between occupational norms and legal violations could represent a fruitful line of inquiry. See Earl R. Quinney, "The Study of White Collar Crime: Toward a Reorientation in Theory and Research," *Journal of Criminal Law, Criminology, and Police Science* 55 (June, 1964), pp. 208-214.

18. *Sharon* (Pa.) *Herald* (February 6, 1961). Reprinted with permission.

19. *New York Times* (February 7, 1961). Reprinted with permission.

20. Earlier, a witness had quoted his superior as saying: "I have the industry under my thumb. They will do just about as I ask them." This man, the witness said, "was known as Mr. Switchgear in the industry."

21. Schenectady, N.Y., *Union-Star* (February 10, 1961).

22. *Hearings,* pt. 27, p. 17076. A contrary view is expressed in Alan J. Dershowitz, "Increasing Community Control over Corporate Crime—A Problem in the Law of Sanctions," *Yale Law Journal* 71 (December, 1961), footnoted material pp. 287-289. It has been pointed out that *Time* (February 17, 1961, pp. 64ff) reported the conspiracy in its business section, whereas it normally presents crime news under a special heading of its own. Donald R. Taft and Ralph W. England, Jr., *Criminology,* 4th edition (New York: Macmillan, 1964), p. 203.

23. See Edwin H. Sutherland, "Is 'White Collar Crime' Crime?" *American Sociological Review* 10 (April, 1945), pp. 132-139.

24. Sutherland, *White Collar Crime,* pp. 234-257.

25. Ibid., p. 70.

26. Ibid., p. 10.

27. Ibid., p. 54.

28. Ibid., p. 247.

29. John Kenneth Galbraith, *The Affluent Society* (Boston: Houghton Mifflin, 1958), p. 84. See also Richard Hofstadter, "Antitrust in America," *Commentary* 38 (August, 1964), pp. 47-53.

30. Max Weber, *The Theory of Social and Economic Organization,* trans. by A.M. Henderson and Talcott Parsons (New York: Oxford University Press, 1947), pp. 367-373.

31. See Donald R. Cressey, *Other People's Money: The Social Psychology of Embezzlement* (New York: The Free Press, 1953); Gresham M. Sykes and David Matza, "Techniques of Neutralization: A Theory of Delinquency," *American Sociological Review* 22 (December, 1957), pp. 664-670.

4

Introduction to
White-Collar Criminal

A sense of injustice, provoked by examples of inequities in the legal treatment of the powerful and the weak, has often led to imprecations against the crimes and sins of members of the upper classes—persons in government, business, and the professions. Often, those in power and those with professional training and social position are held to higher standards than their less fortunate brethren, on the ground that their background demands added social responsibility. It is these ideas, coupled with the view that no behavior is beyond scrutiny and appraisal, that have provided much of the impetus for the study of acts now grouped as *white-collar crime, occupational crime,* and *economic crime.*

It is an intriguing enterprise to attempt to locate in different historical periods the sources of the most powerful forms of social criticism directed against the entrenched classes. Nay-saying prophets, as well as disenchanted members of the ruling classes and free-swinging muckrakers, have at various times led crusades against those they believed were deviating from acceptable standards of conduct.

In the United States social censure and caricature have long been the territory of novelists. If, for instance, Mark Schorer's biography of Sinclair Lewis is an accurate appraisal, some of these writers, exiles from a world to which they longed to belong, stood outside, jeering and casting diabolically well-aimed brickbats. Others, undoubtedly motivated by a sincere desire for social reform, found the literary license of fictional creation the most hospitable milieu for the advocacy of their ideals.

Rather subtly, however, the function performed by novelists in the United States began to be assumed by sociologists, members of a newly emergent academic discipline. Writers of fiction then turned more toward clinical dissection of individual motivation and toward portraiture of their protagonists—people responding to given social conditions which, however deplorable they might be, nonetheless demanded their due and, failing to exact it, took their reasonable psychic and social toll.

The early sociological scholars came together from a wide diversity of sources, but few would miss the strong ministerial tone that pervaded their ranks. They were persons of evangelical bent who believed that they had

From *White-Collar Criminal: The Offender in Business and the Professions.* (New York: Atherton Press, 1968), pp. 1-19.

found the resolution of man's difficulties in a moral fervor buttressed by the dictates and metaphors of science. They were marked by a distaste of fuzzy speculation, a devotion to principles that can best be called "quasi-empirical," and by an insistent thrust to the roots of society where they intended to work their will, fortified by the tools of their trade and the trappings of their academic positions.

In 1896, when sociology was barely out of swaddling clothes, Edward A. Ross, author of the first significant sociological statement made in the United States about white-collar crime, could condescendingly describe sociology before his time as "a turgid mass of stale metaphysics, dark sayings, random historical illusions, and mawkish ethical raptures."[1] Ross' intense interest in social reform is clearly evident in his tribute to Lester F. Ward, his uncle by marriage, and the first president (1906-1907) of the American Sociological Society. "Suckled on the practicalism of Ward," wrote Ross, "I wouldn't give a snap of my fingers for the 'pussyfooting' sociologists."[2]

Sociology was a field, Ross noted, that "does not meekly sidle in among the established sciences dealing with the various aspects of social life"; it "aspires to nothing less than suzerainty."[3] In his turn, Ward told how the new science would operate: Society, he wrote, "should not drift aimlessly to and fro, backwards and forwards, without guidance. Rather, the group should carefully study its situations, comprehend the aims it desires to accomplish, study scientifically the best methods for attainment of these, and then concentrate social energy to the task set before it."[4] In these terms, Ward found agencies such as legislatures well on their way toward senescence. Perhaps they would have to be maintained, he noted, "but more and more they will become a merely formal way of putting the final sanction of society on decisions that have been worked out in the . . . sociological laboratory."[5] For Albion W. Small, a third pioneering sociologist, even the question of social values was readily susceptible to resolution by means of science. "The most reliable criterion of human values which science can propose," Small wrote, "would be the consensus of councils of scientists representing the largest possible variety of human interest, and cooperating to reduce their special judgments to a scale which would render their due to each of the interests of the total calculation."[6]

It is from this heritage that the present-day study of white-collar crime emerged. Edwin H. Sutherland, who in 1940 gave white-collar crime its label and a set of postulates, reflects both the early traditions of sociology and its subsequent development. Sutherland's approach was clearly one of scientific muckraking. Though he eschewed melioristic statements and stressed that his interest lay not in the reform of society but merely in reform of criminological theory, no contemporary reader is apt to regard this as anything other than a patent disingenuousness very similar to the disclaimers of eighteenth-century satirists faced with ostracism or excommunication were their professional heresies to become manifest.

Sutherland was, in fact, also deeply interested in making an impress on criminological theory; he had a vested interest in supporting his "differential association" theory, and in protecting its special vulnerability by demanding that a theory of crime explain *all* crime. It was Sutherland's felt professional obligation to present a facade of disengagement that merits special note, however, because the history of the ethos of sociology runs parallel to the history of study of white-collar crime, and the latter cannot readily be understood without comprehension of the former.

The early rationale of sociology, arising from "that general groping for social betterment produced by the misery that came in the wake of the industrial revolution and the factory system,"[7] was to be ridiculed by later sociologists as a preoccupation with "sex, sin, and sewage."[8] By 1939, Ward's biographer could plaintively label him "A Buried Caesar" and note that "most American teachers of sociology will smile tolerantly at the mention of his name as one who lived in the dim nineties and has been left far behind."[9] "As far as American sociology is concerned," another writer stated, "Ward was dead long before he died."[10] The work of Small and Ross was similarly denigrated. Of Small it was said that his "permanent influence upon sociology through his writings will ultimately prove slight and ephemeral as compared with the impress of his personality and personal activities upon the development of the sociological movement."[11] So, too, it was believed unlikely that Ross' "system as such will ever have a great deal of importance for formal social theory."[12] The nontheoretical work of the early sociological mainstays received even shorter shrift; it was an ephemeral kind of output, beneath comment. Sociologists were now beginning to accord respect to the work of those later caricatured by David Riesman as pedants who, "with no philosophical training, consume their time affixing exact degrees of significance to insignificant correlations and never get around to discovering anything new about society."[13]

The polemical and theoretical return of American sociologists to matters of immediate social concern coincided with the conclusion of World War II; this approach has gained considerable momentum in the 1960s, though the tendency marked by Riesman also remains a major motif in a field of study now able to absorb relatively comfortably a panorama of working ideologies. The postwar ethos was aptly indicated by Louis Wirth in a survey of sociological developments between 1895 and 1947:

> In recent years sociology seems to have begun to move into a phase closely resembling the period of initial enthusiasm for sociology in America. This phase is marked by a return to the original interest of sociologists in the actual problems of man in society. The presently emerging orientation of sociology differs from that of a generation ago, however, in several impor-

tant respects: In Small's day the passion for solving the practical problems of society was supported by little more than faith that sociology could discover a scientific foundation for ethics and social policies and was guided in its investigations largely by unproved but intuitively plausible broad philosophical notions concerning human nature, the social order, and social dynamics.

The contemporary return of sociology to the original interest of its intellectual progenitors in contrast is distinguished by more tempered expectations . . . Rather than aspiring to the role of value-setter, the contemporary sociologist is increasingly sensitive to the fact that science, or at least science alone, cannot set values.[14]

Explanations for the shift in stress may be found in changes in the surrounding political and social atmosphere, conditions which inevitably influence what subjects are studied and how they are approached. Matters of personnel recruitment, availability of funds for certain kinds of research, and differentiated rewards from colleagues and others—all play into the formation of a pattern of work in an academic discipline. For sociology, its chronological position vis-a-vis other defined areas of study and its own movement from infancy through adolescence may have aided in eliminating some self-consciousness and contributed to a breakdown of occupational immurement.

These items must be taken into account, at least partially, in reviewing the development and present position of studies of white-collar crime. There are also matters of personal influence, items generally difficult to assess and weigh properly. Much work regarding white-collar crime was clearly generated from a pattern of respect and discipleship accorded to Sutherland.

It is interesting as well, in this respect, to note that some of the writers on white-collar crime rounded out their sociology work with legal studies in order to complement their understanding of the issues involved in matters such as culpability and deterrence, items of basic importance to legal scholarship. Edward A. Ross and Roscoe Pound, the latter perhaps the most pre-eminent legal scholar of his time, were colleagues at the University of Nebraska, and Pound later dedicated one of his books to Ross, while Ross, for his part, pressed hard to obtain the presidency of the University of Wisconsin for Pound. Jerome Hall, the distinguished professor of jurisprudence at Indiana University, and Sutherland, who spent the major part of his academic career at Indiana, engaged in an exchange of information and ideas that enriched study and discussion of white-collar crime.

These personal influences and cross-disciplinary roots have undoubtedly provided studies of white-collar crime with direction and sophistication. The impact of secularization on an intellectual endeavor is like the impact of foreigners on a previously isolated geographical area—a seaport city, for instance, almost invariably becomes more cosmopolitan than its hinterland neighbors. Sociologists have responded to charges of "fatuous liberalism" raised from legal circles by attempting to buttress their conclusions and recommendations with sounder data. Riesman observed that "When a law professor comes to a sociologist because he is worrying about the unequal distribution of justice, and regards legal aid work as a drop in the bucket, the latter's preoccupation with methodology and lack of reformist concern may surprise him and send him back to his own devices";[15] barbs like that exert real suasion on sociological thought. On the other hand, the sociologist's scorn for legal conclusions that appear to be jerry-built on untested and unwarranted assumptions about human behavior and social activity provide pressure for experimental materials and for the acquisition of the complex and delicate skills essential for the collection of impregnable data.

It is developments such as these that have placed the study of white-collar crime in the position it occupies today and which portend the direction in which such studies are apt to move. Many gaps remain to be filled of course. Virtually the only psychological consideration of white-collar crime, for instance, is Walter Bromberg's clinical analysis of Richard Whitney, president of the New York Stock Exchange, who in 1933 was convicted of grand larceny for manipulating corporate funds;[16] such a study needs additional psychological support from other investigations before its conclusions can safely be generalized. Moreover, articulation between inquiries into organization structures and studies of white-collar crime has only barely gotten underway. Finally, the necessity to relate white-collar crime to theories of deviance and to general theories of human behavior has persistently challenged scholars and remains a major issue which must be carefully addressed.

The foregoing are but a few of the currents which have played upon popular and academic discourse regarding white-collar crime. It is important, initially, to realize that Sutherland, by virtue of his position in American sociology, the attractiveness of his terminology, and the illustrations he used to support his views, broadened the horizons of criminological research well beyond their traditional limits. The tendency to generalize about crime and criminals on the basis of the more readily visible forms of criminal activity, such as murder, assault, and robbery, was irreversibly affected by Sutherland's analysis that the propensity to violate the law is not confined to the stereotyped "criminal." That differential opportunities to commit different kinds of crime must be included in criminological analysis represents a major contribution of the Sutherland focus on white-collar offenses and should not be undervalued. In his foreword to the 1961 edition of *White Collar Crime,* Donald R. Cressey also observes that "the lasting merit of this book . . . is its demonstration that a pattern of crime can be found to exist outside both the focus of popular preoccupation with crime and the focus of scientific investigation of crime and criminality."[17] For Cressey, a paramount problem is the determination of why white-collar crime was able to remain beyond popular and criminological purview for so long.

Justice Oliver Wendell Holmes provided an approach to this issue when he pointed out that matters which a society chooses to study and acts which it decides to proscribe are telling indications of fundamental values. "It is perfectly proper to regard and study law simply as a great anthropological document," Holmes noted, continuing:

> It is proper to resort to [law] to discover what ideals of society have been strong enough to reach that final form of expression, or what have been the changes in dominant ideas from century to century. It is proper to study it as an exercise in the morphology and transformation of human ideas. The study pursued for such ends becomes science in its strictest sense.[18]

The same idea has been stated in the metaphorical language of Justice Cardozo: "Life casts the molds of conduct, which will some day become fixed as law," Cardozo wrote. "Law preserves the molds, which have taken form and shape from life."[19]

Few scholars have directed their attention to the charting of circumstances giving rise to statutes designed to discourage and to punish certain derelictions by members of the more powerful and entrenched segments of the society, though many have noted the striking increase in such rules and have marked signposts along the way. Holmes, for instance, has observed:

> When we read in the old books that it is the duty of one exercising a common calling to do his work upon demand and do it with reasonable skill, we shall see that the gentleman is in the saddle, and means to have the common people kept up to the mark for his convenience. We recognize the imperative tone which in our day has changed sides, and is oftener to be heard from the hotel clerk than from the guest.[20]

The growing concentration of statutory law on principles such as *caveat vendor*—"let the seller beware"—undoubtedly represents a function of, among other things, population growth, the development of cities, greater life expectancy, and enhanced technology, the last rich in its potential and awesome in its threat. As Pound has noted, "The points at which the claims and desires of each individual and those of his fellows conflict or overlap have increased enormously. Likewise, new agencies of menace to the general security have developed in profusion."[21]

Two dominant motifs mark the history of response to acts now considered white-collar crime. On the one hand, throughout time there has been a broad sweep of denunciation based almost exclusively on moral principles, usually deemed as self-evident and part of a natural, immutable code. Witness, for example, the diatribes of the Biblical prophets, such as Micah, the yeoman farmer of the eighth century before Christ who bespoke the doom of Judah because of its low ethical level;[22] note, too, the uncompromising verdict of the Book of Ecclesiastes regarding commercial activities:

> A merchant shall hardly keep himself from doing wrong, and a huckster shall not be freed from sin. . . . As a nail sticketh fast between the joinings of the stones, so doth sin stick close to buying and selling.[23]

On the other hand, there has been a rambling and variegated response in the law to conditions such as those denounced in Biblical writings. Part of the explanation for the discrepancy between moral and legal codes can be found in the nature and the function of law. Law, for instance, may be employed to maintain the status quo as well as to establish new ground rules. The latter situation, as de Tocqueville has pointed out, is not likely to occur when conditions are at their worst, but rather when they are in the process of change to the better.[24] It is then that people come to taste potential gains and to stir restively about the rate of change. Through most of history, with highly segmented and compartmentalized class patterns and strong authoritarian rule, those on the lower rungs of the social order were not likely to insist that they be treated fairly or decently or that their resources not be unreasonably exploited.

The reading of the legal record, however, is not merely a question of rote perusal of provisions with the assumption that absence equals indifference. Failure to outlaw certain behavior may represent espousal of goals likely to be compromised if lesser aims are accentuated. Legal statements may also stand for quite fanciful positions, and the discrepancy between the law on the books and the law in fact may be substantial. In addition, the oft-repeated dictum that law tends to be a reflection, however belated, of customary conditions fails to do justice to the basic question of *whose* customary ways will prevail and for what reason they will do so.

In such terms, a major thesis regarding white-collar crime is that the legal delineation of such offenses can be said to represent, though not in a direct or simple manner, social views that, for complex reasons, have come to be embodied in official codes. One facet of this development may be briefly summarized by reference to extension of the law of theft into white-collar realms.

Anthropological evidence makes clear that a sense of rightful possession of private property is far from an innate human characteristic. Sociologists have suggested that for Western civilization the doctrine of predestination, arising with notable intensity in countries persuaded to Calvinistic dogma, became translated into a belief that material possessions indicated divine approval, manifest in their bestowal.[25] Extratheological precepts also obviously contributed to a belief in the sovereignty of ownership. In the United States, the early entrenchment of this thesis is marked in the ringing words of John Adams, the country's second President:

> Property is surely a right of mankind as really as liberty . . . The moment the idea is admitted into society, that property is not as sacred as the laws of God, and that there is not a force of law and public justice to protect it, anarchy and tyranny commence.[26]

It was from such an ideological perspective that the law of fraud, fundamental in white-collar crime, emerged. In his meticulous tracing of this development in *Theft, Law, and Society,* Jerome Hall concentrates initially upon the decision in the Carrier's Case in 1473, a decision which for the first time included within the definition of theft the appropriation of goods by a middleman. Prior to 1473, virtually all theft involved cattle, and the law covered only direct acts. By the time of the Carrier's Case, however, manufacturing had begun to replace the feudal system. The new middle class had started to take shape, and its trade interests coincided with those of the Crown. In addition, the Carrier's Case involved wool and textile products, and these goods had recently become England's most significant exports. It was these conditions which coalesced in 1473 to change the Anglo-Saxon definition of theft.[27]

The slow, erratic, but nonetheless inexorable expansion of the concept of commercial fraud during the almost half-millenium since the Carrier's Case provides fascinating material on the interplay between those in possession of goods seeking to protect them and place themselves in a position to acquire more and other groups seeking their own advantage—with the state in the middle attempting to set rules by which the game will be played.

A few landmarks along the way may be noted briefly.[28] The thirteenth-century English courts, for instance, provided that there was to be "no remedy for the man who to his damage had trusted the word of a liar."[29] Even in the eighteenth century, a British Chief Justice could rhetorically ask: "When A got money from B by pretending that C had sent for it, shall we indict one man for making a fool of another?"[30] It was only in 1757 that a statutory provision for the punishment of "mere private cheating" was placed into English law. It was such judicial sentiments that led Jonathan Swift to locate an ancient Hebrew tradition in a land visited by Gulliver:

> [The Lilliputians] look upon fraud as a greater crime than theft, and therefore seldom fail to punish it with death; for they allege that care and vigilance, with a very common understanding, may preserve a man's goods from theft, but honesty has no defense against superior cunning.[31]

In the United States, the law of fraud developed too, and was fought each step of the way by those who held the view, expressed in the words of Chief Justice Stone, that "any interference with the operation of the natural laws of greed" was "subversive of liberty."[32] Some of the underlying factors that encouraged state interference with commerce provide keys to present enactments against white-collar crime. Herman Mannheim noted some of these items: (1) movement from an agricultural to a commercial and industrial society; (2) increasing inequality in the distribution of property, and the amassing of great wealth by the few; (3) the growing need to leave property in the hands of other persons; (4) transformation of ownership of visible property into intangible powers and rights, such as corporate shares, including a system of social security in place of ownership of goods; and (5) passage of property from private to corporate ownership.[33]

The present state of this movement—a movement that demands concentrated attention from students interested in understanding the roots of white-collar crime—is epitomized by a recent popular panegyric on the relationship between the activities of federal regulatory agencies and the better life that we presumably all live: "You may never meet an investigator for the United States Government," it begins, "but you are safer, more comfortable, and more secure because thousands of Federal agents labor unceasingly in the background of American life." It proceeds to praise "kilocycle cops" who patrol radio and television airwaves, guardians of drug and advertising standards, enforcers of wage-and-hour laws, and similar federal agents.[34] It requires only a comparison between such sentiments and John Adams' equally self-righteous view on private property and its divine attributes to appreciate the extraordinary social revolution that provides the historical background of acts now designated as white-collar crime.

Use of white-collar crime statistics and case studies to take the moral temperature of the nation is a tempting enterprise. *Life* magazine, for instance, declared that white-collar crime represents a "moral lightheadedness" that "whatever its cause, is potentially far more dangerous than any number of juvenile 'rumbles.' "[35] C. Wright Mills also thought he discerned great social malaise in reactions to announcements of white-collar crimes. "As news of higher immoralities breaks," Mills wrote, "people often say, 'Well, another one got caught today,' thereby implying that the cases disclosed are not odd events involving occasional characters but symptoms of widespread conditions."[36]

The accuracy of such statements and their basic meaning is not readily apparent. Note, for instance, a Biblical commentator's summary of conditions at the time that Micah was inveighing against the scandals he saw in Hebrew life:

Morals were appallingly low. Government officials were dishonest. A low ethical level prevailed in most areas of life. Because the nation had lost her moral integrity, she had become sinful, soft, and ripe for conquest.[37]

The tone has not changed in almost three thousand years, and the following observations can be made about contemporary American society:

There is much evidence of a widespread apathy toward the traditional values of American life. The ideas of strict honesty have become out of date in many fields of endeavor, public as well as private. The fall of certain television quiz heroes led to a widespread suspicion that a sick industry built them up, and that the commercialism which underwrites its programs is cynical and defiant. The crass disregard of the elemental essentials of straightforward dealing has invaded many areas of our society. One investigation after another reveals blunted moral sensibilities on the part of certain public officials and some of the agents of private enterprise who deal with them. Furthermore, the accused seem genuinely to feel justified in their actions, proclaiming one after another that no wrongdoing was involved nor intended. The victims of the deception, while diverse in their reactions, show surprisingly little moral indignation.[38]

In the same vein, early Greece, we are told, had its predators who in violation of its codes bought up land that they had learned would subsequently be acquired by the government; the Alcmaenoids, a leading Greek family, are reported to have contracted to build a solid marble temple, but instead to have employed concrete, veneering it with marble.[39] It is a rather long step, however, to maintain that ancient precursors of present-day white-collar crime underlay the demise of the Greek state, unless one employs such data to fill out Durant's skeletal commentary, built on an analysis of the bones of departed civilizations, that "a nation is born stoic and dies epicurean,"[40]— which, if translated into white-collar crime terms, indicates that self-indulgent, exploitative, and unprincipled behavior ultimately dooms a society. The paradox implicit in Durant's observation is that stable, stoic societies, while they may persist longer than their epicurean counterparts, often do so at the expense of items such as vitality and enterprise, freedom and opportunity for self-determination. On the other hand, societies providing scope for such values, all of which in some measure are considered fundamental in American life, also appear to encourage deviation, variation, and innovation among some persons often at the expense of others.

The necessity for historical and comparative cross-cultural studies of white-collar crime, relating its forms and its intensity to measures of social vitality, is clearly indicated before a better evaluation can be made of the meaning of such crime for a nation's survival or demise.

The relationship between white-collar crime and "ordinary" or "traditional" kinds of crime seems somewhat better established than that between white-collar crime and cultural well-being. Perceptions regarding the ubiquitous nature of white-collar crime are said to have consequences for other kinds of crime, particularly in terms of permitting an individual to "rationalize" or "neutralize" his behavior; that is, to provide an explanation for his offense satisfactory to himself and to his presumed or real accusers. Lacking such an explanation, the offender may be forced to regard himself as an alien and abject creature, unable to control his behavior and incapable of acting in a manner which he has introjected as desirable. The role of white-collar crime in the rationalization of traditional crime is summarized by Gibbons:

> It is not unlikely that the existence of white-collar criminality, along with differential handling of the individuals involved in it, provides run-of-the-mill offenders with powerful rationalizations for their own conduct. The latter can argue that "everyone is crooked" and that they are the "little fish" who are the victims of a corrupt and hypocritical society. In the same way, some rather obvious problems for treatment of conventional offenders may arise from their perception of widespread illegality among individuals of comfortable economic standing. Although definitive evidence on this matter is lacking, it is possible to gather up an abundance of statements by articulate criminals and delinquents in which these individuals allude to the facts of white-collar crime as one basis for their grievances against "society."[41]

Perhaps the best-known piece of research on this subject is by Sykes and Matza; they categorized the rationalizations of delinquents into several types, including an "appeal to higher loyalties" (loyalty to gang friends, for instance, is considered a more important moral obligation than respect for private property) and "condemnation of the condemners."[42] It is with this latter explanation, insisting that the delinquent is but one among many predators in the society, that the issue of white-collar crime comes into focus. Well-versed in newspaper reports of chicanery in high places, the juvenile may maintain that he is no worse, and in some respects much better, than so-called respectable citizens, who not only commit crimes but also compound their offenses by being hypocritical about them. A personalized version of this phenomenon is found in the remarks of one delinquent gang member:

> Wherever you look, wherever you turn, authority is there in the shape of parents, teachers, priests, and policemen, social workers and truant officers—a great Greek chorus of do's and dont's chanting about how you goofed and you've failed. And man, you can't stand that for long. After a while you've got to cut out or go nuts—or turn it all around and tell yourself that it's you who are right and the Greek chorus that is wrong. That's easy enough to do because half the time the chorus doesn't practice what it preaches anyway.[43]

The same point is made more formally by Sheldon and Eleanor Glueck, noted investigators of juvenile delinquency, who point out that "the demands made upon the growing boy by every vehicle of modern life are numerous, involved, often subtle, sometimes inconsistent." The Gluecks draw the following implications from this situation:

> The child is told that he must be honest, non-aggressive, self-controlled, but on every hand he runs into vivid contradictory attitudes, values, and behavior in an environment that—both in and out of politics—seemingly rewards selfishness, aggression, a predatory attitude and success by any means. It does not require the wisdom of a Seneca to convince the child, as it convinced that wise statesman, that "successful and fortunate crime is called virtue."[44]

Research probes into the less favored economic segments of the society reinforce the suggestion that in such groups individuals tend to regard others as exploitative and hostile, and to take comfort in such perceptions as justification for their own behavior. Cohen and Hodges, for example, found the ideas that "people are no good" and that the world "resembles a jungle" pervading responses to a questionnaire given persons in the "lower-blue-collar" class. Particularly notable was the cynicism concerning merchandising and service occupations. Economic and occupational success, they most often agreed, is accomplished by "friends or connections," "luck or chance," "pull or manipulating," or "cheating or underhanded dealing."[45]

Lower-blue-collar class members were found to be the most credulous members of the society regarding the accuracy of the written or printed word. Cohen and Hodges believe that limited experience, both direct and vicarious, makes such individuals particularly vulnerable to messages seeming to emanate from trustworthy sources. The researchers suggest that there is no conflict between their findings of credulity and misanthropy. "It is one thing to feel a generalized distrust of human beings, their motives and their claims," they write. "It is another to form an attitude on a specific claim or message where one has few independent criteria for evaluating the content of the message, little awareness of specific alternatives and little disposition to weigh evidence."[46]

The data necessary to refine the observations presented by Gibbons are as yet not available. It would be informative to learn about the perceptions regarding the prevalence of white-collar crime that are held by different kinds of traditional offenders and to determine the views on white-collar crime among individuals raised in social strata which produce a disproportionately high percentage of traditional offenders—and to do so *before* such individuals separate into essentially law-abiding or criminal categories. An informal California survey suggests the possibility that prison inmates in that state usually do not have recourse to white-collar crime as justification for their own offenses.[47] Persistent demands by the state parole board that offenders accept categorically their own guilt and personal responsibility for their acts—a thesis based upon Freudian principles of therapeutic grace—may condition verbal responses by prisoners. Group therapy, widely practiced in California correctional institutions, tends to divert attention from expressions of social cynicism and concentrate it upon psychic inadequacies. The California study, for instance, found expressions such as "I do my own number" and "I have myself to worry about" the most common answers to questions regarding the influence of knowledge and beliefs concerning white-collar crime upon the individual's own violation.

Most causal explanations of white-collar crime derive from an "evil causes evil" view based on the belief that only deplorable conditions of person or place can give rise to criminal behavior. There is neglect of the fact that perfectly adequate human beings and perfectly adequate social situations, judged by reasonable criteria, may produce untoward consequences, in the manner that both kindness and murder kill.

One of the earliest and hardiest explanations of white-collar crime is suggested by Aristotle in *Politics*. "Men may desire superfluities in order to enjoy pleasure unaccompanied with pain, and therefore they commit crimes," he noted. "The greatest crimes are caused by excess and not by necessity."[48] Sutherland, however, in perhaps the most telling of his observations on crime causation, laid to rest the Aristotelian postulate and its contemporary kin. "Though criminal behavior is an expression of general needs and values," Sutherland emphasized, "it is not explained by those general needs and values, since non-criminal behavior is an expression of the same needs and values."[49] The financially pressed corporate executive, Sutherland's view points out, may embezzle or he may move to a cheaper house, send his wife to work, himself take a weekend job, or borrow money from an uncle. Each of these alternatives may be able to satisfy his necessity adequately. The need alone, shared by untold numbers of other individuals who resolve it both legally and illegally, offers little clue to the precise method that will be selected for its satisfaction.

Notes

1. Edward A. Ross, Review of Giddings, "Principles of Sociology," *Educational Review* 12 (June, 1896), p. 92.

2. Edward A. Ross, *Seventy Years of It* (New York: Appleton-Century, 1936), p. 180.

3. Edward A. Ross, *Foundations of Sociology,* 5th edition (New York: Macmillan, 1926), p. 8.

4. James Quayle Dealey, "Lester Frank Ward," in ed. Howard W. Odum, *American Masters of Social Science* (New York: Holt, 1927), p. 82.

5. Lester F. Ward, *Applied Sociology* (Boston: Ginn, 1906), pp. 338-339.

6. Albion W. Small, *The Meaning of Social Science* (Chicago: University of Chicago Press, 1910), p. 242.

7. Harry Elmer Barnes, "The Development of Sociology," in eds. Harry Elmer Barnes, Howard Becker, and Frances Bennett Becker, *Contemporary Social Theory* (New York: Appleton-Century, 1940), p. 3.

8. Howard Becker, "Anthropology and Sociology," in ed. John Gillin, *For a Science of Man* (New York: Macmillan, 1954). p. 145.

9. Samuel Chugerman, *Lester F. Ward: The American Aristotle* (Durham: Duke University Press, 1939), pp. 67, 70.

10. John C. Burnham, *Lester Frank Ward in American Thought* (Washington, D.C.: Public Affairs Press, 1956), p. 10.

11. Harry Elmer Barnes, "Albion Woodbury Small: Promoter of American Sociology and Expositor of Social Interests," in ed. Harry Elmer Barnes, *An Introduction to the History of Sociology* (Chicago: University of Chicago Press, 1948), p. 788.

12. William L. Kolb, "The Sociological Theories of Edward Alsworth Ross," in ibid., p. 831.

13. David Riesman, *Thorstein Veblen: A Critical Interpretation* (New York: Scribner, 1953), p. 48.

14. Quoted in Leon Bramson, *The Political Context of Sociology* (Princeton: Princeton University Press, 1961), pp. 93-94.

15. David Riesman, "Law and Sociology," in ed. William M. Evan, *Law and Sociology* (New York: The Free Press, 1962), pp. 30-31.

16. Walter Bromberg, *Crime and the Mind* (New York: Macmillan, 1965), pp. 384-389.

17. Donald R. Cressey, Foreword, in *White Collar Crime* (New York: Holt, Rinehart, and Winston, 1961), p. xii.

18. Oliver Wendell Holmes, "Law in Science and Science in Law," in *Collected Legal Papers* (New York: Harcourt, Brace, 1921), p. 212.

19. Benjamin N. Cardozo, *The Nature of the Judicial Process* (New Haven: Yale University Press, 1921), p. 64.

20. Holmes, "Law in Science," pp. 213-214.

21. Roscoe Pound, *Criminal Justice in America* (New York: Holt, 1930), p. 12.

22. Micah 1:1-16 and 2:1-12.

23. Ecclesiastes 27:2.

24. Alexis de Tocqueville, *The Old Regime and the French Revolution,* trans. by Stuart Gilbert (Garden City, N.Y.: Doubleday, 1955), pp. 176-177.

25. Max Weber, *The Protestant Ethic and the Spirit of Capitalism,* trans. by Talcott Parsons (London: G. Allen, 1930).

26. John Adams, *Works,* vol. 6 (Boston: Little, Brown, 1853), pp. 8-9.

27. Jerome Hall, *Theft, Law and Society,* 2d edition (Indianapolis: Bobbs-Merrill, 1952), pp. 1-33.

28. Much of this material is drawn from Hermann Mannheim, *Criminal Justice and Social Reconstruction* (London: Routledge, 1946), sec. 3; and Hermann Mannheim, *Comparative Criminology* (Boston: Houghton Mifflin, 1967), chap. 21.

29. Frederick Pollock and Frederic William Maitland, *History of English Law,* vol. 2 (Boston: Little, Brown, 1909), p. 535.

30. Quoted by Hermann Mannheim, *Criminal Justice and Social Reconstruction,* p. 121.

31. Jonathan Swift, "A Voyage to Lilliput," in *Gulliver's Travels,* pt. 1, chap. 6 (1735).

32. Alpheus T. Mason, *Harlan Fiske Stone: Pillar of the Law* (New York: Viking, 1956), p. 380.

33. Mannheim, *Criminal Justice and Social Reconstruction*, pp. 86-87.

34. Miriam Ottenberg, *The Federal Investigators* (Englewood Cliffs, N.J.: Prentice-Hall, 1962), pp. xi-xii.

35. Frank Gibney, "The Crooks in White Collars," *Life* 43 (October 14, 1957), p. 176.

36. C. Wright Mills, *The Power Elite* (New York: Oxford University Press, 1956), pp. 343-344.

37. Rolland W. Wolfe, "The Book of Micah," in *The Interpreter's Bible,* vol. 6 (Nashville: Abingdon Press, 1951), pp. 898-899.

38. Leroy Bowman, *Youth and Delinquency in an Inadequate Society* (New York: League for Industrial Democracy, 1960), p. 21.

39. John McConaughy, *From Cain to Capone: Racketeering down the Ages* (New York: Brentano's, 1931), p. 24.

40. Will Durant, *Our Oriental Heritage* (New York: Simon and Schuster, 1954), p. 259.

41. Don C. Gibbons, *Changing the Lawbreaker* (Englewood Cliffs, N.J.: Prentice-Hall, 1965), p. 271.

42. Gresham M. Sykes and David Matza, "Techniques of Neutralization: A Theory of Delinquency," *American Sociological Review* 22 (December, 1967), pp. 664-670.

43. Kitty Hanson, *Rebel in the Streets* (Englewood Cliffs, N.J.: Prentice-Hall, 1964), p. 132.

44. Sheldon Glueck and Eleanor Glueck, *Ventures in Criminology* (Cambridge, Mass.: Harvard University Press, 1965), p. 20.

45. Albert K. Cohen and Harold M. Hodges, Jr., "Characteristics of the Lower Blue-Collar Class," *Social Problems* 10 (Spring, 1963), p. 323.

46. Ibid., p. 325.

47. The conclusions were reached by James H. Crosby in 1966 after more than a dozen discussions of the subject with groups of inmates of a California prison.

48. Aristotle, *Politics,* trans. by J.F.C. Welldon (London: Macmillan, 1932), book II, chap. 7, p. 65.

49. Edwin H. Sutherland and Donald R. Cressey, *Principles of Criminology,* 7th edition (Philadelphia: Lippincott, 1966), p. 82.

5 Deterring Corporate Crime

An active debate is underway in the United States concerning the use of imprisonment to deal with crime.[1] Enlightened opinion holds that too many persons are already incarcerated, and that we should seek to reduce prison populations. It is an understandable view. Most prisoners today come from the dispossessed segments of our society; they are the blacks and the browns who commit "street crimes" for reasons said to be closely related to the injustices they suffer. But what of white-collar criminals, and the specific subset of corporate violators? If it is assumed that imprisonment is unnecessary for many lower-class offenders, it might be argued that it is also undesirable for corporation executives. In such terms, it may appear retributive and inconsistent to maintain that a law-violating corporation vice president spend time in jail, while advocating that those who work in his factory might well be treated more indulgently when they commit a criminal offense.

I do not, however, find it incompatible to favor both a reduction of the lower-class prison population and an increase in upper-class representation in prisons. Jail terms have a self-evident deterrent impact upon corporate officials, who belong to a social group that is exquisitely sensitive to status deprivation and censure. The white-collar offender and his business colleagues, more than the narcotic addict or the ghetto mugger, are apt to learn well the lesson intended by a prison term. In addition, there is something to be said for *noblesse oblige*, that those who have a larger share of what society offers carry a greater responsibility also.

It must be appreciated, too, that white-collar crimes constitute a more serious threat to the well-being and integrity of our society than more traditional kinds of crimes. As the President's Commission on Law Enforcement and Administration of Justice put the matter: "White-collar crime affects the whole moral climate of our society. Derelictions by corporations and their managers, who usually occupy leadership positions in their communities, establish an example which tends to erode the moral base of the law. . . . "[2]

"Deterring Corporate Crime" was originally published in slightly different form in *Corporate Power in America*, edited by Ralph Nader and Mark Green. Copyright © 1973 by Ralph Nader. Reprinted by permission of Viking Penguin Inc., New York.

Corporate crime kills and maims. It has been estimated, for example, that each year two hundred thousand to five hundred thousand workers are needlessly exposed to toxic agents such as radioactive materials and poisonous chemicals because of corporate failure to obey safety laws. And many of the two and a half million temporary and two hundred and fifty thousand permanent worker disabilities from industrial accidents each year are the result of managerial acts that represent culpable failure to adhere to established standards.[3] Ralph Nader has accused the automobile industry of "criminal negligence" in building and selling potentially lethal cars. Nader's charges against the industry before a Congressional committee drew parallels between corporate crime and traditional crime, maintaining that acts which produce similar kinds of personal and social harm were handled in very different ways. He maintained that if there are criminal penalties for the poor and deprived when they break the law, then there must be criminal penalties for the automobile industry when its executives knowingly violate standards designed to protect citizens from injuries and systematic fraud.[4] Interrupted by a senator who insisted that the witness was not giving adequate credit to American industry for its many outstanding achievements, Nader merely drove his point deeper: "Do you give credit to a burglar," he asked, "because he doesn't burglarize 99 percent of the time?"[5]

Death was also the likely result of the following corporate dereliction recounted in the *Wall Street Journal* which, if the facts are as alleged, might well be regarded as negligent manslaughter:

> Beech Aircraft Corp., the nation's second-largest maker of private aircraft, has sold thousands of planes with allegedly defective fuel systems that might be responsible for numerous crash deaths—despite warnings years in advance of the crashes that the system wasn't working reliably under certain flight conditions.
>
> Though Beech strongly denies this, it is the inescapable conclusion drawn from inspection of court suits and exhibits in cases against Beech, from internal company memoranda, from information from the Federal Aviation Agency and the National Transportation Board, and from interviews with concerned parties.[6]

After 1970, the fuel systems in the suspect planes were corrected by Beech at the request of federal authorities. Before that, the company had been found liable in at least two air crashes and had settled two other cases before they went to the jury. In one case, tried in California and now under appeal, a $21.7 million judgment was entered against Beech. Of this, $17.5 million was for punitive damages, which generally are awarded in the state only when fraud or wanton and willful disregard for the safety of others is believed to exist. At the moment, suits are pending which involve the deaths of about twenty other persons in Beech planes.[7]

Those who cannot afford a private plane are protected against being killed in a crash of a Beech aircraft, but nothing will help the urban resident from being smogged.[8] Corporate crime also imposes an enormous finanical burden on society. The heavy electrical equipment price-fixing conspiracy alone involved theft from the American people of more money than was stolen in all of the country's robberies, burglaries, and larcenies during the years in which the price fixing occurred.[9] Yet, perhaps it can be alleged that corporate criminals deal death and deprivation not deliberately but, because their overriding interest is self-interest, through inadvertence, omission, and indifference. The social consciousness of the corporate offender often seems to resemble that of the small-town thief, portrayed by W.C. Fields, who was about to rob a sleeping cowboy. He changed his mind, however, when he discovered that the cowboy was wearing a revolver. "It would be dishonest," he remarked virtuously as he tiptoed away.[10] The moral is clear: since the public cannot be armed adequately to protect itself against corporate crime, those law enforcement agencies acting on its behalf should take measures sufficient to protect it. High on the list of such measures should be an insistence upon criminal definition and criminal prosecution for acts which seriously harm, deprive, or otherwise injure the public.

Obstacles to Public Outrage

The first prerequisite for imposing heavier sanctions on corporate criminals involves the development of a deepening sense of moral outrage on the part of the public. A number of factors have restricted public awareness of the depth and cost of white-collar crime. That the injuries caused by most corporate violations are highly diffused, falling almost inperceptively upon each of a great number of widely scattered victims is undoubtedly the greatest barrier to arousing public concern over white-collar crime. "It is better, so the image runs," C. Wright Mills once wrote, "to take one dime from each of ten million people at the point of a corporation than $100,000 from each of ten banks at the point of a gun." Then Mills added, with wisdom: "It is also safer."[11] Pollution cripples in a slow, incremental fashion; automobile deaths are difficult to trace to any single malfunctioning of inadequately designed machinery; antitrust offenses deprive many consumers of small amounts, rather than the larger sums apt to be stolen from fewer people by the burglar. It is somehow less infuriating and less fear-producing to be victimized a little every day over a long period of time than to have it happen all at once. That many very small losses can add up to a devastating sum constitutes impressive mathematical evidence, but the situation lacks real kick in an age benumbed by fiscal jumboism.

Take, as an example, the case of the Caltec Citrus Company. The Food and Drug Administration staked out the Company's warehouse, finding sugar, vitamin C, and other substances not permitted in pure orange juice being brought into the plant. Estimates were that the adulteration practices of the Company cost consumers one million dollars in lost value, thereby "earning" the Company an extra one million dollars in profits.[12] For the average customer, the idea of having possibly paid an extra nickel or dime for misrepresented orange juice is not the stuff from which deep outrage springs—at least not in this country at this time.

There are additional problems stemming from the class congruence between the white-collar offender and the persons who pass official judgment on him. The judge who tries and sentences the criminal corporate official was probably brought up in the same social class as the offender, and often shares the same economic views. Indeed, one Washington lawyer recently told a study group examining antitrust violations that "it is best to find the judge's friend or law partner to defend an antitrust client—which we have done."[13] Also, the prosecutor, yearning for the financial support and power base that will secure his political preferment, is not apt to risk antagonizing entrenched business interests in the community. In addition, the corporate offender usually relies upon high-priced, well-trained legal talent for his defense, men skilled in exploiting procedural advantages and in fashioning new loopholes. The fees for such endeavors are often paid by the corporation itself, under the guise that such subsidies are necessary to protect the corporate image, to sustain employee morale, and to provide an adequate defense. Finally, in the extremely unlikely event that he is sentenced to imprisonment, the corporate offender is much more apt to do time in one of the more comfortable penal institutions than in the maximum-security fortresses to which *déclassé* offenders are often sent.

White-collar criminals also benefit from two prevalent, although contradictory, community beliefs. On the one hand, neighbors of the corporate criminal often regard him as upright and steadfast; indeed, they will probably see him as solid and substantial a citizen as they themselves are. Witness, for example, the following item in the hometown newspaper of one of the convicted price fixers in the 1961 heavy electrical equipment antitrust case:

> A number of telegrams from Shenango Valley residents are being sent to a federal judge in Philadelphia, protesting his sentence of Westinghouse executive John H. Chiles, Jr. to a 30-day prison term. . . . The Vestry of St. John's Episcopal Church, Sharon, adopted a resolution voicing confidence in Chiles, who is a member of the church. . . . Residents who have sent telegrams point out Chiles was an outstanding citizen in church, civic and community affairs and believe the sentence is unfair.[14]

At the same time there is a cynicism among others about white-collar crime in general, a cynicism rooted in beliefs that the practices are so pervasive and endemic that reformative efforts are hopeless. Wearied by expected expose, citizens find that their well of moral indignation has long since run dry.[15] This lack of indignation can clearly benefit the white-collar criminal.[16]

These are some of the barriers to generating public concern; what are the forces that need to be set in motion to surmount them?

Foremost, perhaps, is the firm assurance that justice can prevail, that apathy can be turned into enthusiasm, dishonesty into decency. History notes that corruption was rampant in English business and government circles until in the late 1800s, when an ethos of public honesty came to prevail, largely through the efforts of dedicated reformers.[17] Similarly, at their origin the British police were a rank and renegade force; today they are respected and respectable. In fact, at least one writer believes that the decency of the English police is largely responsible for the mannerly and orderly behavior shown by the general public.[18] Thus, change can be achieved, and such change can have eddylike effects on other elements of social existence.

Following this alteration in the psychology of the polity, the facts of corporate crime must then be widely exposed and explained. This process requires investigation, analysis, pamphleteering, and continual use of mass media outlets. It is a formidable task, but one made easier by the fact that the ingredients for success are already present: corporate offenses are notorious and their victims—especially the young—are increasingly concerned to cope with such depredations.[19] Also, when confronted with a problem, Americans respond by taking action to resolve the difficulty, an approach quite different from, say, that of the Chinese. As Barbara Tuchman has noted, the Chinese, at least in pre-Communist times, regarded passivity as their most effective tactic on the assumption that the wrongdoer ultimately will wear himself out.[20] The ideological basis of the American ethos was set out by Gunnar Myrdal in his now classic analysis of racial problems in the United States. We had to work our way out of the "dilemma" involved in the discrepancy between our articulated values and our actual behavior, Myrdal believed;[21] that resolution has proceeded, largely through the use of legal forces, though at a painfully slow and sometimes erratic pace.

So too, perhaps, with corporate crime. Part of the public may be unduly sympathetic, and part cynical, toward revelations of such crime, but a latent hostility is also evident. The Joint Commission on Correctional Manpower, for instance, found from a national survey a strong public disposition to sentence accountants who embezzle more harshly than either young burglars or persons caught looting during a riot.[22] Similarly, a 1969 Louis Harris Poll reported that a manufacturer of an unsafe automobile was regarded by respondents as worse than a mugger (68 percent to 22 percent), and a businessman who illegally fixed prices was considered worse than a burglar (54 percent to 28 percent).[23]

Corporate offenses, however, do not have biblical proscription—they lack, as an early writer noted, the "brimstone smell."[24] But the havoc such offenses produce, the malevolence with which they are undertaken, and the disdain with which they are continued, are all antithetical to principles we as citizens are expected to observe. It is a long step, assuredly, and sometimes an uncertain one, from lip service to cries of outrage; but at least principled antagonism is latent, needing only to be improved in decibels and fidelity. It should not prove impossible to convince citizens of the extreme danger entailed by such violations of our social compact.[25]

It should be noted that Americans are perfectly willing to outlaw and to prosecute vigorously various kinds of behavior on social grounds; that is, in the belief that the behaviors constitute a threat to the social fabric rather than a threat to any prospective individual victims. Thus, possession of narcotics, abortion, homosexuality, and a host of other "victimless" crimes[26] are proscribed as threats to the moral integrity of our civilization. A reading of historical records indicates without question that class bias and religious intolerance were the predominant forces which gave rise to the laws against such "immoral" behavior.[27] It is now time that the rationale offered for prosecution of victimless crimes—that they threaten the integrity of the society—be applied to where it really belongs: to the realm of corporate offenses. This rationale did not work with victimless crimes because there was no reasonable way to convince nonperpetrators, often members of the perpetrators' general social groups, that what the offenders were doing was wrong. Therefore, eventually and inevitably, the logic of the perpetrators' position moved other groups either to take on their behavior (for example, the smoking of marijuana) or to take their side (for example, the performance of abortions). But the rationale *can* work vis-à-vis corporate crime, given its quantifiable harm actually imposed on nonparticipating victims. Also, there is the possibility of isolating the offender from reinforcement and rationalizations for his behavior, of making him appreciate that nobody morally sanctions corporate crime; of having him understand, as the English would put it, that "these kinds of things simply are not done by decent people." It is a standard defensive maneuver for criminals to redefine criminogenic behavior into benign terms. "Businessmen develop rationalizations which conceal the fact of crime," Edwin H. Sutherland wrote in 1949 in his classic study, *White Collar Crime.* "Even when they violate the law, they do not conceive of themselves as criminals," he noted, adding that "businessmen fight whenever words that tend to break down this rationalization are used."[28]

By far the best analysis of this process—and the way to combat it—is by Mary Cameron on middle-class shoplifters caught in Chicago's Marshall Field's. Store detectives advised that Field's would continue to be robbed unless some assault on the shoplifters' self-conceptions as honorable citizens was undertaken. The methods used toward this end are described by Cameron:

> Again and again store people explain to pilferers that they are under arrest as thieves, that they will, in the normal course of events, be taken in a police van to jail, held in jail until bond is raised, and tried in court before a judge and sentenced. Interrogation procedures at the store are directed specifically and consciously toward breaking down any illusion that the shoplifter may possess that his behavior is merely regarded as "naughty" or "bad". . . . It becomes increasingly clear to the pilferer that he is considered a thief and is in imminent danger of being hauled into court and publicly exhibited as such. This realization is often accompanied by dramatic changes in attitudes and by severe emotional disturbance.[29]

The most frequent question the middle-class female offenders ask is: "Will my husband have to know about this?" Men express great concern that their employers will discover what they have done. And both men and women shoplifters, following this process, cease the criminal acts that they have previously been routinely and complacently committing."[30]

The analogy to the corporate world is self-evident. As a law professor has observed, "Criminal prosecution of a corporation is rather ineffective unless one or more of the individual officers is also proceeded against."[31] A General Electric executive, for example, himself not involved in the price-fixing conspiracy, said that although he had remained silent about perceived antitrust violations, he would not have hesitated to report to his superiors any conspiracy involving thefts of company property.[32] Corporate crimes simply are not regarded in the same manner as traditional crimes, despite the harm they cause, and they will not be so regarded until the criminals who commit them are dealt with in the same manner as traditional offenders.

Harrison Salisbury tells of Leningrad women taking a captured German pilot to a devastated part of the besieged city during the Second World War, trying to force him to understand what he had been doing.[33] Persons convicted of drunken driving sometimes are made to visit the morgue so that they might appreciate the kind of death they threaten. Corporate criminals, though, remain insulated from their crimes. F. Scott Fitzgerald made the point well in *The Great Gatsby*: "They were careless people, Tom and Daisy—they smashed up things and creatures and retreated back into their money or their vast carelessness, or whatever it was that kept them together, and let other people clean up the mess they had made."[34]

How can this situation be changed? Taken together, a number of possible strategies involve widespread dissemination of the facts, incessant emphasis on the implications of such facts, and the methods by which the situation can be improved. Specific tactics might include regular publication of a statistical compilation of white-collar crime, similar to the FBI's *Uniform Crime Reports*, which now cover traditional offenses. It is well to recall that in its earliest days the FBI concentrated mostly on white-collar offenses, such as false purchases and sales of securities, bankruptcy fraud, and antitrust violations;[35] it was not until later that it assumed its "gangbuster" pose. Well publicized by the media, these FBI statistical reports form the basis for a periodic temperature-taking of the criminal fever said to grip us. Numerical and case history press releases on corporate crime would publicly highlight such incidents. It is perhaps too much to expect that there will some day be a "Ten Most Wanted" white-collar crime list, but public reporting must be stressed as a prerequisite to public understanding.

Another possibility is the infiltration of criminally suspect corporations by agents of the federal government trained for such delicate undercover work. It would be publicly beneficial to determine why and how such corporations disdain the criminal statutes they are supposed to obey. The cost would be minimal, since the infiltrators would likely be well paid by the corporation, and the financial yield from prosecutions and fines would undoubtedly more than offset any informer fees involved in the operation. To some this tactic may appear too obnoxious, productive of the very kind of social distrust that the corporate crimes themselves create. But so long as infiltration remains a viable FBI tactic to combat political and street crime, its use cannot be dismissed to combat white-collar crime. But perhaps, as an alternative, large companies should have placed in their offices a public servant who functions as an ombudsman, receiving public and employee complaints and investigating possible law violations.

There are, of course, other methods of uncovering and moving against corporate crimes, once the will to do so is effectively mobilized. Mandatory disclosure rules, rewards for information about criminal violations (in the manner that the income tax laws now operate), along with protections against retaliation for such disclosures, are among potential detection procedures. The goal remains the arousal of public interest to the point where the corporate offenses are clearly seen for what they are—frontal assaults on individuals and the society. Then, journals of news and opinion, such as *Time*, will no longer print stories dealing with the antitrust violations under the heading of "Business," but rather will place the stories where they belong, in the "Crime" section.[36] And judges and prosecutors, those weathervanes of public opinion, will find it to their own advantage and self-interest to respond to public concern by moving vigorously against the corporate criminal.

Alternative Kinds of Sanctions

Sanctions against corporate criminals, other than imprisonment, can be suggested; they are milder in nature and perhaps somewhat more in accord with the spirit of rehabilitation and deterrence than the spirit of retribution. While perhaps less effective instrumentalities for cauterizing offending sources, they at least possess the advantage of being more likely to be implemented at this time.

Corporate resources can be utilized to make corporate atonement for crimes committed. A procedure similar to that reported below for dealing in Germany with tax violators might be useful in inhibiting corporate offenses. "In Germany a taxpayer upon whom a fraud penalty has been imposed is required to make a public confession, apparently by newspaper advertisement, of the nature of his fraud, that a penalty has been imposed, that he admits the fact, and will not do it again."[37] A former FTC Chairman has said that "the Achilles heel of the advertising profession is that you worship at the altar of the positive image."[38] The same is true of corporations; thus the value of the public confession of guilt and the public promise of reform.

There is, of course, the sanction of the heavy fine. It has been argued that the disgorgement of illegal profits by the corporation—in the nature of treble damages or other multiplicated amounts—bears primarily upon the innocent shareholders rather than upon the guilty officials. This is not very persuasive. The purchase of corporate stock is always both an investment and a gamble; the gamble is that the corporation will prosper by whatever tactics of management its chosen officers pursue. Stockholders, usually consummately ignorant about the details of corporate policy and procedure, presume that their money will be used shrewdly and profitably. They probably are not too adverse to its illegal deployment, provided that such use is not discovered or, if discovered, is not penalized too heavily. It would seem that rousing fines against offending corporations will at least lead to stockholder retaliations against lax or offending managerial personnel, and will forewarn officials in other corporations that such derelictions are to be avoided if they expect to remain in their posts. The moral to widows dependent upon a steady income will be to avoid companies with criminal records; just as they are well advised to keep their money out of the grasp of other kinds of shady entrepreneurs and enterprises. Then, perhaps, sanctions against white-collar criminality can be built into the very structure of the market place itself.

What of corporate offenders themselves? The convicted violator might be barred from employment in the industry for a stipulated period of time, just as union leaders are barred from holding labor positions under similar circumstances.[39] All ex-convicts ought to be helped to achieve gainful employment, but surely nonexecutive positions can be found which would still be gainful. It has been noted that business executives in general enjoy the greatest material rewards available in the world today, and that the six-figure salaries at the top might be called "piratical" in any other sphere of activity.[40] A brief retirement by corporate officials from what in other forms of work is disparagingly called the "trough" does not seem to me to be an unreasonable imposition. Why put the fox immediately back in charge of the chicken coop? I recall some years ago the going joke at the Oklahoma State Penitentiary—that Nannie Doss, a woman who had a penchant for poisoning the food of her husbands, was going to be assigned duty as a mess-hall cook and then released to take a job in a short-order cafe. It was a macabre observation, except that similar things happen all the time with corporate criminals.

There have been suggestions that the penalties for corporate crime might be tailored to the nature of the offenses. Thus, the company president who insists that he had no knowledge of the crime could, if found culpable for negligent or criminal malfeasance, be sentenced to spend some time interning in the section of his organization from whence the violation arose. The difficulties inhere, of course, in the possibility of creating a heroic martyr rather than a rehabilitated official, and in problems relating to the logistics of the situation. Yet, veterans on major league baseball teams are dispatched to Class C clubs because of inadequate performance; they then attempt to work their way back to the top. The analogy is not precise, but the idea is worth further exploration.

The Issues of Deterrence

The evidence gleaned from the heavy electrical equipment case in 1961 represents our best information on the subject of deterrence of corporate crime; no antitrust prosecution of this magnitude has been attempted since, and very few had been undertaken earlier. Government attorneys were then convinced (I interviewed a number of them when I was gathering information on the subject for the President's Commission on Law Enforcement in 1966) that the 1961 antitrust prosecutions had been dramatically effective in breaking up price-fixing schemes by many other corporations. By 1966, however, they felt that the lesson had almost worn off. Senate hearings, conducted after the heavy electrical equipment conspirators had come out of jail, shed further light on the subject of deterrence. One witness before the Senate Antitrust and Monopoly Subcommittee who had done jail time stated with some certainty that he had learned his lesson well. "They would never get me to do it again. . . . I would starve before I would do it again," said the former General Electric executive.[41] Another man, from the same organization, was asked: "Suppose your superior tells you to resume the meetings; will they be resumed?" "No, sir," he answered with feeling. "I would leave the company rather than participate in the meetings again."[42]

These penitents were the same men who had earlier testified that price fixing was "a way of life" in their companies. They had not appreciated, they said, that what they were doing was criminal (though they never used *that* word; they always said "illegal"); and if *they* had not met with competitors, more willing and "flexible" replacements were available. They were men described by one of their attorneys in a bit of uncalculated irony as not deserving of jail sentences because they were not "cut-throat competitors," but rather persons who "devote much of their time and substance to the community."[43] O. Henry's Gentle Grafter, speaking for himself, had put it more succinctly: "I feel as if I'd like to do something for as well as to humanity."[44]

The corporate executives were model prisoners in the Montgomery County jail. The warden praised them as the best workers he had ever had on a project devoted to reorganizing the jail's record-keeping system. Thus, to the extent that they conduct themselves more honestly within the walls than they have outside, corporate offenders might be able to introduce modern business skills into our old-fashioned penal facilities. The imprisoned executives refused to have their families see them during the time, slightly less than a month, that they were jailed.[45] It was shame, of course, that made them so decide—shame, a sense of guilt, and injured pride. These are not the kinds of emotions a society ought cold-bloodedly and unthinkingly try to instill in people, criminals or not, *unless* it is found necessary to check socially destructive behavior.

What of the sanctions? That the corporations still felt the need to alibi and evade before the public was noteworthy for its implication that loss of goodwill, more than loss of money or even an agent or two, might be the sanction feared most. Note, for instance, the following verbal sleight of hand by General Electric about the case that involved flagrant criminal behavior. At its first annual meeting following the sentencing of the price-fixing conspirators, General Electric dismissed suggestions that further actions might be taken to cleanse itself. The idea, advanced by a stockholder, that the Company should retrieve sums paid to the conspirators as "incentive compensation" was said to "ignore the need for careful evaluation of a large number of factors." These factors—the expense of litigation and the morale of the organization—boiled down to a concern that "the best interests of the Company are served."[46] The president of Westinghouse demanded that employees adhere to the antitrust laws *not* because failure to do so was a crime or because it damaged the public. Rather, such behavior was discouraged because "any such action is—and will be considered to be—a deliberate act of disloyalty to Westinghouse."[47]

GE president Ralph Cordiner observed in 1961: "When all is said and done, it is impossible to legislate ethical conduct. A business enterprise must finally rely on individual character to meet the challenge of ethical responsibility." But by then the president had come to understand how the public might achieve what the Company could not: "Probably the strong example of the recent antitrust cases, and their consequences, will be the most effective deterrent against future violations," he decided.[48]

So the lesson had been learned—but only partly. It was much like the mother who scolds her children about stealing by saying that their behavior upsets her and might hurt the family's reputation in the neighborhood. After several such episodes, however, and a few prison terms or similarly strong sanctions against her offspring, she might suggest that a more compelling reasons for not stealing is that it is a criminal offense, and that when you get caught you are going to suffer for it. When such an attitude comes to prevail in the corporate world, we will have taken a major step toward deterring corporate crime and protecting its innocent victims.

Notes

1. My views on prison reform are set out in *Saturday Review* (December 11, 1971), pp. 47-48, 56.

2. President's Commission on Law Enforcement and Administration of Justice, *Crime and Its Impact—An Assessment* (Washington, D.C.: U.S. Government Printing Office, 1967), p. 104.

3. *New York Times* (December 27, 1971).

4. *Los Angeles Times* (May 11, 1971).

5. Ibid. Similarly, Nader has been quoted as saying, "If you want to talk about violence, don't talk of Black Panthers. Talk of General Motors." (Quoted in "White-Collar Crime," *Barron's*, March 30, 1970, p. 10.)

6. G. Christian Hill and Barbara Isenberg, "Documents Indicate 4 Beech Models Had Unsafe Fuel Tanks," *Wall Street Journal* (July 30, 1971), pp. 1, 6.

7. Ibid. See also *Warnick v. Beech Aircraft Corp.,* Orange County Superior Ct., File #174046 (Calif. 1971).

8. Ralph Nader, Foreword, to John Esposito, *Vanishing Air* (New York: Grossman, 1970), p. viii.

9. Nicholas Johnson, quoted in Morton Mintz and Jerry S. Cohen, *America, Inc.* (New York: Dial Press, 1971), p. 81.

10. Brooks Atkinson, *Broadway* (New York: MacMillan, 1970), pp. 315-316.

11. C. Wright Mills, *The Power Elite* (New York: Oxford University Press, 1970), p. 95.

12. James S. Turner, *The Chemical Feast* (New York: Grossman, 1970), p. 63.

13. Mark Green, et al., *The Closed Enterprise System* (mimeograph, 1971), p. 319.

14. *Sharon* (Pa.) *Herald* (February 8, 1961). Reprinted with permission.

15. *Supra* note 11, pp. 343-344.

16. Gay Talese, *Honor Thy Father* (New York: World, 1971). p. 479. Note also:

> Last year in Federal court in Manhattan . . . a partner in a stock brokerage firm pleaded guilty to an indictment charging him with $20 million in illegal trading with Swiss banks. He hired himself a prestigious lawyer, who described the offense in court as comparable to breaking a traffic law. Judge Irving Cooper gave the stockbroker a tongue lashing, a $30,000 fine and a suspended sentence.
>
> A few days later the same judge heard the case of an unemployed Negro shipping clerk who pleaded guilty to stealing a television set worth $100 from an interstate shipment in a bus terminal. Judge Cooper sentenced him to one year in jail.
>
> In fact, some judges don't think of white collar criminals as criminals, legal experts say.

Glynn Mapes, "A Growing Disparity in Criminal Sentences Troubles Legal Experts," *Wall Street Journal* (September 9, 1970).

17. Ronald Wraith and Edgar Simpkins, *Corruption in Developing Countries* (New York: W.W. Norton, 1964), pp. 65-70.

18. Geoffrey Gorer, "Modification of National Character: The Role of the Police in England," *Journal of Social Issues* 11 (1955), pp. 24-32.

19. It has been noted that the corruption of the robber baron days was more direct, and that officials made straight deals for big kickbacks and usually admitted they were wrong when caught. Now, it is claimed, the deals are comparatively small and oblique, and all proclaim innocence at the end. James Reston, "Washington: The Supreme Court and the Universities," *New York Times* (May 18, 1969).

20. Barbara W. Tuchman, *Stillwell and the American Experience in China* (New York: Macmillan, 1970), chap. 11.

21. Gunnar Myrdal, *An American Dilemma* (New York: Harper, 1944).

22. Joint Commission on Correctional Manpower and Training, *The Public Looks at Crime and Corrections,* February 1968, pp. 11-12.

23. "Changing Morality: The Two Americas," *Time* (June 6, 1969), p. 26.

24. E.A. Ross, "The Criminaloid," in ed. G. Geis, *White-Collar Criminal* (New York: Atherton, 1968), p. 36.

25. Quoted in Congressional Record, vol. 111, pt. 4 (March 10, 1965), p. 4631.

26. See generally Edwin M. Schur, *Crimes Without Victims* (Englewood Cliffs, N.J.: Prentice-Hall, 1965).

27. See, for example, Richard J. Bonnie and Charles H. Whitebread II, "The Forbidden Fruit and the Tree of Knowledge: An Inquiry Into the Legal History of Marihuana Prohibition," *Virginia Law Review* 971 (1970), p. 56.

28. Edwin H. Sutherland, *White Collar Crime* (New York: Dryden Press, 1949), pp. 222, 225.

29. Mary O. Cameron, *The Booster and the Snitch: Department Store Shoplifting* (New York: Free Press, 1964), pp. 160-162.

30. Ibid., p. 163.

31. Glanville Williams, *Criminal Law—The General Part,* 2nd edition (London: Stevens, 1961), p. 865.

32. U.S. Senate, Committee on the Judiciary, Subcommittee on Antitrust and Monopoly, *Administered Prices,* 87th Cong., 2nd Sess., 1961, pt. 28, pp. 17223-17232, 17287-17288.

33. Harrison Salisbury, *The 900 Days: The Siege of Leningrad* (New York: Avon, 1969), p. 445.

34. F. Scott Fitzgerald, *The Great Gatsby* in *Three Novels of F. Scott Fitzgerald* (New York: Scribners, 1925), pp. 180-181.

35. Max Lowenthal, *The Federal Bureau of Investigation* (New York: Sloane, 1950), p. 12.

36. *Time* (February 17, 1961), p. 84.

37. Harold C. Wilkenfield, "Comparative Study of Enforcement Policy in Israel, Italy, the Netherlands, the United Kingdom, and Other Countries" unpublished manuscript, Internal Revenue Service, October 7, 1965.

38. Paul R. Dixon, quoted in *New York Times* (February 10, 1966).

39. Joseph E. Finley, *Understanding the 1959 Labor Law* (Washington, D.C.: Public Affairs Institute, 1960), p. 24.

40. Hugh Crossland, "Confessions of a Business Dropout," *Wall Street Journal* (December 13, 1967).

41. U.S. Senate, *Administered Prices, supra* no. 32, pt. 27, p. 16790.

42. Ibid, p. 16694.

43. *New York Times* (February 7, 1961).

44. W.S. Porter, "The Chair of Philanthromathematics," in *The Gentle Grafter* (New York: McClure, 1908), p. 48.

45. *New York Times* (February 25, 1961).

46. General Electric Company, *Notice of Annual Meeting of Share Owners,* March 17, 1961, pp. 17-27.

47. *Sharon* (Pa.) *Herald* (February 12, 1961).

48. Ralph J. Cordiner, "Comments on the Electrical Antitrust Cases," at Ninth Annual Management Conference, Graduate School, University of Chicago, March 1, 1961, p. 9.

6 Upperworld Crime

Upperworld crime provides clues to a wide range of issues important to the understanding of criminal behavior and the relationship of such behavior to the social system in which it occurs. The study of upperworld crime is revealing in the following ways, among others:

1. Upperworld crime challenges the more banal kinds of explanations of criminal activity. To say that poverty "causes" crime, for instance, fails utterly to account for widespread lawbreaking by persons who are extraordinarily affluent.

2. Upperworld crime indicates the distribution of power in our society. An examination of statute books shows which kinds of occupational acts of the wealthy have come to be included within the criminal codes and which go unproscribed. The enactment of laws curbing the activities of certain classes of persons demonstrates that, at least for a time, other persons with other interests had the power to prevail legislatively.

3. Upperworld crime portrays the way in which power is used in our society. A review of upperworld violations, and the manner in which they are prosecuted and punished, tells who is able to accomplish what in American society.

4. Upperworld crime pinpoints elements of hypocrisy. It is hypocrisy, for instance, when fraud among the lower classes is punished by law while upper-class deception is dismissed as "shrewd business practice." Hypocrisy may be seen as leverage by means of which the society can be forced toward congruence between its verbal commitments on the one hand and its actual conduct on the other.[1]

5. Upperworld crime illustrates changes in social and business life. Thus the old-time grocer, dealing on a personal basis with his customers, may have had less inclination and less opportunity to defraud. Today's supermarkets, engaged essentially in the rental of shelf space to commodity manufacturers, epitomize commercial impersonality and its consequences for the emergence of upperworld crime in the form of consumer fraud.

6. Upperworld crime furnishes material helpful for an understanding of changes in social values. New laws demanding that foods be uncontaminated and that pollution be controlled reflect a belief that humans

should be accorded every reasonable opportunity to remain alive and healthy until cut down by uncontrollable forces. In the future, additional forms of upperworld crime will be declared, as support grows for enunciation of the right of each human being to achieve his or her full potential, as such potential comes to be defined.

There are, besides these, many other considerations associated with the study of upperworld crime—or, *white-collar crime,* as Edwin H. Sutherland first called it.[2] We can notice the use of rationalization by "respectable" persons as they struggle to maintain their self-esteem in the face of attempts to label them as criminals. We can watch responses in suburbia as "respectable" citizens strike a posture of self-righteous indignation over the disclosed depredations of their neighbors. We can also examine the impact of the traditional processes of criminal justice on the upperworld offender and determine, among other things, how constitutional guarantees won by the rapist and the robber are used by the corporate-class criminal conspirator. We can, in addition, consider the impact of punishment, especially incarceration, upon upper-class violators who are accustomed to think of prisons as places where "bad" people, and certainly none such as themselves, are deposited for safekeeping.

Defining Upperworld Crime

Difficulties in delineating with precision the realm of upperworld crime are a function of the problem of defining adequately the two components of the designation—*upperworld* and *crime.* We must therefore try to indicate when an act might reasonably be regarded as a crime and then attempt to draw some boundaries that will set off the upperworld from the rest of the world.

When Is a Crime a Crime?

It needs to be noted, initially, that it is perfectly reasonable to provide any definition that one chooses for terms, so long as what is being discussed is clearly specified. The goal, however, ought to be a definitional state of grace that will move others to exploration of the same concept; otherwise, one is apt to be engaged in an idiosyncratic and dead-end enterprise. It is possible, for example, to maintain that the rate of infant mortality in the United States is so shocking (as indeed it is, with this country as far back as thirteenth in international statistics) that every member of the medical profession must stand convicted of criminal negligence. Such a position, I would maintain, makes fine polemics but rather bad social science. For one thing, there is (however unfortunately) no law against the inadequate diffusion of medical services. For another, it would be impossible to demonstrate that all doctors have acted with the intent to violate standards that might be designed to punish those responsible for the death of so many infants before their first birthday. There is a further difficulty. If all doctors can be regarded as criminal because of the infant mortality rate, then presumably all citizens, by the same stroke of semantic justice, could be said to have been criminal because of the Vietnam War, or because of some similar event whose perpetration offends us. If the concept of crime is going to have discriminatory and analytical strength, it will have to be tied more firmly to a set of delimited criteria.

I would maintain that the label *upperworld criminal* ought to be confined to persons who commit acts in violation of criminal statutes, that is, statutes designated by lawmakers as criminal and providing for fines, terms of imprisonment, or similar disabling penalties. I would reject the over-delicate stipulation of Paul Tappan that to be an upperworld criminal a person must be *convicted* of such violations.[3] It seems unreasonable to maintain that an unapprehended armed robber or an undiscovered antitrust violator, for instance, is not a criminal. Under such rules, only the more unlucky or the more inept fit the category, rather than all who have engaged in the stipulated behavior. Tappan's concern, of course, was that the opprobrium of the social epithet *criminal* not be loosely attached to persons innocent of violation of the criminal law. This concern, certainly an important one, can be met by stipulating clearly that unconvicted persons designated criminal may not be legally guilty of the offense alleged against them. It should be noted, in turn, that convicted criminals might not in fact be guilty of the offenses for which judgment was pronounced against them.

This kind of dictum, however, addresses but one aspect of the definitional dilemma. What about upperworld acts that could be prosecuted as criminal violations but are handled by other adjudicatory and punitive methods? The issue here is intricate, but some resolution might again be obtained by reference to the procedures employed with more traditional kinds of offenses. It seems clear, for instance, that Al Capone might reasonably have been regarded as a person performing acts classifiable under the heading of organized crime. Yet Capone's major criminal conviction was not for extortion or for murder, both acts that it seems highly likely he committed, but for income tax violation. This, too, was of course a criminal conviction. But suppose Capone had been dealt with instead under civil law. I would argue that he still might reasonably have been considered a key member of a group engaging in the patterned form of behavior known as organized crime, and that his activities in organized crime included extortion and murder as well as income tax evasion. In the same manner, upperworld offenders who are handled, because of administrative decisions, by means other than criminal statutes—though such statutes might have been employed—can be regarded as upperworld criminals.

It is true, of course, that the administrative decisions are neither whimsical nor haphazard (though, on occasion, they may be both) but represent, rather, the considered judgment of the relevant government agency regarding the offense and the offender and a variety of other factors. The basis for such judgment should be part of the criminologist's analytical material, and it seems perfectly proper to second-guess the administrators. After all, such second-guessing is routine among administrators themselves. Shifts in internal power, and changes in the coloration of political leadership, can mean the sudden movement of cases from criminal to civil categories as well as their total elimination from court or administrative agency calendars. For the criminologist, the problem should be this: "Such an act, being considered part of the category of upperworld crime, fits the definition of criminal activity in the statutes. The act apparently was not so prosecuted because . . . " The *because* might be that the person in authority, believing the behavior under review to be negligible, decided that justice would be better served by ignoring the matter, just as the officer on the street may decide to ignore behaviors that violate laws defining juvenile delinquency.[4] Perhaps the explanation is more invidious, and based on political, social, or economic favoritism. But since the law exists, I think we may reasonably classify the person violating it as an upperworld criminal, though we should look further to determine why in fact he was not officially so classified. We could also attempt to differentiate between those who are acted against officially and those who are treated more benignly. In such a manner, we may gain insight into the wellsprings of power and decision making that lie at the heart of the criminal justice system—and should be at the core of criminological study.

What may we say, then, about acts not outlawed by criminal statutes but seemingly harmful to individuals and/or the social system, acts that are engaged in deliberately (perhaps even diabolically) by members of the upperworld who are aware of the detrimental consequences of their behavior? Acts such as—the selection depends upon one's political and social viewpoints—writing advertising copy for cigarettes, manufacturing automobiles with built-in obsolescence, mercilessly harassing one's wife or husband, or endlessly haranguing one's children? Or, perhaps, giving examinations to college classes that cause "irreparable" damage to the self-esteem of students?

It seems to me that we will slide into definitional quicksand if we include such behaviors—on such grounds—as part of the realm of upperworld crime. For one thing—and a very important thing—the perpetrators of the acts cannot be aware of official definitions of their behavior as criminal (since no such definitions exist) and therefore cannot bring to the acts that state of mind required for most (though, it should be said, not for all) criminal acts. For another thing, there seems little chance of achieving agreement among investigators regarding the kinds of acts that ought to be included within such amorphous categories as infliction of "social injury" or "personal harm." It should be of concern to the sociologist and to the political scientist to determine why particular acts are not included in the criminal statutes despite an inherent element of harm. But it must be remembered that the reasons for such omissions are multifarious. For instance, certain acts universally regarded as vile and reprehensible may not fall under criminal law because the criminal law is not seen as an effective weapon for dealing with them. It is also true that they may be omitted because of more nefarious reasons, such as bribery of legislators or social brainwashing brought about by massive advertising campaigns.

It may be observed, in this connection, that no law lies against failure to warn a blind man that he is about to walk off a cliff, even if the onlooker can easily do so without any risk to his own safety. (The onlooker would be liable if he were related to the blind man, had an agreement to protect him, or had previously undertaken to forewarn him against danger.) We might want to know what components of the power system, what elements of the democratic ethos, and indeed, what requirements of criminal justice procedure have led to the exclusion of behavior such as this from the criminal law. And we might want to determine what interests appear to be served by allowing high infant mortality rates, deficient automobiles, and detrimental advertising to exist beyond the concern of criminal statutes. This would appear to be about as far as the boundaries of criminology might legitimately be extended. For criminologists going much further, the danger is that they will be neither adequate social scientists nor responsible citizens if they are not excruciatingly clear as to just what they are about and what criteria they are using to select material and to reach conclusions.

Criminologists may of course, if they choose, insist that car manufacturers ought to be considered upperworld criminals because of their failure to go beyond their legal responsibility in adopting safety precautions. Or they may maintain that legislators ought to be regarded as upperworld criminals for their failure to proscribe various car manufacturing techniques. But criminologists taking such a line should not be surprised if others, for their part, regard *them* as persons who ought to be called upperworld criminals for their failure to stay within the bounds of fair comment and to observe fundamental due process principles, even though the accusations no more violate the criminal law than do the acts of those used as object lessons.

The heart of such definitional problems lies in the fact that criminology, by its very name, deals with behaviors that, once they are included in its realm, brand their perpetrators with a label carrying derogatory connotations. The aim of social justice would seem to be to see to it that all persons performing similarly objectionable acts share equivalently in the label. The pinning of the label, however, is a function of the power system of the society, and criminology, by accepting the official labels in part (though not necessarily altogether), reinforces such labels. A partial saving grace is that power in the United States, however ill-distributed, can be a multifaceted phenomenon. And however ill-distributed power might be, some room tends to be allowed for dissent and reform efforts; otherwise, we would not be discussing abuses by the powerful. It might be argued, however, that our discourse is only permitted by those in control because they know that such efforts to change things in any significant way are likely to be ineffectual and are little more than cathartic flailing exercises and verbal jousts.[5]

What Part of the World Is the Upperworld?

For Sutherland, white-collar crime was defined "approximately" as "a crime committed by a person of respectability and high social status in the course of his occupation,"[6] a definition posing a number of analytical problems. Consider, for example, the crimes of two corporate managers, one respected, the other not (say the second is a former organized crime boss, now gone righteous, but still far from country club material). Both might commit the same offense—perhaps an antitrust violation—in the course of their occupation. One of the violators presumably would satisfy Sutherland regarding his credentials as a bona fide white-collar criminal; the second, lacking respectability, apparently would not. Thus it is neither the action nor the particular statute that has been violated that is the reference point for classification but, rather, the social position of the actor. It seems to me, in this regard, unrewarding to differentiate between, say, income tax violators in the more "respectable" segments of society and income tax violators in the less "respectable" segments of the society; it is, indeed, odd to do so if, as could happen, both groups cheated in similar amounts on their returns.

Indeed, Sutherland's most extensive discussion of his concept of white-collar crime is, as has been observed, a "model of obfuscation:"[7]

> Perhaps it should be repeated that "white-collar" (upper) and "lower" classes merely designate persons of high- and low-socioeconomic status. Income and amount of money involved in the crime are not the sole criteria. Many persons of "low" socioeconomic status are "white-collar" criminals in the sense that they are well-dressed, well-educated, and have high incomes; but "white-collar" as used in this paper means "respected," "socially accepted and approved," "looked up to." Some people in this class may not be well-dressed or well-educated or have high incomes,

although the "upper" classes usually exceed the "lower" classes in these respects, as well as in social status."[8]

In this chapter, the term *upperworld* is meant as no more than a very rough contrast to *underworld.* It points at a group of people engaged in a variety of acts contrary to the law; in this sense, the term is used as a publicist or a muckraker would use it. It is employed to call attention to a wide range of lawbreaking that usually escapes public attention and indignation, and to persuade that such offenses as advertising fraud, antitrust violation, and water pollution ought to be regarded as serious crimes; their perpetrators ought to suffer the public indignity of the label *criminal* and ought to benefit or suffer from whatever action appears necessary and reasonable to bring them within the ranks of the law-abiding.

Most fundamentally, in respect to upperworld crime, we are interested in various *offenses,* regardless of who commits them. These offenses mostly are perpetrated by persons who, because of their position in the social structure, have been able to obtain specialized kinds of occupational slots and/or skills essential for their commission. Thus anybody with the physiological capacity can murder, but only a limited number of persons are in a position to violate the antitrust laws. Dentists and carpenters, Rotary Club members and ministers, as well as the unemployed can (and sometimes do) commit forcible rape, but to violate the statute forbidding pollution of navigable waters with factory refuse it is necessary to have some decision-making power within a factory.

To repeat, the term *upperworld* is not a scientific criminological designation but rather a label designed to call attention to the violation of a variety of criminal statutes by persons who at the moment generally are not considered, in connection with such violations, to be the "usual" kind of underworld and/or psychologically aberrant offenders. Such persons often possess a number of qualities that differentiate them from violators of other statutes, just as burglars tend in some ways to be different from murderers. But we lack sufficient information to discern a persistent patterning among them; and we have yet to uncover an interlocking array of circumstances of sufficient homogeneity to merit a separate criminological nomenclature to embrace these upperworld offenders and their offenses. Nor do we really have enough useful information about individual kinds of upperworld crimes. Someday, however, we undoubtedly will be able to devote major criminological attention to polluters and to misrepresenters, in the same manner that we now attend to such offenders as robbers and arsonists. We likewise soon should be able to formulate patterns for what might be called *occupational crime, economic crime,* or *corporate crime*—patterns that will provide us with the same level of insight as the study of such entities as professional crime and organized crime.

Consequences of Upperworld Crime

In spite of the prod supplied by Sutherland's pioneering work, upperworld crime long remained a relatively neglected area of criminological investigation. One reason appears to be that criminological research is done primarily by sociologists, who tend to have sparse training in economics and law and hence find the intricacies of upperworld business manipulations difficult to comprehend. In more recent years, however, with the growing politicalization of sociology, upperworld crime has come in for greater attention, as sociologists have become more willing to attack entrenched interests and to buttress their attacks with studies of criminal activity by such interests. In particular, attention is now being paid to the consequences of upperworld crime, such as (1) financial costs; (2) social costs, including ghetto distress, political turmoil, and public cynicism; and (3) spin-off costs—for example, rationalization of their crimes by lower-class offenders, who say that unpunished lawbreaking is endemic in the upper classes.

Detailing Recent Developments

Behavioral science work on upperworld crime was further spurred by the Vietnam War protests and by the Watergate scandals. Vietnam seriously undermined unquestioning acceptance of the wisdom and well-meaning nature of government actions and the logic of official proclamations defending such actions. Watergate spotlighted lawbreaking, chicanery, lying, and deceit at the highest levels of the political structure. Both Vietnam and Watergate were effectively challenged, largely by persons and groups without official standing or strong power bases: the student movement in the case of Vietnam, and investigative journalists in the case of Watergate. The potential for useful social critique and social reform was made more promising. The result has been greater focus on upperworld crime during the past five years than throughout the previous twenty-five.

This work has been spurred also by revelations of blatant disregard by powerful persons and by huge corporations of the health and safety of consumers and the general public. The Three-Mile Island nuclear reactor leakage in Pennsylvania in 1979 alerted people to the possible carcinogenic consequences of energy-producing plants if adequate safeguards are not maintained because of government or company negligence or malfeasance. Indeed, the leakage raised the fundamental question of whether a press for corporate profits was instrumental in the construction of nuclear plants that are inherently likely to wreak lethal damage at some time or other. Frauds against government health programs appeared to be almost endemic. Unnecessary surgery, said to be done for the fees involved, is believed to lead to thousands of avoidable deaths of patients, and some critics have equated such medical acts to manslaughter. The Equity Funding scandal[9] highlighted the new threat of computers. Employers and employees in the commercial world can manipulate access to such new technology to reap huge gains at the expense of the public. In 1979, an Indiana indictment of the Ford Motor Company for reckless homicide in regard to the manufacture of allegedly unsafe automobiles, based on the charge that the company had permitted the Pinto model "to remain on Indiana highways, knowing full well its defects," pointed to increasing recourse to newer forms of criminal law to reach ends defined as socially protective. Previously, under older common law, corporations could not be charged with crimes against the person, such as homicide.

In the first thoroughgoing update of Sutherland's work, Marshall Clinard and Peter Yeager examined federal administrative, civil, and criminal actions taken against the 624 largest American corporations and their subsidiaries during a two-year period. It was found that a majority of the corporations suffered such actions, and that the failing fiscal health of an organization seemed to be related to the likelihood that it would violate the law—or at least, that it would be caught in such a violation.[10]

The task of Clinard and Yeager was aided by the fact that the Freedom of Information Act of 1974 permits access to a good deal of data about corporations that previously was not available to researchers. On the other hand, it remains true that the corporate world is largely inaccessible to scrutiny. Tom Wicker, a *New York Times* columnist, has noted that the huge corporations are the most glaring example of contemporary institutional forces that have been "little scrutinized and mostly unchallenged in print or on the airwaves."[11] The absence of satisfactory mass media coverage of corporations is particularly troublesome if one agrees with Tawney's observation that "the man who employs governs. He occupies what is really a public office."[12]

Costs of Upperworld Crime

Estimating the cost of any type of crime is a hazardous undertaking. For one thing, it is difficult to decide what shall be included and what omitted from the balance sheet. For another, there are factors such as emotional harm and pain and suffering that do not readily translate into financial terms.

The early suggestion by Sutherland that, in the United States, the financial cost of upperworld crime is probably several times greater than the cost of all crimes customarily regarded as the "crime problem" is probably as accurate as any estimate is apt to be. Sutherland pointed out that an officer of a chain grocery store embezzled $600,000 in one year, or six times more than the losses that chain suffered during the year from burglaries and robberies.[13]

There are far subtler costs of upperworld crime, however, than those calculable in dollars and cents. British historian Arnold J. Toynbee, for instance, has asserted that modern advertising (at least some of which undoubtedly violates criminal statutes) represents a greater threat to Western civilization than totalitarianism. Advertising, Toynbee insists, has forced Americans to waste ability, time, and resources in obtaining goods "we should never have dreamed of wanting if left to ourselves."[14]

It illustrates the power of advertising that national brands of aspirin—an item where one brand is basically the same as another—are able to sell at considerably higher prices than local products only because, as Donald Turner, former chief of the antitrust division of the Department of Justice, has noted, "producers have convinced a large number of consumers that their product is different."[15] Undertaking a more overt kind of deception, the advertising agency for the Libbey-Owens-Ford Glass Company once attempted to show the difference between the company's safety plate glass and sheet glass by filming television commercials through an open or rolled down automobile window instead of through the advertiser's product.[16]

To control advertising, as demanded by a growing reaction against upperworld excess, the federal government now can require advertisers to provide proof of product claims. The need for such a requirement was pointed out by Ralph Nader and an associate, who mentioned that only three out of fifty-eight companies had chosen to respond to a request for documentation of advertising claims, such as that by Ralston Purina that "good" dogs had selected their product "six to one in a recent test."[17]

In a more general sense, the consequences of upperworld crime are suggested by an assistant United States district attorney in the Fraud Division: He believes that people should be able to trust one another and they should know that laws designed to punish those who abuse trust are being enforced effectively. Otherwise, he maintains, "everything starts falling apart."[18]

Upperworld crime may also create anger among persons who find themselves deprived of what they regard as the essentials for decent living, while all about them they hear reports of dishonesty and exploitation by those in positions of power. The National Commission on Causes and Prevention of Violence spoke of a pervasive suspicion among the poor that "personal greed and corruption are prevalent among even the highest public officials."[19] C. Wright Mills made the same point, noting the casual way in which Americans react to upperworld crime:

> Many of the problems of "white-collar" crime and of relaxed public morality, of high-priced vice and of fading personal integrity, are problems of structural immorality. They are not merely the problem of the small character twisted by the bad milieu. And many people are at least vaguely aware that this is so.[20]

A term used by Al Capone sums up the underworld view of upper-world criminal activities. They are, Capone said, "the legitimate rackets." An articulate explanation of how one professional thief views upperworld "rackets" is found in the comments of Robert Allerton:

> Take the case of a jeweler. He's a businessman, and he's in the game to make money. O.K., so I'm a business man too, and I'm also out to make money. We just use different methods. The jeweler makes a profit—and often a very big profit—out of what he sells. On top of that he fiddles the income tax and the purchase tax, and even the customs duty if he can get away with it. That's considered all right by him and others like him, and if he makes enough to buy himself a big house and posh car everyone looks up to him as a clever fellow, a shrewd business man. But how's he got his money? By rooking people, taking advantage of soft young couples getting engaged to sell them a more expensive ring than they can afford, and fiddling the authorities whenever he can. But at least he didn't steal it. Well, what's in a name? Tell me exactly where the line is between thieving and "shrewd business" and I might believe it. What's more, the jeweler can insure himself against people like me going and pinching his stock. But I can't insure against the police nicking me. The Law's on one side only, the side of the pretenders, that's all.[21]

Consumerism: The Work of Nader's Raiders

At least two factors, sometimes present in combination, can be recognized in the social malaise generated by upperworld crime: (1) moral outrage over the violation of fundamental principles of human decency[22] and (2) jealousy that others are commanding more of the wherewithal of the society. Little research has been directed toward the kinds of social climates in which attention tends to be paid to upperworld crime. It is possible that such concern goes in cycles, recurring when things get badly out of hand, then abating until a later crisis arises. Or perhaps affluence and leisure are directly related to the growth of social concern with exploitative behavior by socially entrenched persons. Certainly, an element of security from decimating reprisal must be present before reform movements can make headway.

Whatever its source, concern with upperworld crime seems to be at a high point in the United States today. Such concern undoubtedly is epitomized by the work of Ralph Nader, head of the Center for the Study of Responsive Law—a group known in the vernacular as Nader's Raiders. "The real challenge," one of Nader's associates has said when describing the group's work, "is going into a courtroom against a corporation and having the establishment's own judge come down on your side and say the other guy is wrong. That does more to shake up the corporate structure than destroying some buildings."[23]

Investigation by a Nader study group of the work of the Food and Drug Administration (FDA) demonstrates how the Raiders come to grips with upperworld offenses. They rely primarily on (1) research, (2) use of legal processes, and (3) publicity. The legal process is employed, for instance, to make certain that the investigators are given access to relevant materials. Research undergirds their case, and publicity hits at the upperworld's special sensitivity to notoriety.[24]

The Nader teams work on the premise that industry will take advantage of virtually any opportunity to exploit the consuming public, and will desist from such exploitation only when forced to do so by governmental organizations goaded into action by the pressure of public opinion. The focus of the Nader work, therefore, has been on documentation of the failure of federal and state regulatory agencies to control practices that Congress gave them the power to regulate.

The Nader survey of the FDA begins with an overview of the food industry, which, according to Nader, has become concentrated into "fewer and fewer corporate hands," with the following result:

> The competition, such as it is, has focused heavily on massive promotional expenditures (between 16 and 18 percent of gross revenues), on brand-name identification, wasteful nonprice competition, and other marketing expenses that do not provide added value for the consumer but simply increases food prices. In addition, the food companies have one of the tiniest research budgets (for nutrition and food quality) of any United States industry.[25]

The probe into the work of the FDA, conducted largely by college students and recent graduates, found that rather than launch campaigns against major firms that routinely break the law, the FDA pursues small and inconsequential violators so as to give the appearance of activity and produce a record of successful prosecution while allowing major depredators to proceed unmolested. Even when successful the FDA is said to be hampered by an archaic penalty structure.[26]

Nonetheless, the Nader team was not convinced that it was limited enforcement power that primarily hamstrung the FDA; if the FDA allowed the public to be bilked, the cause was its own apathy and indifference. "As long as the FDA believes that the food industry wishes to provide the safest, highest-quality food possible to the American people," the team concluded, "no amount of legislation, manpower, or money will turn the agency into an effective food regulator." The Nader group found the FDA's faith in the industrial self-regulation "ludicrous, if not tragic." The food industry, it insisted, "has vigorously set about its task of making profits." Therefore it was time that the FDA set about "its assigned task of insuring that profits made by the food industry are not the result of fraud, deception, adulteration, or misbranding.'' Otherwise, the public interest would continue to be mauled by the food industry's "callousness, ignorance, and greed."[27]

In some measure because of the work of Nader and his associates, the number of acts defined as upperworld crime has grown considerably in recent years. Nader's book *Unsafe at Any Speed*[28]—developed from a third-year paper written while he was a student at the Harvard Law School—was instrumental in bringing about passage of the National Traffic and Motor Vehicle Safety Act of 1966. A year later, national legislation was passed to insure that the states come up to federal meat inspection standards, so that the public might be protected from so-called 4-D meat—meat derived from dead, dying, disabled, or diseased animals. Testimony by federal meat inspectors told of packing plants where "abscessed beef and pork livers and parasitic infected livers were mixed with edible products" and where meat was dragged across floors on which there were vermin droppings. The Fair Packaging and Labeling Act went into effect in mid-1968, and by the following year it was reported that, among other things, the number of different kinds of packages for toothpaste had been reduced from fifty-seven to five, and of peanut butter from twenty-nine to twelve.[29] Today, particular attention is being focused on criminalizing such things as air and water pollution, unsafe noise conditions, reckless disposal of hazardous chemicals, and dangerous workplace conditions. In the political realm, new laws strive to reduce conflicts of interest and to control influence peddling.

Upperworld Crime and the Criminal Justice System

One of the difficulties that the criminal justice system in the United States faces in dealing with upperworld offenders is that there is a monetary price on justice, so that, to some extent, justice can be bought. The wealthier the defendant, the more apt he is to command resources permitting him to bring about a judicial conclusion favorable to his interests.[30] As Solon noted very long ago, "laws are like cobwebs, for if any trifling or powerless thing fell into them, they held it fast; while if it were somewhat weightier, it broke through them and was off."[31]

"Justice delayed is justice denied," a federal attorney has noted in regard to what seemed an endlessly postponed trial of an affluent upperworld criminal. "That's what they say about the junkies, but not about these guys."[32] In court, the upperworld offender presents an appearance that helps shield him against the more severe sentence that might be given to a defendant who looks "disreputable." Another consideration, of course, is that upperworld criminals usually do not represent a recidivistic threat. If they are embezzlers, for instance, they are not again likely to obtain positions of financial trust for further defalcations. Besides, they are apt to be

older persons, whose attorneys tell the court that two years in the penitentiary—given the background and sensitivity of their client—would be
equivalent to a death sentence. Another difficulty involved in prosecuting
upperworld criminals is victim embarrassment at being duped.[33]

Even when imprisoned, upperworld offenders are apt to be sent to the
cozier kinds of institutions, those in which security is minimum, since they
are not considered escape threats. Thus, for a federal offense, the upperworld criminal is likely to go to the penitentiary at Lewisburg, Pennsylvania,
the traditional offender to the penitentiary at Lorton, Virginia. The difference? "I'd much rather serve two years at Lewisburg," says a federal
prosecutor, "than two months at Lorton."[34]

The irony of disproportionately lighter sentences for upperworld crime
lies in the fact that upperworld offenders seem to be a good deal more responsive to tougher penalties than their underworld counterparts. For this
reason, tough sentences against discovered upperworld criminals would
seem to be particularly effective deterrents to potential offenders. "The imposition of jail sentences," the President's Commission on Law Enforcement and Administration of Justice noted in regard to upperworld crime,
"may be the only way adequately to symbolize society's condemnation of
the behavior in question. . . . And jail may be the only sanction available
which will serve as an adequate deterrent."[35] These views are corroborated
by the experience of the director of the Fraud Division of the Department of
Justice, who noted that "similar sentences in a few cases each decade would
almost completely cleanse our economy of the cancer of collusive price fixing, and the mere prospect of such sentences is itself the strongest available
deterrent to such activities."[36]

To argue that indications of the deterrent value of prison terms justify
"unreasonable" sentences for upperworld offenders is like arguing that the
more sensitive rapist ought to be given a longer sentence than the callous
one because he seems more likely to be responsive to the aim of reform
through incarceration. But it is noteworthy that the social response that
might be more effective with upperworld offenders and offenses is the one
least employed.

There appears to be an urgent need, if upperworld offenses are to be
subject to the same obloquy as the more traditional kinds of violations, for
the public to come to regard upperworld offenses and offenders in terms of
stronger abhorrence.

Criminology of Upperworld Crime

The study of upperworld crime has been the precursor of the contemporary
swing of criminology toward more penetrating investigation of the political

processes by which certain behaviors become defined as criminal. Studies of such offenders as robbers and rapists were apt to concentrate on individual psyches and to reflect what Schur saw in criminology as "a general disdain of political, economic, and historical considerations."[37]

Upperworld crime, however, cannot very readily be analyzed in terms of its participants and their psychological experiences. For one thing, the upperworld offender, not being imprisoned or otherwise readily accessible, usually is unavailable for direct investigation. Thus such data as his I.Q. and his responses to items on an investigator's inventory are lacking. In addition, the usual psychiatric explanations for traditional crime are patently inappropriate for upperworld offenses.

Partly out of necessity, therefore, explanations for upperworld crime have focused on the value system of the society and upon the processes through which certain kinds of behavior come to be singled out for attention by the system of criminal justice. This line of inquiry has led to a reexamination of social values and to repudiation of the common, and rather banal, causal explanations of criminal activity. The absence of tabulations of upperworld crime in the FBI's *Uniform Crime Reports* is characteristic. To date, upperworld crime remains too loosely defined, inadequately investigated, and inexpertly assessed in regard to causality and consequences. But in large part because of its failure to fit readily into earlier molds of definition and explanation, growing attention to upperworld crime is today rejuvenating the entire study of criminal behavior.

Notes

1. See Gunnar Myrdal, *An American Dilemma* (New York: Harper, 1944).

2. Edwin H. Sutherland, "White-Collar Criminality," *American Sociological Review*, 5 (February 1940), pp. 1-12. All quotes reprinted with permission.

3. Paul W. Tappan, "Who is the Criminal?" *American Sociological Review*, 12 (February 1947), pp. 96-102.

4. Suzanne Weaver, *Decision to Prosecute: Organization and Public Policy in the Antitrust Division* (Cambridge, Mass.: MIT Press, 1977); Nathan Goldman, *The Differential Selection of Juvenile Offenders for Court Appearance* (New York: National Research and Information Center, National Council on Crime and Delinquency, 1963), pp. 17-22.

5. David M. Gordon, "Capitalism, Class, and Crime in America," *Crime and Delinquency*, 19 (April 1973), pp. 163-168.

6. Edwin H. Sutherland, *White Collar Crime* (New York: Dryden Press, 1949).

7. Virginia S. Lewis, "A Theoretical Critique of the White-Collar Crime Concept," unpublished master's essay, California State College, Los Angeles, 1970, p. 6.

8. Sutherland, "White-Collar Criminality," p. 4.

9. William E. Blundell, "Equity Funding: I Did It for the Jollies," in eds. John M. Johnson and Jack D. Douglas, *Crime at the Top* (Philadelphia: Lippincott, 1978), pp. 153-185.

10. The final report has not yet been published. A preliminary statement appears in Marshall B. Clinard and Peter C. Yeager, "Corporate Crime," *Criminology*, 16 (August 1978), pp. 255-272.

11. Tom Wicker, *On Press* (New York: Viking, 1978), p. 17.

12. Ross Terrill, *R.H. Tawney and His Times* (London: André Deutsch, 1973), p. 46.

13. Sutherland, "White-Collar Criminality," pp. 4-5.

14. *United Press International* (June 11, 1961).

15. *New York Times* (February 8, 1967).

16. *Associated Press* (March 1, 1960); see further Arthur A. Leff, *Swindling and Selling* (New York: Free Press, 1976).

17. *Wall Street Journal* (December 14, 1970).

18. Quoted in Harvey Katz, "The White Collar Criminal," *Washingtonian Magazine*, 5 (May 1970), p. 65.

19. *To Establish Justice, to Insure Domestic Tranquility*, National Commission on the Causes and Prevention of Violence (New York: Bantam 1970), pp. 57-58.

20. C. Wright Mills, *The Power Elite* (New York: Oxford University Press, 1956), pp. 343-344.

21. Tony Parker and Robert Allerton, *The Courage of His Convictions* (New York: Norton, 1962), pp. 98-99.

22. John C. Watkins, Jr., "White-Collar Crimes, Legal Sanctions, and Social Control," *Crime and Delinquency*, 23 (July 1977), pp. 290-303.

23. James S. Turner, quoted in *Wall Street Journal* (November 19, 1970).

24. See, generally, Francis E. Rourke, "Law Enforcement Through Publicity," *University of Chicago Law Review* 24 (Winter 1967), pp. 225-255.

25. Ralph Nader, Foreword, to James S. Turner, *The Chemical Feast* (New York: Grossman, 1970), p. vii.

26. Turner, *The Chemical Feast*, p. 63.

27. Ibid., pp. 85-86.

28. Ralph Nader, *Unsafe at Any Speed* (New York: Grossman, 1965).

29. *New York Times* (March 9, 1969).

30. August Bequai, "White-Collar Crime: A Losing War," *Case & Comment*, 82 (September-October 1977), p. 10.

31. Diogenes Laertius, *Lives of Eminent Philosophers*, trans. R.D. Hicks (Cambridge, Mass.: Harvard University Press, 1959), vol. 1, p. 59. Solon's words, slightly paraphrased, find their way into the mouth of Daniel Drew, "a pious old fraud," in Sutherland's *White Collar Crime*, p. 47.

32. *Washington Post* (November 2, 1969).

33. Ralph Ogden, quoted in Katz, "White Collar Criminal," p. 62.

34. Ibid., p. 64.

35. *Crime and Its Impact—An Assessment*, President's Commission on Law Enforcement and Administration of Justice (Washington, D.C.: U.S. Government Printing Office, 1967), p. 105.

36. Gordon B. Spivak, "Antitrust Enforcement in the United States: A Primer," *Connecticut Bar Journal*, 37 (September 1963), p. 382.

37. Edwin M. Schur, "Theory, Planning, and Pathology," *Social Problems*, 6 (Winter 1958-1959), p. 227.

7

The Psychology of the White-Collar Offender

Robert F. Meier and
Gilbert Geis

In 1941, two thirds of the nation's industrial assets were held by the country's one thousand largest corporations; by 1971, this same proportion was held by two hundred corporations.

Between 1969 and 1971, sales by the nation's largest corporations increased 12.5 percent, but employment in these companies dropped by 5.2 percent.

In 1969, the corporate share of the federal income tax was about 35 percent; it fell to about 26 percent in 1972.[1]

Such results might have occurred as the consequence of perfectly normal, and legal, business practices. But the foregoing facts document the enormous concentration of wealth and power in our society today. That power offers opportunities for abuse by persons who make decisions in the corporate world. It is the criminality of such persons—as well as the criminal behavior of other affluent and successful people—that constitutes the subject-matter of this chapter.

There are two noteworthy characteristics of literature on white-collar crime. First, in line with the interests of Ralph Nader and other consumer advocates, the aim is to identify and to control acts, not to analyze and understand their dynamics. Second, there has been a conspicuous absence of sociological and social-psychological theory to guide and orient questions for white-collar crime research.

"Correcting" White-Collar Crime

The correctional expert is informed and motivated by the purpose of ridding society of deviance. In his discussion of correctionalism, David Matza observed: "The correctional perspective is reasonable enough, perhaps even commendable, except that it makes empathy and understanding difficult and sometimes impossible."[2]

Modern correctionalism permeates the work of Ralph Nader. The most explicit example occurs in his foreword to the papers presented at the Conference on Corporate Responsiblity in Washington, D.C., in 1971:

> We have long been familiar with the often adverse ways corporations affect people, but specific structural remedies to correct corporate abuses have not been forthcoming. The aim of the conference and therefore this book is to push beyond diagnosis to prescription, to emphasize not merely what is wrong, but ways to right it.[3]

An associate of Nader, Mark Green, addressed the same theme when he asked, "How does government enforcement actually work—or not? And, if not, why not?"[4]

These issues have become identified as *the* issues with respect to white-collar crime today. And it was precisely the same kinds of issues that initially were identified and articulated by the pioneers in criminology who began looking at white-collar crime a quarter of a century ago.

Although Edwin H. Sutherland, the originator of the term *white-collar crime*, is not generally thought to be a muckraker in his approach to the subject, his work on closer scrutiny fits into the genre in certain respects. Karl Schuessler, one of Sutherland's former graduate students, has noted that " . . . Sutherland was concerned with a scientific criminology that might, because of its capacity for prediction, have some practical value for purposes of social engineering."[5] For Sutherland, any potential conflict between these values was resolved by regarding them as compatible means to the same end: the advancement of scientific criminology was seen as advancing the control of crime. Sutherland was willing to merge scientific and correctional issues, but he was aware that others did not share his viewpoint. He therefore took utmost pains to disclaim anything other than a scientific approach to his subject. In the first sentences of the preface to his monograph he says:

> This book is a study in the theory of criminal behavior. It is an attempt to reform the theory of criminal behavior, not to reform anything else. Although it might have implications for social reform, social reforms are not the objective of the book.[6]

Sutherland's major research contribution on professional theft was more sympathetic to the offender than his view of white-collar crime.[7] While not condoning theft, Sutherland clearly was intrigued by it. Jon Snodgrass has observed, "Sutherland seemed to have a quiet admiration and genuine respect for professional thieves. He tended to ennoble their occupation."[8] Sutherland's appreciation for professional thieves, however, does not extend to his attitudes regarding white-collar and corporate offenders.

Over time, Sutherland came to regard white-collar criminals as the upper-world counterparts of professional thieves. In both groups, Sutherland maintained, illegal activity was an integral part of occupational effort, and for both groups there was no loss of prestige among colleagues because of criminal involvement. Both sets of activities also required considerable training, tutelage, and specialized skill. There was, however, a significant difference between professional theft and white-collar criminality, a difference that shifts Sutherland's perspective. This difference lies in the self-concept of offenders. "Professional thieves, when they speak honestly, admit that they are thieves," Sutherland observed, while white-collar criminals "think of themselves as honest men."[9] This alleged hypocrisy and false virtue of white-collar criminals drew Sutherland's severe reprobation. It is evident that Sutherland came to admire and glamorize the professional thief, and to loathe the white-collar criminal, a loathing that translated into his claim that businessmen were the most subversive force in America,[10] and his equating of the advertising tactics of the power and light utility companies to the propaganda of German Nazis.[11] Not only must white-collar behavior be controlled, Sutherland insisted, but the public must come to appreciate what criminologists had understood for some time—that white-collar and corporate offenses are serious criminal depredations.

Correcting Correctionalism

In studies of white-collar crime, attention usually has been concentrated on persons of prestige, but logic suggests that the designation embrace all individuals who violate laws regulating their occupational activities, such as grocers who shortweight and factory workers who knowingly are negligent in the construction of products whose faults might cause consumer injuries or deaths.[12] Violators of antitrust laws, pharmacists who break criminal laws dealing with the writing of prescriptions, and politicians who accept bribes are also among those criminal offenders who appear on the white-collar crime roster.

The social and psychological factors that might govern so diverse a range of human behaviors would, if enunciated, prove too amorphous to be useful for scientific or policy purposes. Analytically, the offenses must be broken down into homogeneous categories so that productive ideas can be generated regarding underlying mechanisms. The categories that might be employed would depend, of course, on the ends being sought. The researcher may group by occupation, task, offender status, the legal definition of the violation, or in terms of any other approach that might likely serve his purposes.

Sutherland himself, contrary to this view, chose to regard white-collar offenses as part of general criminal activity, *all* of which (from arson to illegal zymurgy) was to be explicable by a single theory, which he labeled *differential association*.[13] The theory consists of a set of postulates which describe rather simplistically the manner in which people introject ideas and values and then behave in terms of what they have absorbed. The most powerful influence on human behavior, Sutherland suggested, is the primary group, those individuals who share most intimately in a person's life. From such sources, the person acquires views of what is right and what is wrong, permissible and impermissible, legal and illegal. The slum youngster of the Depression period may learn that it is admirable to foray for coal in railroad yards or to swipe milk bottles from stoops in the wealthier neighborhoods, and he may argue that the most important characteristic of both acts is their contribution to the survival or well-being of his family.

The individual also develops a set of rationalizations or neutralization techniques;[14] these allow him to regard as reasonable behavior that others might find unacceptable. Fee-splitting by a medical doctor becomes in this manner a legitimate process of reward for services rendered, a system that has been outlawed only because of wrong-headed "socialistic" sentiments or legislative ignorance about the necessary nature of actual medical practice. Antitrust violations are defined as imperative in order to stabilize an errant market situation and/or as compassionate acts aimed at keeping on the job employees who otherwise might have been laid off. At worst, such crimes are regarded as "technical" violations of obfuscatory regulations.

Lest these modes of thought appear unusual, readers might well examine their own feelings about running through a stop sign near their house at two o'clock on a traffic-free morning, helping themselves to supplies where they work, using the office telephone for personal business, or showing someone else's identification card to obtain an alcoholic beverage defined as illegal for such as themselves. All these acts, like white-collar (as well as traditional) offenses, can be seen by some "sensible" persons as acceptable actions.

Sutherland's social psychological postulates are particularly compelling as signposts warning us away from rote dependence upon shibboleths about the causation of criminal activity, ideas which suggest that poverty, broken homes, Oedipal complexes, and similar things cause crime. What we learn combines with what we are (Sutherland rather neglects this second item) to determine what we do—this is the essence of differential association. This formula may prove useful for predicting that we speak with a Southern accent if we are born in Biloxi and spend our life there and that, as Americans, we are apt to find snakes unpalatable. But it does not carry us very far toward understanding why some persons with deep indoctrination favoring lawbreaking avoid doing so, while others, with contrary experiences, violate the law. It is obvious enough that human beings can be inventive, or to suppose that contradictory currents have sifted into what misleadingly appeared to be impermeable social or personal systems. Such hypotheses caution us to keep our predictions suitably general, so that we say, "All things being equal, it is likely that a person who entertains a keen desire for financial gain, who perceives that he will not be caught, and who has not adequately learned inhibitions about criminal behavior, will cheat when a suitable opportunity arises." The last item in the equation offers proof enough of the pitfalls of prediction on an individual basis, for the chance to commit a specific crime often depends on luck and circumstance.

In the first edition of his criminology textbook, published more than half a century ago, Sutherland concluded a review of crime causation with the observation that "the most important thing to know about crime is the mechanisms by which it is produced, and . . . such knowledge can be secured best by the individual case studies."[15] Later criminologists suggest that such a formulation addresses but part of the major issues. It is essential also to understand why certain behaviors are singled out for attention by the criminal law, while others, though they seemingly produce as much or more harm, are neglected.[16] Criminologists also want to investigate patterns of law enforcement—who, among the universe of perpetrators, is caught, tried, and convicted? And how do sentences differ?[17]

These are requisite ingredients of a cosmopolitan criminology. Sometimes, however, the currently popular approach camouflages a reductionist concept: Without the law, it suggests, there would be no crime; therefore the cause of crime is the criminal law. The suggestion that the fundamental cause of crime is capitalism suffers when confronted with the existence of criminal activities in all precapitalistic societies of any complexity and the appearance of such activity in contemporary noncapitalistic systems, such as the Soviet Union, Cuba, and China. In the Soviet Union, for instance, a fiddling taxi driver sounds very much like his American counterparts:

> The cheating's wrong, I know that . . . I cheat because everyone else does. The Party high-ups live like kings—on the people's money. Factory directors take a share of their plant's profits. Foremen take wage "kickbacks," workers smuggle out what raw materials they can under their coats, shop assistants water the wine. . . . Why should I be a martyr? I would if it would help, but it wouldn't change a single thing.[18]

Types and quantities of crime may vary in terms of dominant economic arrangements within social systems, but laws and law-breaking apparently are endemic to human organizations. It seems reasonable, therefore, to follow Sutherland's suggestions, and using case studies, to concentrate some continuing attention on the attributes of criminal behavior itself.

White-Collar Offenders

In Finance

The most extensive clinical analysis of a single white-collar offender is that of Richard Whitney by Walter Bromberg.[19] Whitney's obituary notice observed that he "seemed to be one of those privileged patricians upon whom Providence could only smile."[20] He had purchased a seat on the New York Stock Exchange at the age of twenty-three, and soon became a principal broker for J.P. Morgan and Company. But Whitney fell deeply into debt through speculation, and turned to thievery to cover himself, embezzling funds entrusted to him by the Exchange and by the New York Yacht Club, of which he was treasurer. After being found out, he was sentenced to five-to-ten-years imprisonment for grand larceny. In prison, both guards and fellow convicts always deferentially referred to him as "Mr. Whitney."

For Bromberg, Whitney's behavior is understood in terms of a "fantasy of omnipotence." He notes that the psychological examination of Whitney found him scoring 174 on the Army Alpha intelligence test, a result placing him above the ninety-ninth percentile. Whitney reacted to the psychiatric probes, Bromberg notes, "in an urbane and sportsmanlike manner. The picture emerging . . . was sharp and definitive, with no smudges of neurotic inferiority, depressive reactions, or other defenses against inner conflicts."[21] The examiners found Whitney to be markedly egocentric, and they were surprised by his statement that he never imagined he would run afoul of the law, despite his long administrative experience on the Stock Exchange. Bromberg summarizes this case and others like it in the following terms:

> [O]ffenders display little guilt; their consciences have become identified with the common business ideal of success at any price. Beguiled by the need for success, their fantasies of omnipotence and wealth, indistinguishable from the reality of their financial world, outrun their judgment. On the base of a narcissistic character structure, a dichotomy develops insidiously between practical judgment and daydreams of conquest. Self-advancement through fraud easily enters the hiatus thus created; the transition from successful manipulation to larceny occurs unobtrusively.[22]

Some of the foregoing is platitudinous, however fancily dressed in the verbal costume of its discipline. Some is tautological, not useful for prediction. At the same time, though, Bromberg tells us, in a very rare report based on actual contact with white-collar criminals, that their environment is criminogenic and that its values subtly corrupt. He offers a framework for more precise and detailed social psychological investigation.

Some further insights may be gleaned from parts of the very considerable literature on white-collar crime which caters to public interest in large-scale frauds. Note, for instance, Shaplen's observation about Ivar Krueger, one of the most sensational high-finance swindlers of our time: "The more he tempted, the more contemptuous he became of those who gave, and it was this human frailty of his, as much as anything, that ultimately defeated and destroyed him."[23] In his recent presidential address to the Society for the Psychological Study of Social Issues, Ezra Stotland stressed the same matter as a particularly promising line of inquiry for psychologists seeking to comprehend white-collar crime and criminals. The offender often makes a fool of his victims, Stotland notes, and the offender's feeling of satisfaction may be increased if victims do not know that they have been swindled. Stotland also points to laudatory words used to describe some white-collar crime and criminals. We talk of con *artists* and the *sharp* trader; or the *smart* thing to do. We also speak of the *skill* of the defrauder, of his imagination, rather than of his sneakiness.[24]

In Business

The only book-length work by a convicted white-collar criminal who fits into the genre of criminal-authors is that by W.E. Laite, Jr., a three-time member of the Georgia State Assembly who was sent to prison for failing to pay proper overtime wages to his workers, not fulfilling the terms of a government contract, and stealing or misusing federal property. Laite's response to the situation is self-pitying:

> I felt wronged, mistreated—here I was going into custody several years after the offense had *allegedly* occurred. The punishment seemed unrealistic and severe. I felt I had been punished enough already—by the publicity and harrassment, by the financial drubbing that had my family economically drained.[25] (Italics added.)

The remainder of the prison inmates are described by Laite as "foul-mouthed, sadistic riff-raff." He found them "different from me in a very basic and dangerous way." Later, with a note of pride, much like that of a society columnist with a good catch, Laite presents the credentials of other white-collar criminals at the facility to which he was transferred: "Five bank presidents, the president of a life insurance company, and a sheriff from Tennessee. There was also a Catholic priest from Miami."[26]

Willard Gaylin's fine study of conscientious objectors, made while they were incarcerated,[27] offers a prototype of the kind of study that ought to be conducted with white-collar offenders. Such offenders are accessible, since they generally are placed in special institutions, those that are the most likely to be described in the media as "country clubs." Gaylin observed the poignant difficulties of the war objectors as they sought to reconcile their intense moral convictions with the yawning indifference to such matters within the prisons. Should they continue to protest, rather pointlessly, and lose "good time," or should they capitulate and finish out their sentence as graciously and as quickly as possible? Researchers working with white-collar criminals might locate other kinds of themes that mark the nontraditional offender as he (perhaps) struggles to bring into alignment what he has done, the society's response to it, and his past and present condition and future prospects.

In Politics

The Watergate crimes and the concurrent investigation of Vice President Agnew for accepting bribes spawned considerable public soul-searching among participants in the scandals.[28] Very little social-psychological research has been devoted to the Watergate and Agnew cases, perhaps because so much has been written in the media that behavioral scientists believe their observations likely to be redundant, second hand, and/or trite. But these cases provide a voluminous data base that can be reinterpreted with social-psychological constructs. The work of Herbert C. Kelman offers an excellent example of how such a task might be handled. Kelman seeks "conceptual handles" for understanding " the conditions under which systemic abuses of power became possible and probable." He locates an answer that strikingly resembles that proferred by Bromberg following his analysis of the case of Richard Whitney:

> Through processes of authorization, the situation becomes so defined that standard moral principles do not apply and the individual is absolved of responsibility to make personal moral choices. Through processes of routinization, the action becomes so organized that there is no opportunity for raising moral questions and making moral decisions. Through processes of dehumanization, the actor's attitudes toward the target and toward himself become so structured that it is neither necessary nor possible for him to view the relationship in moral terms.[29]

The triumvirate of key terms in the analysis receives further elaboration. *Authorization* refers to the idea that "when immoral, criminal, or corrupt acts are explicitly ordered, implicitly encouraged, tacitly approved, or at least permitted by legitimate authorities, people's readiness to commit or condone them is considerably enhanced." Kelman notes that many witnesses before the Senate Watergate committee expressed an orientation to authority based on unquestioning obedience to superior orders. *Routinization* is seen to have two levels, one individual, the second organizational. At the individual level, the job is broken down into discrete steps, most of them carried out in automatic, regularized fashion. At the organizational level, the task is divided among different offices, each of which has responsibility for only a small portion. This arrangement limits the scope of decision making and diffuses responsibility. Finally, *dehumanization* refers to the idea that "targets of action are deprived of their human status so that the principles of morality no longer apply to them." Opponents are defined as "foreign, subversive, and dangerous," not entitled to the protection of sympathy expressed to other human beings. These considerations, taken together, vitiated the capacity of the Watergate conspirators to behave as moral beings, according to Kelman.

What should society do in the face of behavior such as the Watergate crimes and white-collar offenses in general? Kelman pits his scruples opposing punishment against a deeper consideration—"that failure to take action in the face of a great evil—allowing the evil to stand unchallenged and unrighted—is tantamount to acceptance of the evil and thus inherently dehumanizing." On this basis, he opts for some kind of meaningful social retaliation against the offenders, though he is willing to settle for acts of restitution on their part, acts which might "existentially affirm . . . the very principles that the original crime had violated."

White-Collar Crime in Context

It is a moot point whether doctors are more or less honest than the average person—or the average professional person—in the United States. What is not arguable is that medical practitioners have been caught in innumerable kinds of white-collar crime, and that their social and vocational positions are related to their law-breaking.[30]

Systematic study of medical white-collar crime with a social-psychological focus is nonexistent. One excellent journalistic article describes widespread law-breaking by doctors,[31] and there is considerable literature on medical quackery.[32] Newspapers document relentlessly, almost monotonously, criminal charges against doctors. Medical offenses involve not only financial predation, but also crimes against the person, such as unwarranted surgery, which reasonably might be defined as a form of assault. In addition, as Stotland has observed, trepidation in government circles about medical fiscal venery undoubtedly has inhibited establishment of a national health service, to the detriment of large segments of the population.[33] It should be noted, in this regard, that the United States lags far behind more than a dozen countries in terms of life expectancy and infant mortality, two sensitive indices of national health.[34]

The litany of medical crime need only briefly be sampled to establish its pervasiveness. The American College of Surgeons, for instance, has charged that about half of the operations performed in American hospitals are performed by unqualified doctors, largely because of fee-splitting, under which referring doctors receive an illegal kickback from the doctor performing the surgery.[35] A 1966 Government lawsuit charged that the 4,500 doctors who own medical laboratories overcharge the public for tests and conspire illegally to keep everyone but themselves out of the medical laboratory business.[36] In 1970, the Internal Revenue Service said that about half of the 3,000 doctors who received $25,000 or more in Medicare or Medicaid payment failed to report a substantial amount of their income.[37] A 1976 study by Cornell University investigators maintained that from 11 to 13 percent of all surgery in the United States is unnecessary, a function of diagnostic incompetence or of greed stemming from the lure of high fees for surgery. There are about twenty million operations performed in the United States annually: the Cornell researchers believed that at least two million or more were unwarranted.[38] A later survey found that the rate of surgery on the poor and near-poor—financed by Medicaid—is twice that for the general population. It was estimated in this survey that the cost of unnecessary surgery in the United States is $3.92 billion.[39]

Three factors offer grounds upon which it might be predicted that medical practitioners would *not* commit illegal acts:

1. Physicians, by reasonable standards, are able to fulfill their personal needs legally. On the basis of the evidence of their white-collar criminality, we can more readily appreciate that greed is not a class-specific trait, but a relative concept emerging from the standards of a person's reference group. We know that upper-class individuals jumped from windows during the Depression, though their remaining assets exceeded by far the wherewithal of lower-class persons who faced continued existence with equanimity. Cressey's classic study of embezzlers similarly tells of the "nonsharable problem"—the demand that the person puts upon himself and for which, twist as he may, he cannot find a resolution other than through violation of the criminal law.[40]

2. Physicians, by reasonable standards, appear to have a "proper" upbringing: good schools, friends, and social advantages. The pleasure of clinical analysis, of course, is that it can retroactively take any life and find within it indications of maladjustment, a father either "too stern" or "too easy going," or even "too normal" in the face of other family conditions. The evidence from physician law violation only further assures us that there is no single set of child-rearing principles that guarantees subsequent conformity to changing social and legal norms.

3. Physicians in training are exposed to professional socialization, a process that emphasizes the interests of others, such as patients, above their own interests. The patent violation of such standards indicated by the roster of criminal acts committed by medical doctors suggests that professional

socialization refers, at best, to an ambiguous and oftentimes contradictory collection of attitudes and values.[41] Indeed, such attitudes and values, when they mesh with other factors, may be conducive to deviance rather than conformity.

It seems evident that there are very considerable pressures generated in medical practice toward acquisition of wealth. It is because they are such powerful incentives that economic rewards are entrenched in capitalist—and many socialist—countries.[42] Firms offer vacations, prizes, and cash bonuses with the reasonable expectation that people will work harder to achieve these carrots.

But such kinds of incentives are not *supposed* to operate as reinforcements for the professional person. Self-aggrandizement is incompatible with the professional orientation. Physicians are not expected to be concerned with their patients' ability to pay bills—what should matter is the nature of their illness and how it best may be cured. This is what is supposed to be taught, along with proper skills to reach the goals. Why, in many cases, doesn't the training produce the results desired?

Socializing Doctors

There have been a number of studies of the process by which young men and women are molded into a professional cadre that shares to a high degree a body of attitudes and values, in regard both to professional matters and toward larger social issues. Studies indicate that medical school provides an encompassing environment in which the subculture of the profession is intensively stressed.[43] There is a heavy emphasis on the "right way of doing things." In school and in the teaching hospital, faculty and supervisors monitor both professional and personal behavior closely. Technical skills are evaluated; so is the degree to which students have assimilated the professional *role* of physician.

The self-image of the medical student alters as he or she proceeds through training. A study comparing students in each of the four years in the medical school sequence found that 31 percent of the first-year group thought of themselves primarily as physicians, as did 30 percent of the second-year class, and 59 percent of the third-year class. By the fourth year, 83 percent of the graduating cadre had internalized the role model.[44] Particularly interesting were the 17 percent of the seniors who still did not view themselves as "real" physicians. These people had not, as had their fellows, taken on the mantle so assiduously woven for them. With graduation, however, the period of supervision, critique, and control for most medical students is over.

Two of the major settings in which doctors practice their calling can be examined to indicate how pressures toward law-violation swamp the socialization process—the individual or solo practice of medicine, and the autonomous professional organization.[45] In the latter setting, supervision from older physicians may prevail, though hardly to the extent that it existed during the period of the student's education. Whitman's investigation indicates that, as in the corporate world, group medical practice may impose strong pressures toward law-breaking, since senior personnel already may have established illegal practices, and the newcomer is in a weak position to resist on ethical or other grounds.[46] The ethos of medical work, in addition, even in group practice, tends to inhibit close scrutiny of one's colleagues. Thus, a study by Freidson and Rhea found that many medical clinic physicians were unable to rate their colleagues' level of competence, on the ground that they felt unable or unwilling to judge "good" medical practice in areas of specialty other than their own.[47]

In solo practice, the doctor finds himself virtually without formal supervision and accountability, having been thrust into a business role that only peripherally (if at all) was examined in medical school. Here, to succeed, the doctor must attract and retain patients. Since the attraction of patients takes place in a competitive environment, "enterprise may be more important than medical knowledge and skill."[48] Carlin, studying lawyers, thought he located the forces pushing the attorney in solo practice into law-breaking in conditions which offered little freedom of choice of clients, type of work, or conditions of practice. It is not unlikely that some similar combination of factors operates in the same manner for entrepreneurial doctors.[49]

Stigma and Status

There are, in addition, two particular problems regarding white-collar crime that may be illuminated by insights from the social-psychological literature. These concern (1) how the white-collar offender fails to perceive the seriousness of his act; and (2) how others around the white-collar offender fail to appreciate the act's seriousness.

1. White-collar offenders usually deny, distort, defuse, or deflect the reasonable interpretations of their criminal behavior. Businessmen, for example, claim that there is a "very fine line" between law violations and acceptable business practice. Physicians claim that the border between incompetence resulting in an unfavorable malpractice verdict or a criminal charge and reasonable professional judgment is similarly gray. One of the most consistent findings is the essentially noncriminal self-concept of the white-collar offender, regardless of the occupational context in which his behavior takes place.[50]

There are at least two major reasons for this failure of the offender to think of himself as a criminal, or, in sociological terms, to be "labelled." First, the legal process, with its usual inattention to white-collar crime, reinforces the idea that this is not serious behavior.[51] In addition, the offender must undergo a process of dissonance reduction based on the fact that his social roles are valued and "respectable"—community leader, member of the PTA, and Elk, good family provider, respected citizen, on the board of directors of the local hospital, active in the political arena, and so on. Obviously, roles such as these are not consistent with the appellation *criminal*. Festinger suggests that the need to reduce dissonance pushes toward denial of the less-acceptable label; in this instance the offender denies that he or she is indeed a criminal.[52]

2. White-collar crimes do not generate substantial public outrage and concern.[53] Nor are the careers of white-collar offenders much changed if they are prosecuted for law-breaking. Of the fifteen persons who were fired from General Electric in the wake of heavy equipment antitrust prosecutions, twelve were reemployed at higher levels elsewhere.[54] Some of these persons may have been fearful about their lives after release from incarceration, but their apprehensions were unfounded. Similarly, a study of fifty-eight physicians losing malpractice suits found that none reported negative effects on their practice, and five actually reported an expanded practice. The heaviest financial loser also had the largest gain in practice. He thought that other physicians felt sorry for him and had increased their rate of referrals.[55]

The unwillingness to stigmatize white-collar offenders is consistent with Heider's balance theory. Heider posits relationships between two persons and an impersonal entity—an object, idea, or event.[56] If we view criminality as the event, the white-collar offender as one person, and another individual as the third member of the triad, we see the need to balance or reconcile criminality (which would receive a negative evaluation) with the interpersonal bond between the individuals. The offender may be liked by the other, but he has committed a criminal act. Denying the illegality of the act makes the behavior more consistent with previous valuations of the offender. In this manner, a state of congruity can be achieved by the individuals.[57]

Another useful perspective is that of social exchange theory.[58] Interpersonal relations, this theory posits, are a function of the relative costs and rewards that accrue to the participants in a relationship. Unless certain expectations remain unfulfilled, the rewards persons give one another in the course of social interaction will serve to maintain mutual attraction and continued association.[59] An upper-class individual, by virtue of his position, power, and wealth, could be expected to be able to offer more rewards to others, such as gifts, employment, or other tangible things. His status thus insulates him from bearing the full burden of his illegal behavior.

Concluding Observations

There is a parochialism about much behavioral science research. Violence is defined by popular opinion in the United States as street crime, such as mugging, raping, and forms of assault. Psychologists uncritically accept definitions such as this, though it is obvious that some forms of death-dealing violence also involve white-collar criminals—knowingly cutting corners on required safety devices, failing to deliver medical care.[60] The time seems overdue for social psychology to break some of its ties to the laboratory, to unloose the bonds of parochialism, and to turn more of its professional talents to the investigation of socially significant matters.

A fundamental part of our thesis is that the phenomenon of white-collar crime represents just such a matter.

What sparse research currently exists offers only fragmentary clues about control mechanisms for white-collar crime, while those materials advocating particular preventive tactics, such as the works of the Nader group, tend to be built on unexamined premises. We need to reconcile, for instance, the strong movement for decarceration of many traditional kinds of offenders with the regular calls for imprisonment of white-collar criminals. We do not know whether adequate philosophical or empirical grounds exist to support such a distinction, or whether the distinction is based largely on common anti-business feelings within the academic community, and a general malaise about professionals such as doctors on the part of their patients, based in some measure on public perception of them as "money-hungry."[61]

Paradoxically, social psychological research suggests that if white-collar crime is to be reduced it is essential that it be defined in heavily invidious terms by the public at large and by members of the reference group with whom the offender identifies. It also seems necessary that the rationalizations of the offender be penetrated and that offenders be made to confront less palatable interpretations of what they have done.

Nonetheless, the leverage of tactics concentrating on individual offenders, either for purposes of specific or general deterrence, should not be overrated. Gurr's comprehensive survey of crime in four cities—London, Stockholm, Calcutta, and Sydney—over several centuries led him to conclude that it was not matters susceptible to criminological manipulation, such as legislation or penal policy, that bore most directly upon criminal activity, but items of a more abstract and fundamental nature, such as the economic condition of a jurisdiction and its general ethos.[62] This is not to say that short-term and limited improvements cannot be realized in regard to white-collar crime, particularly in regard to its identification and condemnation. It does suggest, however, that much criminal activity is responsive to the kinds of things for which we stand. Individualism, hedonism, materialism—these are criminogenic social values: they may have utility for the production of many social and individual boons; and they may be preferable on some grounds to different social emphases. But they have their price, and part of that price clearly appears to be the phenomenon of white-collar crime.

Notes

1. Donald R. Cressey, "Restraint of Trade, Recidivism, and Delinquent Neighborhoods," in ed. James F. Short, *Delinquency, Crime, and Society* (Chicago: University of Chicago Press, 1976), p. 211.

2. David Matza, *Becoming Deviant* (Englewood Cliffs, N.J.: Prentice-Hall, 1969), pp. 15-17.

3. Ralph Nader, Preface, in eds. Ralph Nader and Mark J. Green, *Corporate Power in America* (New York: Grossman, 1973), p. vii.

4. Mark J. Green, *The Closed Enterprise System* (New York: Grossman, 1971), p. xviii.

5. Karl Schuessler, Introduction, in Edwin H. Sutherland, *On Analyzing Crime* (Chicago: University of Chicago Press, 1973), p. x.

6. Edwin H. Sutherland, *White Collar Crime* (New York: Dryden Press, 1949), p. v.

7. Edwin H. Sutherland, *The Professional Thief* (Chicago: University of Chicago Press, 1937).

8. Jon Snodgrass, "The Criminologist and His Criminal: The Case of Edwin H. Sutherland and Broadway Jones," *Issues in Criminology*, 8 (Spring 1973), p. 8.

9. Sutherland, *On Analyzing Crime*, pp. 95-96.

10. Ibid., p. 92.

11. Sutherland, *White Collar Crime*, p. 210.

12. Joseph Bensman and Israel Gerver, "Crime and Punishment in the Factory: The Function of Deviancy in Maintaining the Social System," *American Sociological Review*, 28 (1963), pp. 588-598.

13. Edwin H. Sutherland and Donald R. Cressey, *Principles of Criminology*, 4th edition (Philadelphia: Lippincott, 1947).

14. Gresham M. Sykes and David Matza, "Techniques of Neutralization: A Theory of Delinquency," *American Sociological Review*, 22 (1957), pp. 664-670.

15. Edwin H. Sutherland, *Criminology* (Philadelphia: Lippincott, 1924), p. 15.

16. Frank Pearce, *Crimes of the Powerful* (London: Pluto Press, 1976).

17. Richard Quinney, *Class, State, and Crime: On the Theory and Practice of Criminal Justice* (New York: McKay, 1977).

18. Walter D. Connor, *Deviance in Soviet Society: Crime, Delinquency, and Alcoholism* (New York: Columbia University Press, 1972).

19. Walter Bromberg, *Crime and the Mind* (New York: Macmillan, 1965), pp. 384-389.

20. Albin Krebs, "Richard Whitney, 86, dies; headed Stock Exchange," *New York Times* (December 6, 1974).

21. Bromberg, *Crime and the Mind*, p. 388.

22. Ibid., p. 389.

23. Robert Shaplen, *Krueger: Genius and Swindler* (New York: Knopf, 1960), p. 10.

24. Ezra Stotland, "White Collar Criminals," *Journal of Social Issues*, 33 (1977), p. 187.

25. W.E. Laite, Jr., *The United States vs. William Laite* (Washington, D.C.: Acropolis Books, 1972), p. 23.

26. Ibid., p. 191.

27. Willard Gaylin, *In the Service of their Country: War Resisters in Prison* (New York: Grossett and Dunlop, 1970).

28. John Dean, *Blind Ambition* (New York: Simon and Schuster, 1976); Jeb Magruder, "Watergate Reflections," *New York Times Magazine* (May 19, 1974), pp. 31, 103-112.

29. Herbert C. Kelman, "Violence without Moral Restraint: Reflections on the Dehumanization of Victims and Victimizers," *Journal of Social Issues*, 29 (1973), p. 381. Reprinted with permission. See also Kelman, "Some Reflections on Authority, Corruption, and Punishment: The Social-psychological Context of Watergate," *Psychiatry*, 39 (1976), pp. 303-317.

30. P. Atkinson, M. Reid, and P. Sheldrake, "Medical Mystique," *Sociology of Work and Occupations*, 4 (1977), pp. 243-280.

31. Howard Whitman, "Why Some Doctors Should be in Jail," *Colliers*, 132 (October 30, 1953), pp. 23-27.

32. J.H. Young, *The Medical Messiahs* (Princeton: Princeton University Press, 1967).

33. Stotland, "White Collar Criminals," p. 182.

34. Martin L. Gross, *The Doctors* (New York: Dell, 1967).

35. *New York Times* (October 4, 1961).

36. *New York Times* (July 7, 1966).

37. *Wall Street Journal* (September 22, 1970).

38. *New York Times* (May 3, 1976).

39. *New York Times* (September 1, 1977).

40. Donald R. Cressey, *Other People's Money* (New York: Free Press, 1953).

41. Robert Merton, *Sociological Ambivalence and Other Essays* (New York: Free Press, 1976).

42. John P. Clark and Richard R. Hollinger, "On the Feasibility of Empirical Studies of White-Collar Crime," in ed. Robert F. Meier, *Theory in Criminology* (Beverly Hills: Sage, 1977), pp. 139-158.

43. Howard S. Becker, Blanche Geer, Everett C. Hughes, and Anselm L. Strauss, *Boys in White: Student Culture in Medical School* (Chicago: University of Chicago Press, 1961).

44. M. Huntington, "The Development of a Professional Self-Image," in ed. Robert Merton, Leo Reader, and Patricia Kendall, *The Student-Physician* (Cambridge, Mass.: Harvard University Press, 1957).

45. Robert Hall, *Occupations and Social Structure*, 2nd edition (Englewood Cliffs, N.J.: Prentice-Hall, 1975).

46. Whitman, "Why Some Doctors."

47. Eliot Friedson and B. Rhea, "Knowledge and Judgment in Professional Evaluation," *Administrative Science Quarterly*, 10 (1965), pp. 107-124.

48. O. Hall, "Stages of a Medical Career," *American Journal of Sociology*, 53 (1948), pp. 327-336.

49. Jerome Carlin, *Lawyers on their Own* (New Brunswick: Rutgers University Press, 1962).

50. Marshall B. Clinard and Richard Quinney, *Criminal Behavior Systems: A Typology*, 2nd edition (New York: Holt, Rinehart and Winston, 1973), pp. 191-192.

51. Alan M. Dershowitz, "Increasing Community Control over Corporate Crime: A Problem in the Law of Sanctions," *Yale Law Journal*, 71 (1961), pp. 289-306.

52. Leon Festinger, *A Theory of Cognitive Dissonance* (Stanford: Stanford University Press, 1957).

53. Peter Rossi, Emily Waite, C. Bose, and Richard Berk, "The Seriousness of Crimes: Normative Structure and Individual Differences," *American Sociological Review*, 39 (1974), pp. 224-237.

54. Richard Heilbroner, *In the Name of Profit* (Garden City, N.Y.: Doubleday, 1972), p. 36.

55. Richard D. Schwartz and Jerome H. Skolnick, "Two Studies of Legal Stigma," *Social Problems*, 10 (1962), pp. 133-142.

56. Fritz Heider, *The Psychology of Interpersonal Relations* (New York: Wiley, 1958).

57. C.E. Osgood and P.H. Tannenbaum, "The Principle of Congruity in the Prediction of Attitude Change," *Psychological Review*, 62 (1955), pp. 42-55.

58. Peter Blau, *Exchange and Power in Social Life* (New York: Wiley, 1964); George Homans, *Social Behavior: Its Elementary Forms*, rev. edition (New York: Harcourt Brace Jovanovich, 1974).

59. Albert Lott and Bernice Lott, "The Role of Reward in the Formation of Positive Interpersonal Attitudes," in ed. Ted L. Huston, *Foundations of Interpersonal Attraction* (New York: Academic Press, 1974).

60. Gilbert Geis and John Monahan, "Social Ecology of Violence," in ed. Thomas Lickona, *Moral Development and Behavior* (New York: Holt, Rinehart and Winston, 1976).

61. Esther Haar, Victor Halitsky, and George Stricker, "Patients' Attitudes towards Gynecological Examination and to Gynecologists," *Medical Care*, 15 (September 1977), pp. 787-795.

62. Ted R. Gurr, Peter N. Grabosky, and R.C. Hula, *The Politics of Crime and Conflict* (Beverly Hills: Sage, 1977).

8

Criminal Enforcement of California's Occupational Carcinogens Control Act

Gilbert Geis and
Thomas R. Clay

Statutes aimed at eliminating or reducing the presence of carcinogens at workplace sites raise a host of social, scientific, political, and juridical issues.[1] A fundamental question concerns the right of the state to interfere with the property of employers, particularly when such interference is based upon arguable consequences of the proscribed workplace conditions. Should not workers be informed of the risks they are likely to experience at the workplace and then be allowed to make up their own minds, just as they must do in regard to whether to smoke cigarettes? Or is it true that the threat of cancer seems too remote and too unreal to deter what must be regarded as masochistic behavior on the part of employees, behavior against which a decent state is obligated to protect them? Is it correct to maintain, as do the Marxists, that the power and the resources of the employer so outweigh the bargaining position of the worker that in the final analysis proletarians will be "forced" to accept employment under dangerous conditions because alternatives, such as welfare status, are even more meretricious in their eyes?[2]

There are, beyond these, intricate questions concerning the right of agents of the state to gain access to workplace sites for inspection purposes. In addition, questions arise regarding state use of information that is discovered when state agents are permitted to scrutinize freely occupational premises. Should inspections that might result in criminal charges be allowed only if a judge issues a warrant specifying the precise nature of the objectionable circumstances? If so, how can this information be secured without prior scouting expeditions? How much reliance should be placed upon workplace informers? Should law enforcement and regulatory agencies plant their own personnel in factories and other job sites in order to ascertain covertly whether violations exist?

Such regulatory statutes also give rise to unanswered questions pertaining to economic issues. How much money will a particular company be willing to spend to make "more certain" that cancer is not transmitted through

Gilbert Geis and Thomas R. Clay, in *Temple Law Quarterly*, 53 (1980), pp. 1067-1099. Reprinted with permission.

neglect of specified workplace precautions? The elimination of factors which may contribute to the illness and death rate is always measured against monetary costs, as well as against competing social preferences and political priorities. For example, we allow highway travel at fifty-five miles per hour because we believe it more worthwhile to reach places more rapidly than to try to reduce traffic fatalities by driving more slowly. Furthermore, most jurisdictions in the United States allow motorcyclists to decide whether to wear helmets although we know that there is an increased likelihood of injury and death if they fail to opt for such protection. We do not want to interfere with the freedom of motorcyclists to do as they please despite predictable lethal consequences.[3]

These matters are complicated further by the symbolic and real nature of the malignancy of cancer, a macabre, terrifying disease. The victim often desperately seeks a "logical explanation" for his or her fate. Blame may be directed at negligent workplace conditions which supposedly contributed to this illness. However, translating that blame into scientific proof can be a complicated and arduous task. Cancer is a time-fuse disorder; its seeds often linger in a quiescent condition in the body for long periods of time before making their lethal presence known. In the time interval between exposure to an unhealthy environment and overt illness, an almost infinite number of other things can happen to the sufferer that may contribute to, or even cause, the cancerous condition. For example, epidemiologists may determine that a cohort of humans who shared a common experience, employment in a particular factory during a specified time span, later show statistically significant higher rates of cancer than might have been anticipated, given their demographic traits. However, not all members of the cohort will develop cancer. There must be some other factor that inhibits or fails to inhibit the appearance of the malignancy in persons who shared the particular work experience. Is it possible or fair to make legal determinations of responsibility and to impose sanctions on the basis of this kind of evidence?

A civil case being tried at the time of this writing serves to highlight this problem. A forty-year-old former pipefitter is seeking unspecified damages from two manufacturers for their failing both to warn him of the hazards of inhaling asbestos fibers and to advise him to take precautionary measures to prevent development of the disease of asbestosis. This is the first trial of more than one thousand local lawsuits against asbestos manufacturers which are now pending. The manufacturers deny that the plaintiff has the disease, maintaining that x-rays do not substantiate what should be its marked progression over the past five years if the illness truly is asbestosis. Lawyers for the corporate defendants also argue that the scarring on the plaintiff's lungs is "consistent with" pneumonia, which he suffered in 1978, and that his chronic cough could be related to his smoking habits.[4] After six days of deliberations following a six-week trial, the jury decided for the plaintiff and awarded $1.2 million in general damages. The trial judge later ordered the plaintiff to accept a reduced verdict of $250,000 or face a new trial, stating that the jury's verdict was based on "either passion, prejudice or speculation" and was "more than four times the amount that in good conscience could be permitted in the light of the fault of the defendants [asbestos manufacturers] and the comparative fault of the plaintiff" who had smoked up to two packs of cigarettes a day for twenty-five years.[5]

The choice of an enforcement strategy after violations have been detected also poses a variety of perplexing questions. Should the courts allow employers to rectify faulty workplace conditions over a reasonable period of time without invoking further penalties, assuming civil remedies may be available to any person who has been injured by demonstrable employer commissions or omissions? Or should more severe measures be employed to guarantee that this violator and others will more effectively conform to regulatory standards? In particular, what use should be made of criminal sanctions, including jail or prison sentences, when persons knowingly, or with reckless ignorance, create or allow to exist conditions proscribed by law? Are such rules desirable? Are they enforceable? Do they serve a deterrent function?

These final questions most particularly will occupy our attention in the present article although they must be regarded in the light of the other issues set forth in the introductory paragraphs. To respond to these matters we will examine in some detail the experience of the state of California in its attempt to regulate workplace conditions said to be cancer-related.

Historical Background

It has taken a long time to attach responsibility onto employers for the maintenance of conditions favoring workplace safety and health. An ethic of "rugged individualism" in the United States had proclaimed that financial success could be achieved by any hard worker and that such opportunity was best accorded under a system of economic laissez faire. Accidents were considered an inevitable risk, part of the wage calculation, and most often were seen as representing failures of the worker, brought on by ignorance or carelessness. Legislatures and courts shielded industry from any burden that might have been imposed for occupational injuries. Courts proved slow to give precedence to human over property rights despite the growing complexity of the manufacturing process and the inability of workers to appreciate harm caused by exposure to dust, gases, and chemicals.

The first research report in the United States on occupational health hazards appeared in 1837.[6] Massachusetts became the first state to pass a safety statute in 1877, requiring the guarding of shafts and gears on machinery; the measure was largely cosmetic. The first federal statute was passed in 1891 when Congress set standards and provided for inspections in the coal mines. Statutes prescribing safety equipment specifications for railroad cars and engines were enacted in 1893. Research and investigative activities were stepped up in 1902 through the creation of the Public Health Service. By 1920, forty states and the federal government had passed workmen's compensation laws, which provided limited relief. Although the workmen's compensation laws shifted part of the cost of industrial accidents from employee to employer, not every worker nor every occupation was covered. For example, the early statutes completely disregarded occupational disease.

Despite the patent shortcomings of the laws designed to promote job safety and to provide compensation for disabled workers, no major advances were made until the 1960s. The economic Depression diminished whatever feeble pressure had been mounted to improve occupational safety and health conditions. Faced with a high rate of unemployment, workers were willing to endure hazards against which they otherwise would have protested. Organized labor, which would later assume a leading role in the occupational safety and health field, was preoccupied with establishing its own foothold during this period. Management's priority was economic survival rather than implementation of nonprofit programs.[7]

The Second World War saw a growth of interest in the problem of workplace conditions, as the government sought to reduce occupational accidents that might adversely bear upon the war effort. Legislation continued to be thwarted, however, for two major reasons. First, federal control over job safety was viewed as an unacceptable encroachment upon states' rights. Second, bureaucratic jealousies intruded, and, as a result, public health officials proved unwilling to grant jurisdiction to state labor departments to deal with matters of occupational health. During the postwar period, however, industry modernized and expanded at a rapid rate. Workers were exposed to an array of newly synthesized materials the effects of which, particularly in the long term, were unknown.

The first Presidential Conference on Industrial Safety was called in 1948 by Harry S. Truman. In reaction to what was considered an abnormally high accident rate, the federal government swiftly enacted laws in the 1950s to regulate mining and maritime safety.

Finally, in 1970 the federal Occupational Safety and Health Act (OSHA) was enacted.[8] The legislative history of the federal law reveals a gradual interest in occupational safety and health which developed out of a series of congressional hearings, progressively disclosing the dire failures of past federal and state efforts to assure healthy work environments.[9] Curiously, at the time the legislation was proposed, there was no mass media expose of dangerous working conditions nor was there pressure from organized labor in the wake of job-related disasters, events which are often necessary to prod legislatures into remedial action. Rather than a gradual legislative process culminating with the passage of remedial legislation, the more common rule seems to be that a gigantic, well-publicized tragedy is often the impetus for such a statute's passage.

In its final form, OSHA substantially altered the responsibilities of agencies dealing with job safety and health and included provisions for the establishment of uniform national standards, the development of a national system of inspection of workplace sites, and the allocation of federal funds for research. The Act allowed states to regain jurisdiction over safety and health standards provided they fulfilled certain requirements and secured approval from the Department of Labor. To secure approval, the investigative, enforcement, and penal provisions of a state plan would have to be "at least as effective" as the federal OSHA requirements.

Cal-OSHA and the OCCA

At the time the federal law was passed, California already had an extensive occupational safety and health program. The state submitted its plan to the United States Department of Labor on September 27, 1972, and the Cal-OSHA law went into effect in October, 1973.[10] In 1976, the California Occupational Carcinogens Control Act (OCCA), designed specifically to regulate carcinogenic substances used in the workplace, was passed.[11]

Passage of the OCCA was generated by a high level of medical concern and moral indignation regarding alleged cancer-producing substances which were used in various industrial processes purportedly without adequate protective care. The Health and Welfare Committee of the California State Senate, chaired by Arlen Gregorio, who introduced the measure, had as its legal counsel from 1970 to 1973 Larry Agran, who during the time was preparing a book on the relationship between occupational conditions and ensuant cancer.[12] Agran's concern had been aroused by a crescendo of media publicity spotlighting horror stories about the consequences of uncontrolled production of diverse chemical products, such as DDT, saccharine, vinyl chloride, dye stuff, and asbestos.[13] State Senator Gregorio became interested in this issue by an episode, within his district, of employer neglect of safety precautions.[14]

The bill's sponsor adopted a strategy which often appears to be successful in proposals aimed at curbing what are regarded as business excesses. He first introduced a much more stringent measure, and later settled for a compromise proposal. The tougher measure would have mandated licensing of any firm intending to produce certain designated substances believed to have carcinogenic properties. To obtain a license, the company would have to demonstrate beforehand that its procedures were in total compliance with predetermined standards. If serious violations were later proven, the license could be revoked. Industry balked at this proposal. A series of meetings in 1974 and 1975 among legislative aides and business and union representatives resulted in a compromise. Instead of a licensing requirement, users were to register and be subject to periodic inspections. The larger manufacturers were willing to acquiesce to a less stringent inspection system, in part, Agran believes, because they presumed that they could meet its standards, and, in part, because they were not altogether displeased that the stipulations would place a heavy burden upon their smaller competitors, thus affording the larger businesses a marketplace advantage. The sponsors of OCCA also believed that at a later date they could readily make more stringent any bill which they initially secured.

The legislative purpose of OCCA was "to clarify and strengthen the provisions of state law applicable to the use of carcinogens in California." The state would seek to "exercise strong leadership in preventing employees, employers, and other persons from being exposed to carcinogens." Sixteen substances were listed as falling within the law's ambit. The statute required employers who were using identified carcinogens to submit written reports describing such use and documenting any incident which resulted in the release of a potentially hazardous amount of a carcinogen into any area where employees could have been exposed. Mandatory medical examinations for employees involved with stipulated carcinogens were inaugurated under the new law. The heart of the measure provided for periodic inspections at sites where it was believed that employee health might be jeopardized by carcinogens. A fee of between $25 and $500, to be levied no more than once a year, would be charged to the employer to cover the cost of inspection.

The penalty structure, for the most part, did not differ notably from the usual approaches that many commentators have ridiculed as involving no more than slap-on-the-wrist or cost-of-doing-business fines. Failure to report conditions or events when so required were fined by not less than $500. An initial violation of the standards could involve a $1,000 fine; repeated violations would be punishable by a fine of not less than $5,000 nor more than $10,000. Failure to abate a violation in a timely manner could result in a penalty of up to $1,000 per day for each day of noncompliance.

What made the OCCA law different and tougher than Cal-OSHA was a legislative decree that a violation of its standards by definition rose to the level of "serious" acts proscribed under the umbrella Cal-OSHA program. Therefore, employers could be fined up to $5,000 and/or sentenced to six months in jail if they (a) knowingly or negligently committed a violation; (b) did so repeatedly in a manner creating a real and apparent hazard to employees; or (c) failed to comply with a standard, once cited and after the abatement period had expired, thereby creating a real and apparent hazard to employees. Furthermore, the statute permitted prosecutions to be brought against not only the corporate entity but responsible company officials. The OCCA's registration requirement also allowed a presumption of employer knowledge, undercutting possible pleas of ignorance about the dictates of the carcinogens statute. The *mens rea* standard exempted employers from liability if they "did not, and could not with the exercise of reasonable diligence, know of the presence of the violation or if the violation is minor and resulted in no substantial health hazard, as determined by the division [of Occupational Safety and Health, Department of Industrial Relations]."[15]

There is further criminal provision in the overarching Cal-OSHA statute applicable to OCCA cases. A willful violation causing death or prolonged injury to an employee can bring a fine of up to $10,000 and/or six months in jail. If the employer has previously been convicted he or she may be punished by a fine of up to $20,000 and/or one year in jail.

From 1977, when OCCA went into effect, until March 1979—almost two years later—no criminal sanctions were imposed for violations of the law. This outcome largely was the consequence, it appeared, of the assumption by California officials charged with enforcing the Act that health cases would be difficult, if not impossible, to prosecute. In rather strong contrast, occupational safety violations often are referred for criminal prosecution in California. Absence of attention to possible criminal sanctions under OCCA was not a function of the fact that there were no cases against which such penalties might have been sought; neither was it a function of a high degree of compliance with the mandates of the law. Occupational health inspections during 1977 and 1978 found approximately forty per cent of the companies visited in violation of the standards set by law. During the initial four months of OCCA's operation, sixty-five per cent of the inspections resulted in the issuance of citations for violations. In the fourteen-month period ending March 1979, when the first criminal case went forward, there were thirty-five instances in which employers were cited and fined for serious OCCA violations. This number may be regarded as a minimum figure, since there are not enough industrial hygienists employed under the program to inspect covered companies at better than infrequent intervals.

Work of the Center for Law in the Public Interest

The March 1979 case chosen for criminal prosecution, *People v. Brassbestos Manufacturing Corp.*,[16] represented the first time in the United States that a jurisdiction had referred a violation of occupational health standards to a local district attorney for criminal prosecution. Prior to this time, no employer had been prosecuted at either the federal or the state level. The fines in California that normally had been imposed under OCCA for violations had averaged about $239, an amount that hardly would be regarded as a deterrent to either the offender or others weighing the cost of remedial measures against the risk of a penalty. The path by which the criminal sanction moved to the forefront sheds light upon an issue of fundamental importance in the area of white-collar crime: the mobilization of public and political opinion to support a redefinition of corporate violations in order to promote a consensus that the violations are particularly serious offenses and that the perpetrators should be criminally prosecuted.

The redirection in OCCA enforcement strategy grew out of a series of meetings involving attorneys at the Center for Law in the Public Interest (CLPI), located in Los Angeles, and the Governor and his aides.[17] These meetings were set up largely through the catalytic agency of Tom Hayden and his Campaign for Economic Democracy. These sessions resulted in an agreement to locate OCCA cases suitable for criminal prosecution and to proceed apace with them.

The altered focus was buttressed by a background report and call to action issued in May 1979 by the Center.[18] Created in 1971, largely with the financial help of the Ford Foundation, CLPI had been staffed by attorneys who withdrew from prestigious Los Angeles law firms to focus on what they regarded as important legal issues aimed at advancing the interests of the general public. When Center leaders began to concentrate on industrial health, several young attorneys were assigned to examine the operation of OCCA. Their report, which received widespread mass media attention, first documented what was regarded as a lackadaisical attitude among state officials about strictly enforcing the law, given the particularly harmful consequences of violations. Although the authors of the report acknowledged that "[m]ost companies, when cited and fined for a violation, will abate the violation in good faith," they assumed the sterner position that "some firms apparently do not comply unless compelled to do so; for these companies criminal penalties must be invoked." The authors of the report also maintained that criminal sanctions, especially if used against first offenders, would greatly increase the likelihood that other employers would take quick action to remedy deleterious workplace conditions and would encourage workers to report violations to the state agency.

Since there had been no OCCA criminal prosecutions, the Center's position was, at best, only speculative in suggesting that prosecutions would impel employers or employees to be more vigilant. The evidence for the effectiveness of deterrence by criminal sanctions, which we will review in some detail below, was sketchily alluded to in the Center's report, and then only in terms of a single study. That study, used as a strategy blueprint for the Center's campaign in regard to OCCA, concerned violations of regulations bearing upon nursing homes. Prosecutions for such violations had not been undertaken during the first thirty years of the law's existence. In the first three years of criminal enforcement, twenty nursing home staff members and licensees at twelve facilities had been convicted of misdemeanors. In one case, a charge of fund commingling resulted in a ninety-day jail sentence against an owner of several nursing home facilities. The study concluded that these prosecutions and convictions had served a deterrent function.[19] It is arguable, however, whether the lessons presumably learned from the nursing home experience would be applicable to enforcement of carcinogenic control laws. Most importantly, the basic premise—that enforcement will deter—is not convincingly established by the study. The criterion for success in the nursing home context was a change of management, but there is no reason to believe that subsequent managers were better than their predecessors. In addition, even if the managers were better, improved administration may not have been a consequence of prosecutions. While the anecdotal evidence supplied by the nursing home inspector on which the report relied must be accorded some credence, the data fall well below any reasonable standard of scientific acceptability. On the other hand, many persons studying white-collar violations intuitively feel, as the authors of both the nursing home study and the Center Report on OCCA did, that use of criminal penalties is essential to bring business behavior more in line with legal requirements.

The Brassbestos Case

Despite the theoretical basis for their position, the Center's work paid off with exceeding rapidity. The Governor's command to the bureaucracy that health violation cases be handled by criminal prosecutions resulted in a review of the files in Sacramento and the identification of a number of instances in which it was felt that the factual situation justified criminal procedures against the alleged offender. The Brassbestos Manufacturing Corporation was the first target. The firm, located in Anaheim, manufactures and distributes brake linings. Its use of asbestos required registration under the OCCA. An industrial hygienist employed by the Division of Occupational Safety and Health conducted a compliance inspection at Brassbestos on April 6, 1978. On the basis of this visit, the company was cited for four violations: one serious and three *repeat* serious. The repeat nature of the violations was based on an earlier compliance inspection.

For these four violations, Brassbestos was ordered to remedy the health hazards by October 13, 1978, and to pay a total civil fine of $16,000. The company appealed, and a hearing was scheduled for March 29, 1979. This appeal was suspended when criminal charges were brought on the same evidence. The criminal charge was filed on April 4, 1979, under section 6423(b) of the state Labor Code. Under this section, there is no need to prove a defendant's negligence or awareness of the condition. It need only be established that Brassbestos committed a repeat violation.

The pursuit of the criminal conviction of Brassbestos as a herald of the new OCCA enforcement strategy shortly encountered a variety of roadblocks. In reviewing the record, the district attorney concluded that there were patent inadequacies in the proof needed to support the allegations. The district attorney believed that state inspectors had not notified the defendant after an earlier visit that the violation they discovered constituted a *serious* infraction; Brassbestos claimed that it was told that it was being given only a general warning to take remedial action. Reviewing the entire documentation provided him, the prosecutor concluded that it was not persuasive enough to proceed to trial; instead, he was willing to plea bargain. On May 23, 1979, at the municipal court's Disposition and Resetting session, a nolo contendere plea was accepted, and the company was fined $350. The case against the Brassbestos vice-president was dismissed. The assistant district attorney concluded that this was not a good case; should another, stronger OCCA case be forthcoming at some later date, he was convinced that his office would prosecute it vigorously.[20]

The Salwasser Case

It has become uncertain now whether California OCCA authorities will be able to institute other criminal cases in the wake of the *Brassbestos* debacle. Such a prospect was sidetracked, at least temporarily, when the Fifth District Court of Appeals of California declared in the *Salwasser* case that, absent employer consent, probable cause in the criminal sense was required in order to gain entrance to workplace sites for the purpose of conducting routine inspections of occupational safety and health conditions.[21]

Melvin Salwasser, owner of a business located in southcentral California, twice refused admission of a Cal-OSHA inspector to his plant. The inspector thereafter obtained a warrant that recited, among other things, that he was authorized by law to examine places of employment to enforce compliance with safety regulations. To establish inspection priorities the inspector used a computerized listing of places which showed reported industrial accidents which were believed to be preventable. Salwasser again denied the inspector admittance to his plant and, consequently, was charged with and convicted of a misdemeanor for willfully refusing to permit an inspection lawfully authorized by a warrant.

The California appellate court reversed the lower court's conviction and based its decision on the ground that, unlike the federal OSHA, the California Act was primarily criminal in nature; thus, it was necessary to establish criminal probable cause before a warrant could be issued to permit premise inspections. Criminal penalties were said to "permeate" the California OSHA statute to the point where a person, the court's ruling noted, could be guilty not only for knowing violations, but for mere negligence. These provisions were said to be "extreme departures" from the federal OSHA law, and therefore, under the requirements of the Fourth Amendment of the United States Constitution, the provisions of Cal-OSHA necessitated more stringent standards for search warrants than those allowed by federal courts under the federal OSHA law and under municipal laws equivalent to the federal OSHA.

The reasoning offered to support the *Salwasser* decision is open to serious challenge. It is true that the penalty structure of the California OSHA law is much more criminal in nature than that found in the federal OSHA statute.[22] However, a determination of what standard of probable cause should exist in order to justify the issuance of a search warrant hinges on the purpose underlying the particular search, rather than the nature of the penalty which may potentially be invoked. The express purpose of a search resulting from a warrant issued under the criminal law probable cause standard is the securing of evidence which will lead to the prosecution and conviction of a person or persons. Thus, the purpose of obtaining incriminating evidence necessitates the "higher" probable cause standard prior to the issuance of a warrant. The purpose of an administrative search, on the other hand, is not necessarily to obtain incriminating evidence. The California appellate court in *Salwasser* apparently missed this distinction and misread the thrust of the United States Supreme Court decision in *Marshall v. Barlow's Inc.*,[23] from which it felt compelled to distinguish *Salwasser*. The Court in *Barlow's* agreed with the judgment in *Camara v. Municipal Court* that the right to inspect under a warrant depended only on a showing that "reasonable legislative or administrative standards" formed a basis for the determination of which premises were to be inspected. In *Camara*, the lessee of a San Francisco apartment refused to permit the warrantless inspection of his premises by a housing inspector making a routine annual review. The standard did not require probable cause that would justify a belief that conditions in violation of the act could be found, nor did it emphasize a concern with the possible consequences of the detection of a violation. *Camara* focused instead on "determining reasonableness . . . by balancing the need to search against the invasion which the search entails."[24] *Invasion* presumably had reference to considerations of privacy, interruption of work, and similar immediate employer inconveniences. Similarly, the key to the holding in *Barlow's* is the purpose underlying the administrative search, and not the nature of the penalty which may be imposed, a point clearly missed by the *Salwasser* court.

Federal courts have specifically upheld administrative search warrant procedures with full knowledge that the regulatory laws to which they apply might well be enforced by criminal penalties. In *Camara*, for instance, it was noted:

> Like most regulatory laws, fire, health, and housing codes are enforced by criminal processes. In some cities, discovery of a violation by the inspector leads to a criminal complaint. Even in cities where discovery of a violation produces only an administrative compliance order, refusal to comply is a criminal offense, and the fact of compliance is verified by a second inspection, again without a warrant. Finally, as this case demonstrates, refusal to permit an inspection is itself a crime, punishable by fine or even by jail sentence.[25]

Similarly, the Sixth Circuit Court of Appeals had declared that administrative probable cause was constitutionally satisfactory grounds to secure warrants to inspect under provisions of the Federal Coal Mine Health and Safety Act, although criminal penalties were possible for violations of the Act's provisions. The court took direct notice of the purpose of the Act as undergirding its conclusion:

> Here the public need, recognized as "urgent" by Congress in the preamble to the Act, is the promotion of the "health and safety of [the coal mine industry's] most precious resource—the miner. . . ." The demands of effective enforcement, which may prevent needless injury, disability or death, outweigh the "historic interests of 'self protection'" which would otherwise come into play when the inspector asks "that the property owner open his doors to a search for 'evidence of criminal action' which may be used to secure the owner's criminal conviction."[26]

Nonetheless, however unfounded its legal argument, the *Salwasser* decision posed a significant dilemma for California authorities charged with enforcing the state occupational health and safety laws. While most businesses had been willing as a matter of course to allow inspections, it was possible that, as a result of *Salwasser*, they might resist such incursions. The likelihood of getting information from second-hand sources that would permit the building of a criminal probable cause standard, however unlikely for safety violations, would be particularly remote in carcinogens cases. One of the more obvious remedies for the state authorities was to retreat from criminal sanctions and to adopt a penalty structure more in accord with the federal law, thereby taking advantage of the more favorable rulings on administrative probable cause criteria imposed by the federal courts. At the moment, the response to *Salwasser* has not been determined, although the decision has at least temporarily derailed plans for an intensive effort to bring a barrage of criminal cases against violators of the carcinogenic control workplace standards.

Deterrence

Regardless of the state's adaptation to *Salwasser*, a fundamental unanswered issue remains concerning the value of criminal sanctions, both in white-collar crime cases in general and in OCCA cases in particular. The question focuses on whether criminal penalties against violators of occupational health and safety standards, and particularly those standards set forth in OCCA, induce greater conformity to the guidelines than would be produced by mediation, by civil penalties, such as injunctions and civil fines, or by other approaches, such as a harsh glare of publicity.[27] Perhaps this statement of the matter is too simplistic when in truth each sanction, or combination of sanctions, would be appropriate depending upon the circumstances, with criminal sanctions reserved for the most heinous malevolences.

Occupational health crimes are somewhat different from street crimes, such as robbery and burglary, in one important respect. In the case of street crimes, a term of imprisonment has a true incapacitative effect—the offender during the period of incarceration will not commit depredatory acts upon persons outside of the prison. There is, in this sense, an element of *specific deterrence* involved in the penal response to the act. The only other effective manner for achieving the same outcome would be constant surveillance, a method which, though not impossible,[28] is replete with logistic and civil rights problems. For the workplace violator, however, it is likely that plans can be adopted to assure that the offending situation is immediately remedied. Although such measures may resolve the particular problem, some reasonable scrutiny must be used to make certain that other potential violations do not occur through the willful negligent agency of the offending corporation or persons. Violators, however, can develop techniques to outwit inspectors, so perhaps the matter is not as simple as the text here implies. A chief steward in a Missouri factory told a Senate investigating committee how his company duped the industrial hygienists:

> My company will only make changes when it is forced to make changes. Health, community health[,] plays second fiddle to increased production and bigger profits. For example, a State inspector announces the date of his inspection tour to the company, and it is very easy to cut production that day, cutting back the furnaces; there is no risk of a furnace blowhole to pollute the air. After his trip, the inspector writes a good report and then there is business as usual.[29]

The issue in occupational health cases, then, is one of *general deterrence*, the ability of a criminal sanction to convey to others besides the particular offender a sufficiently forbidding message to encourage adequate attempts to conform to the standards of the law.

Much speculation has surfaced regarding deterrence of white-collar crime, but relatively little unimpeachable research evidence exists. A recent

law review note devoted some 168 pages to the matter of regulating corporate behavior through criminal sanctions, taking heed of the fact that
"[d]uring the last decade . . . in areas ranging from tax . . . to the newer
fields of environmental control [and] safety regulation . . . the federal
government has come to rely more and more on the deterrent effect of
criminal punishment to shape corporate action."[30] But the author could
offer no more substantive data on the utility of criminal penalties against
corporations and/or their officers than an article that appeared the
previous year on the same topic, which concluded: "In short, our
knowledge of the relationship between the theories of criminal punishment
and the nature of the modern corporation is not sufficiently developed to
permit a commitment to a particular sanction for a particular class of
crimes."[31] The author suggested, as have other commentators in the field
of social sciences, that the resolution lay in more and better research. It
was believed necessary to authorize as wide a range of reasonable penalties
as possible and then to examine their effectiveness. Judges, it was argued,
then would be able to adjust sentences for corporate crime both for the circumstances of each case and in regard to the demonstrated utility of the
particular sanction. The author, however, failed to do justice to the
burgeoning cry in criminal justice circles for what is called "just
deserts"—that is, for nondiscretionary, nonindividualized sentences based
on the specifics of behavior, rather than differentiating individual characteristics of offenders.[32] Nor were ethical issues in regard to conducting
research to determine deterrent impact adequately addressed.[33] Such
research can best be accomplished by randomly imposing certain penalties
to determine how they work, although there are other, more inferential,
kinds of strategies. Such randomness, however, may well be regarded as a
violation of the *equal protection* rights of convicted persons.

The evidence that exists would seem to favor the argument that
criminal penalties, particularly those involving incarceration, would prove
effective as general deterrents if leveled against violators of statutes such as
OCCA. The grounds for such a belief are manifold. The United States
Attorney General, speaking before the House of Representatives Subcommittee on Crime of the Committee on the Judiciary, insisted that "heavy
prison terms" should be the rule for white-collar crime because such
offenses "generally involve careful planning . . . and a conscious weighing
of the cost and anticipated benefits in the design of evil intent.[34] Studies of
deterrence by academicians have found that older, more established professional persons are less likely to be recidivists than younger persons.[35] It is
also maintained that for the individual whose initial socialization was largely
conventional, the social costs of labeling are probably higher than for those
whose early socialization was based on deviant norms and values.[36] This
general line of reasoning is summarized in the following terms:

Punishment may work best with those individuals who are "future oriented" and who are thus worried about the effect of punishment on their future plans and their social status rather than being concerned largely with the present and having little or no concern with their status. For this reason gang boys may be deterred by punishment less strongly than the white-collar professional person.[37]

Finally, some commentators enunciate a principle of noblesse oblige, insisting that persons who have reaped the greatest good from the social system owe it a higher obligation than those in less privileged positions. The default of the well-positioned on matters involving the public trust merits more severe disapprobation than similar derelictions by persons less well-situated, such as members of minority groups from whom the largest number of traditional criminals are drawn.[38] Other commentators, on the other hand, argue that criminal sanctions are neither appropriate nor useful for dealing with offenses such as occupational health violations. They state that the statutes generally regulate economic transactions; that violators engage in what one writer has termed *morally neutral* behavior; and that the public has not demanded harsh penalties.[39] The results of a considerable series of studies of public attitudes refute this latter position. All but one of these studies report that public estimates of the seriousness of white-collar crimes and street crimes are virtually identical if the harms are similar. The public also favors similar sentences for similar harms.[40] Critics of these studies might maintain that they pose hypothetical vignettes to respondents, vignettes which assume that guilt is as unequivocal in the white-collar offenses as it is in the street violations. The studies also might be faulted for allowing attitudinal results to be taken too readily to represent the actual kinds of behaviors that the respondents would perform were they to find themselves on juries charged with determining guilt and/or assessing penalties. The guess is that, despite similar harmfulness of their acts, white-collar offenders would fare better than street offenders.

Despite the intense debate, there exists extraordinarily little empirical evidence that might offer comfort to persons on one side of the matter or the other. Ezra Stotland and his colleagues offer some support for the view that militant prosecution of home repair frauds in King County, Washington, reduced the number of such frauds, as measured by the flow of complaints registered by residents.[41] Earlier, the President's Commission on Law Enforcement and Administration of Justice, reporting in 1967, suggested that prison sentences levied against executives of the General Electric Company and other businesses in the wake of flagrant antitrust violations had becalmed such activities, at least temporarily.[42] The Commission also provided some suggestive, but far from definitive, evidence that the rate of prosecutions for income tax violations bore an inverse relationship to the rate of violations in a given jurisdiction.[43]

But sterner sentences for white-collar offenders are not limited to their effect upon the violating party. They involve further matters, such as the inculcation in the citizenry of a sense of justice and fairness, a faith in the integrity of the system, and a trust that the wealthy or powerful are not immune from the legal process and that the system will intervene to protect victims. Viewed from this philosophical and empirical perspective, the argument for criminal penalties against white-collar offenders seems to be particularly compelling.

Conclusion

The impetus in California to apply criminal penalties to violations of the state's statute to control the use of substances alleged to produce cancer has, for the moment at least, been stalled. There are, however, a number of lessons that might be learned from the brief, somewhat frantic, and so far ineffective, venture. By no means are all of the conclusions discouraging.

The California experience reinforces the growing conviction among criminologists that a public and political constituency exists—one latently responsive to calls for heavier sanctions against violators of many of the laws regulating white-collar offenses. This is probably truest when the matter at hand involves real or potential serious harm traceable to a violation of the legal standards. The proliferation of public and academic concern about white-collar crime reflects a variety of social considerations: (1) a relative affluence, which allows talents and emotions to be directed to other things besides the stark earning of a living; (2) the greater degree of education in America and abroad which brings in its wake a lesser willingness to cater to control by those whose credentials are rooted only in economic power; (3) an increasing control of the human life span which engenders a lesser willingness to tolerate life- and health-threatening conditions that might shorten possible longevity; (4) an inflationary trend of a degree sufficient to call into question the goals of the business community in regard to other than its own aggrandizement; (5) a consumer movement that, as it develops, creates an accretive effect; and (6) the Watergate scandals, which created a general cynicism about the honesty of government officials and processes. The work of Ralph Nader and his study teams, the polemics of the Marxists, and the litigation by public interest lawyers also have aroused public concern.

The California OCCA has several conditions making it a good place upon which to focus a strong enforcement effort. In its favor is the dread nature of the harm being attacked. No one is likely to argue that effective efforts to remedy cancer-causing conditions do not warrant serious attention. Furthermore, the inability to demonstrate "success" may in a paradoxical way favor OCCA. Many remedial campaigns are quickly faulted because later statistics do not demonstrate any apparent improvement in the rates at which the targeted ills have declined. For OCCA it will take years before any possible relationship between cancer rates and occupational health conditions might be inferred, and then the matter will remain somewhat speculative. In regard to safety, for instance, research efforts appear to show that the federal OSHA, with a considerable expenditure of funds, has not had a very significant impact on altering the rate of injuries at the workplace.[44] The results of such studies may reflect a flaw in experimental design: the pre- and post-figures do not adequately indicate what would have happened without the law. At best, the reports allow informed guesses by attempting to take into account lesser or more serious dangers involved in newer equipment and similar noncontrolled (in an experimental sense) issues. As is true of many governmental interventions, however, the onus tends to fall on the program to demonstrate its success, rather than upon its opponents to demonstrate its failure. No such "empirical" disputation can proceed very far in regard to OCCA since the definitive data will not be available for some time, if ever.

However, the delayed, time-bomb nature of workplace-induced cancer has to be seen as a strong barrier to effective criminal prosecutions under the OCCA formulation. It is not impossible that a person could be convicted of a violation of standards that, years later, could be demonstrated to have produced none of the harms said to be associated with the offense. As a result, it is juridically clear that the delayed aspect of the cancer harm makes criminal prosecution more difficult in terms of proof and also justification than in cases with a closer juxtaposition of act or neglect and outcome.

The brief biography of the manner in which OCCA came to be singled out for criminal prosecutions is in some regards an object lesson about what not to do. The failure to coordinate prosecution efforts between state authorities and the county district attorneys seems an obvious tactical error. Failure to involve the objects of the crusade in some part of its implementation also may have been a shortcoming. It may be that cooptation of state authorities by business interests, a common condition said to affect federal regulatory agencies,[45] may have occurred. But the idea of mounting a campaign against workplace carcinogens, which included some industrial leaders in its ranks, should have been explored. In particular too, the state bureaucracy might have been involved more thoroughly in the contemplated turn to criminal sanctions, rather than, as our interviews indicate, being dragged into a procedure that its members often regarded as an irritating dictate from above.

It could not have been anticipated that the *Salwasser* decision would undercut so thoroughly the campaign to use criminal enforcement against OCCA violators. That case raises a basic issue in regard to white-collar crime, one that never has been addressed adequately. Anglo-Saxon juris-prudence rests upon a commitment to equal protection before the law. All are entitled to the same guarantees, and, to the best of our limited ability, to the same kinds of resources in pressing or defending suits. Although the doctrine of free will underlies our system of jurisprudence, these tenets of equality may be largely a chimera, an unachievable and even undesirable goal rather than the noble doctrine that we almost invariably take it to be. In the recent ABSCAM cases, critics often raised the matter of entrapment, claim-ing that perhaps it was asking too much that citizens be tested to see if they could resist temptation. Few, if any, commentators seemed to take the posi-tion that resistance to temptation, despite possible entrapment, was none-theless a reasonable standard to which to hold a public official.

The future patterns of enforcement of the OCCA are for the moment unclear. There has been an increase in calls for sterner penalties against white-collar crime, and the media often report minatory remarks by judges imposing sentences on persons in the higher social echelons who have vio-lated laws regulating business, political, or professional conduct. At the same time, the resources available to ferret out and to prosecute white-col-lar crime remain notably slim, and the path to successful prosecution re-mains strewn with sizeable pitfalls. It may be that greater resources will be brought to bear upon such offenses, or it may be that novel steps—par-ticularly those of a legal nature—will be adopted to improve some of the conditions hindering prosecution. On the other hand, the complexities of changing social conditions and moods may undercut the enforcement momentum that seems to have built up in recent years, or strategies of control may evolve that differ from the present use of civil and criminal sanctions. Future developments in regard to OCCA enforcement may well foretell possible outcomes in regard to both occupational health and white-collar crime in general. At the moment, it appears that matters might follow any of the foregoing courses, so uncertain is the relationship among the law, effective and possible tactics for its enforcement, and the public and official aspirations.

Notes

1. See generally Nicholas A. Ashford, *Crisis in the Workplace* (Cam-bridge, Mass.: MIT Press, 1976); Daniel M. Berman, *Doing the Job* (New York: Monthly Review Press, 1979); Paul Brodeur, *Expendable Americans* (New York: Viking, 1974); Lawrence L. Fishbein, *Potential Industrial Car-cinogens and Mutagens* (New York: Elsevier, 1979); John Mendeloff, *Regulating Safety* (Cambridge, Mass.: MIT Press, 1979); Joseph A. Page and Mary-Win O'Brien, *Bitter Wages* (New York: Grossman, 1973).

2. See, for example, Jeffrey H. Reiman, *The Rich Get Rich and the Poor Get Prison* (New York: Wiley, 1979), pp. 65-72.

3. National Highway Traffic Safety Administration, U.S. Department of Transportation, *A Report to the Congress on the Effect of Motorcycle Helmet Use Law Repeal—A Case for Helmet Use* (1980), IV-15.

4. Beauregard v. Johns-Manville, No. C-137466 (Los Angeles Superior Court 1980).

5. *Los Angeles Times* (July 22, 1980), sec. 1, p. 1.

6. Benjamin W. McCready, *On the Influence of Trades, Professions, and Occupations in the United States, in the Production of Disease* (1837) (New York: Arno Press, 1972).

7. An exception was the Walsh-Healey Act, Public Law No. 74-846, 49 Stat. 2036 (1936). The Act regulated wages, hours, and conditions of labor for employees of governmental contractors that manufactured or furnished supplies and equipment in amounts exceeding $10,000.

8. Public Law No. 91-596, sec. 2, 84 Stat. 1590 (1970) (codified at 29 U.S.C. sec. 651-678 (1976)).

9. See John B. Perna, *Occupational Safety and Health Act, 1970: A Bibliography* (1974). This bibliography, prepared by the Library of Congress Law Library, contains references for the extensive legislative history of the federal OSHA. See generally Marjorie E. Gross, "The Occupational Safety and Health Act: Much Ado About Something." *Loyola-Chicago Law Journal,* 3 (Summer 1972), pp. 247-269; Stephen R. Kirklin, "OSHA: Employer Beware," *Houston Law Journal,* 10 (January 1973), pp. 426-449; Michael H. Levin, "Crimes Against Employees: Substantive Criminal Sanctions Under the Occupational Safety and Health Act," *American Criminal Law Review,* 14 (1977), pp. 717-745.

10. See Carol Hunter, "The California Occupational Safety and Health Act: An Overview," *Los Angeles Bar Bulletin,* 50 (June 1975), pp. 303-312; Susan A. Myers, "The California Occupational Safety and Health Act of 1973," *Loyola Law Review,* 9 (1976), pp. 905-960.

11. Calif. Health and Safety Code, sec. 24200-24261 (West Supp. 1980).

12. Larry Agran, *The Cancer Connection* (Boston: Houghton Mifflin, 1977).

13. See generally *New York Times* Information Service, *Industrial and Occupational Hazards* (1979), which provides a selection of news clippings from more than sixty leading U.S. and international publications.

14. Agran, *Cancer Connection,* pp. 35-36. The case involved the Diamond Shamrock Chemical Company in Redwood City, California. Several workers out of a relatively small work force had developed lung cancer, allegedly because of uncontained exposure to bis(Chloromethyl)ether, known as BCME.

15. The propriety and constitutionality of statutes imposing what can amount to strict criminal liability had been affirmed in United States v. Park, 421 U.S. 658, 673 (1975), with the ringing phrase: "Congress has seen fit to enforce the accountability of responsible corporate agents dealing with products which may affect the health of consumers by penal sanctions cast in rigorous terms. . . ."

16. People v. Brassbestos Mfg. Corp., Criminal Complaint No. NM7903777 (N. Orange County Mun. Ct. 1979).

17. See *Wall Street Journal* (October 16, 1975), p. 1, for a discussion of the CLPI. The Campaign for Economic Democracy (CED) began in 1977 as an outgrowth of Hayden's unsuccessful bid for the U.S. Senate. Hayden claims a membership of eight-thousand persons, with five-hundred to one-thousand said to be active in the organization.

18. Aletta d'A. Belin, Geoffrey Cowan, Stephen M. Kristovich, Allegra Hamman, and David Dominguez, "Criminal Enforcement of California's Occupational Health Laws: A Preliminary Analysis of Occupational Carcinogens Control Act Violations," *American Journal of Criminal Law,* 8 (March 1980), pp. 43-89.

19. Aileen Adams and Lynn Miller, "Implementation of a Model Misdemeanor Nursing Home Enforcement Program," *University of West Los Angeles Law Review,* 10 (Summer 1978), pp. 141-158.

20. The assistant district attorney stated that he had to have "a 'makeable' case, where you've got a chance. Then the office would have to get together expert witnesses on carcinogens and feel its way into a novel area." Telephone interview with Terry Hall, Assistant District Attorney, Anaheim, Cal. (August 2, 1979). It is unclear how widely this view is held among other prosecutors. According to attorneys at the Center for Law in the Public Interest, the district attorneys in Los Angeles and Orange Counties are receptive to the idea of criminal prosecutions for OCCA violations.

21. Salwasser Mfg. Co. v. Municipal Ct., 94 Cal. App. 3d 223, 156 Cal. Rptr. 292 (1979). Cf. Comment, "Criminal Probable Cause in Administrative Searches Under California OSHA: Mandated or Preempted?" *Pacific Law Journal,* 11 (July 1980), pp. 1019-1038.

22. The only criminal provision in the federal statute specifies that if an employer willfully violates a provision of the law and if that violation leads to the death of an employee, the employer can be fined up to $10,000 and/or imprisoned for up to six months. The second conviction for such a violation is punishable by a fine up to $1,000 and/or six months' imprisonment. 29 U.S.C. sec. 666 (f) (1976). Giving unauthorized advance notice of an inspection is criminally punishable by a fine up to $1,000 and/or six months' imprisonment. 29 U.S.C. sec. 666 (f) (1976). Making a false statement or filing false documents is punishable by a fine up to $10,000 or imprisonment up to six months or both. 29 U.S.C. sec. 666 (g) (1976).

23. 436 U.S. 307 (1978). See Mark A. Rothstein, "OSHA Inspections after *Marshall v. Barlow's, Inc.*," *Duke Law Journal* (1979), pp. 63-103; Lynn G. Weissberg, *"Marshall v. Barlow's Inc.*: Are Warrantless Routine OSHA Inspections A Violation of the Fourth Amendment?", *Environment Affairs*, 6 (1978), pp. 423-447; Note, *"Marshall v. Barlow's, Inc.*, and the Warrant Requirement for OSHA 'Spot Check' Inspections," *Idaho Law Review* (1978), pp. 187-217; Robert I. Goldfarb, "Constitutional Law—OSHA Searches: A Fourth Amendment Warrant Requirement," *University of Florida Law Review*, 30 (1978), pp. 991-1001.

24. 387 U.S. 523 (1967).

25. Ibid., p. 531 (footnotes omitted).

26. United States v. Consolidation Coal Co., 560 F. 2d 214, 220 (6th Cir. 1977), cert. denied, 439 U.S. 1069 (1979), quoting Camara v. Municipal Ct., 387 U.S. 523, 530 (1967).

27. See generally Brent Fisse, "The Use of Publicity as a Criminal Sanction Against Business Corporations," *Melbourne University Law Review*, 8 (June 1971), pp. 107-150.

28. Ralph Schwitzgebel, *Development and Legal Regulation of Coercive Behavior Modification Techniques with Offenders* (Washington, D.C.: U.S. Government Printing Office, 1971), pp. 15-21.

29. John Esposito, *Vanishing Air* (New York: Grossman, 1970), p. 87.

30. Comment, "Corporate Crime: Regulating Corporate Behavior through Criminal Sanctions," *Harvard Law Review*, 92 (April 1979), pp. 1227-1235.

31. Stephen A. Yoder, "Criminal Sanctions for Corporate Illegality," *Journal of Criminal Law and Criminology*, 69 (Spring 1978), p. 58.

32. See Andrew Von Hirsch, *Doing Justice: The Choice of Punishments* (New York: Hill and Wang, 1976); American Friends Service Committee, *Struggle for Justice* (New York: Hill and Wang, 1971).

33. See Franklin E. Zimring and Gordon Hawkins, *Deterrence: The Legal Threat in Crime Control* (Chicago: University of Chicago Press, 1973), pp. 32-50.

34. Benjamin Civiletti, Statement, in U.S. House of Representatives, Committee on the Judiciary, Subcommittee on Crime, *White Collar Crime: Hearings,* 95th Cong., 2d Sess. (1979), p. 81.

35. Harold G. Grasmick and Herman Milligan, Jr., "Deterrence Theory Applied to Socioeconomic/Demographic Correlates of Crime," *Social Science Quarterly,* 57 (1976), pp. 608-617.

36. John Delamater, "On the Nature of Deviance," *Social Forces,* 46 (June 1968), pp. 445-455.

37. Marshall B. Clinard and Robert F. Meier, *Sociology of Deviant Behavior,* 5th editor. (New York: Holt, Rinehart and Winston, 1979), p. 248.

38. Gilbert Geis, "Deterring Corporate Crime," in eds. Ralph Nader and Mark Green, *Corporate Power in America* (New York: Grossman, 1973), p. 182.

39. Sanford H. Kadish, "Some Observations on the Use of Criminal Sanctions in Enforcing Economic Regulations," *University of Chicago Law Review,* 30 (Spring 1963), pp. 435-440.

40. Laura Schrager and James F. Short, Jr., "How Serious a Crime?: Perceptions of Organizational and Common Crimes," in eds. Gilbert Geis and Ezra Stotland, *White-Collar Crime: Theory and Research* (Beverly Hills: Sage, 1980), pp. 14, 20-30.

41. Ezra Stotland, Michael Brintnall, Andre L'Heureaux, and Eve Ashmore, "Do Convictions Deter Home Repair Fraud?" in eds. Gilbert Geis and Ezra Stotland, *White-Collar Crime: Theory and Research* (Beverly Hills: Sage, 1980), pp. 252, 258-263.

42. President's Commission on Law Enforcement and Administration of Justice, *Crime and Its Impact—An Assessment* (Washington, D.C.: U.S. Government Printing Office, 1967), p. 105.

43. Ibid., pp. 113-115.

44. Robert S. Smith, "The Impact of OSHA Inspections on Manufacturing Injury Rates," *Journal of Human Resources,* 14 (1979), pp. 145-170.

45. See, for example, Gabriel Kolko, *The Triumph of Conservatism* (New York: Free Press, 1963); James Weinstein, *The Corporate Ideal in the Liberal State: 1900-1918* (Boston: Beacon Press, 1968); Andrew Hopkins, "On the Sociology of Criminal Law," *Social Problems*, 22 (1975), pp. 608-619. But see Suzanne Weaver, *Decision to Prosecute* (Cambridge, Mass.: MIT Press, 1977), p. 175.

9

The Abuse of Power as a Criminal Activity: Toward an Understanding of the Behavior and Methods for Its Control

Robert F. Meier and
Gilbert Geis

Newspaper headlines throughout the world daily proclaim that abuses of power are rampant and that they challenge the integrity of social and political existence. Not long ago, for instance, the *New York Times* concluded about a foreign power with which the United States does a good deal of business that ". . . Corruption is Threat to . . .Stability."[1] Another newspaper headline tells of an announcement by an assistant attorney general in the United States: "1,000 Officials Convicted of Corruption." The body of the story details the prosecutions initiated for illegal use of public office during the previous twelve months.[2] Elsewhere, the *China News* notes that "India Cracks Down on Economic Crimes,"[3] while the *Wall Street Journal* observes that " 'Sticky Handshakes' Are Coming Unglued . . ." in an Asian country.[4] The same paper also calls attention to what it headlines as ". . . Currency Smugglers" operating from positions of power in a European nation.[5]

Scholars also pinpoint abuse of power as characterizing many societies. ". . . Corruption . . . seems endemic to public life," one commentator notes in regard to a third world country.[6] Other writers have found abuse of power and corruption in parts of Africa "an omnipresent fact of life,"[7] and they have coined phrases such as "kleptocracy" to describe "a political system ruled by thieves."[8]

Another recent headline proclamation—"White Collar Crimes Called an Epidemic"[9]—seems an accurate depiction of current public belief. It remains arguable whether matters are worse today than they were in earlier times, or whether people have become less willing to tolerate abuses of power. Possible decreasing passivity in the face of exploitation might well be based upon more widespread and better education, and upon better documentation by the media of abuses of power. It might also be a function of better living standards. On the other hand, affluence itself may well

Robert F. Meier and Gilbert Geis. Presented at United Nations' conference on "Crime and the Abuse of Power," San Jose, Costa Rica, 5-9 May 1980.

125

have increased opportunities and temptations which raise the level of abuse. Whatever the explanation for the apparent heightened worldwide level of concern and indignation about abuse of power, it is clear that there are widespread demands for remedial action.

It is not necessary to understand either the causes or the concomitants of an activity in order to control it effectively. Medical research workers often have created satisfactory remedies for illnesses whose etiology was unknown to them. At the same time, it is helpful to comprehend the basis of an activity in order that the proposed curative agenda not prove ineffective or even counterproductive because of a failure to take account of possible alternative outcomes which, had the target been better understood, might have been anticipated. For this reason, we will devote some early attention to characteristics of the abuse of power, though our fundamental focus— and the largest portion of the paper—will concentrate on what we know or need to find out about the containment of such abuses.

Power and Its Abuse

The concept of *power* has been variously defined: perhaps the common denomination of the multifarious definitions has been a recognition that power plays a very great role in human and political interactions. Bertrand Russell noted that "the fundamental concept in social science is Power, in the same sense that Energy is the fundamental concept in physics."[10] Nonetheless, precise delineation of what is meant by power generally has evaded scholars. As Robert Bierstedt has observed:

> In the entire lexicon of social concepts none is more troublesome than the concept of power. We may say about it in general only what St. Augustine said about time, that we all know perfectly well what it is—until someone asks us.[11]

The American criminologist, Edwin H. Sutherland, was the first to popularize in a forceful manner the idea of a distinctive category of criminal activities perpetrated by persons of power, persons who could employ business, professional, or political advantages to exploit others in less advantaged positions. Sutherland called attention to the fact that such persons, whom he labeled *white-collar criminals,* were regarded as "normal" and "well-adjusted" members of the society. Sutherland maintained, on the basis of persuasive evidence, that the impact upon a society of offenses committed by persons in positions of power is of greater magnitude than the effect of such "conventional" crimes as robbery, arson, and murder. The suffering in economic deprivation was for Sutherland only the most obvious outcome of abuses of power: more serious was an erosion of citizen trust and confidence in the decency of the social system and the integrity of its leaders.[12]

In the literature on abuse of power, only Ronald Wraith and Edgar Simpkins have tried to relate nationwide honesty and the integrity of a country's leaders. They ask: "What were the factors which led Britain, a country as corrupt as any, to achieve in a particular century [the nineteenth century] a standard of public integrity which is perhaps without precedent?"[13] They suggest the answer lies in the fact that the country's leaders during the period were persons who had gained large fortunes through commerce that sometimes had been conducted on the periphery of the law. Once the fortunes were secure, their possessors felt impelled to turn their energies to public service, perhaps as a recompense for their depredations, perhaps out of a sense of theological necessity, as an attempt to save their souls.

The lesson from these materials may be that power will not be abused—at least in fiscal terms—if persons who come to possess it are so well off financially beforehand that additional funds seem irrelevant. But such a formulation ignores the force of *relative deprivation,* a term that refers to the fact that no matter what most of us have, we seem to conclude that something additional will make life more satisfying. It may be that the abuse of power can only be controlled when those who possess power have been trained or have internalized moral imperatives that make distasteful the exploitation of others. In this regard, Wraith and Simpkins have noted of those incorruptible nineteenth-century British leaders:

> They were immensely *responsible* people. In considering solid, middle-class Victorian respectability today it is fashionable to emphasize the smugness and hypocrisy which were its darker side, and to pay too little tribute to its enduring achievement, particularly in the creation of a sense of public duty.[14]

On the other hand, overwhelming evidence undergirds the significance of Lord Acton's axiom that "power corrupts," and perhaps only by keeping the exercise of power balanced by alert and countervailing forces can its abuse be kept in check. We shall, as noted, examine propositions such as these as we proceed.

Although the precision and analytical value of Sutherland's original writings about white-collar crime have been severely criticized, the appellation has gained widespread currency in both intellectual and popular circles throughout the world. The phrase *white-collar crime* calls attention to a secondary, inferential characteristic of the offender—his social status and an aspect of his dress that signifies such status. A term such as *abuse of power,* which the United Nations employs, places emphasis more intensively on the political and social leverage that a person can exercise by means of his status. Ultimately, of course, the behaviors of concern will have to be examined in terms of their individual or group characteristics as these become relevant to an understanding of etiology and control. We will have to talk about corruption and its many different forms, and about matters which may be quite distinctive, such as bankruptcy fraud, crimes against creditors, the filing of false financial statements, antitrust or anticombines violations, tax offenses, civil rights crimes, and illegal election procedures. Activist reformers would go even further; they suggest that criminologists attend to any behaviors which violate what they perceive to be fundamental human rights.[15]

It may be regarded either as an irony or as a truism that a community's most serious crimes quite often are committed by the community's most powerful members. Power itself, as Dennis Wrong has indicated, can be viewed as an expansible phenomenon, limited by social arrangements, such as the number of persons over whom it is possible to exercise control.[16] As these arrangements change, so does the amount of power. And as power shifts and alters, so do the potentials for its abuse. Since power is a property of social systems, societies that have the greatest division of labor are prone to be the most power-ridden. Movement from agrarian to industrialized social life brings about a proliferation of occupation titles, and an increase in the number of "service" workers. With the increase in the number and the specialization of roles, there ensue more ways in which power can be abused.

Not that abuses of power are to be found only in those societies with heavy industrialization; it is that such societies will manifest the largest *range* of violations. Developing nations, with more agrarian emphases, can demonstrate patterns of power abuse that have greater serious negative national impacts than their industrialized counterparts. Indeed, concentration of power leads to its abuse affecting more victims, other things being equal. In the United States, for instance, the Watergate crimes, however terrible, remained relatively encapsulated. Few persons were personally affected, whatever the disclosures might have done for the public faith in governmental processes. The Watergate crimes also call attention to an important component of abuse of power: it need not occur only for fiscal purposes, but may primarily be directed at the maintenance of power.

Self-interest and self-serving behavior, we emphasize, can take a variety of behavioral forms, most of them involving competition between diverse individuals and groups for limited resources. A basic task, particularly for a law seeking true justice and fairness, is to separate legitimate from unacceptable exercises of self-determination and self-aggrandizement and to interdict the latter. Then the concern becomes one of arranging and controlling human and institutional acts so that the desirable and decent forms of social life can prevail.

Culture and the Abuse of Power

There is no question but that social learning is the most fundamental in-gredient in determining how different people are going to behave as they proceed through life. We all learn, generally in quite subtle ways, what is permissible—to ourselves and to others—for us to do in order to achieve what we desire. Those things we desire are determined presumably both by biological conditions in general and in particular (that is, by our own genetic makeup), and by the segment of the society into which we are born and the experiences we have there and acquire elsewhere. The foregoing points, once said (and they certainly have been said often enough) seem obvious enough, almost trite. But their implications are profound, and those implications tend to be ignored in discourse on law and policy. The reason for this is simple enough: there is nothing that anybody can do (at least in terms of our present state of knowledge) to alter biologically determined human nature, and there is precious little that truly can be accomplished, at least very quickly, that will change the basic ethos of a social system so that the values transmitted and the mores observed conduce to more desirable ways of behaving. There are, to be sure, grand schemes of one or another kind that insist that this or that form of economic or political rearrangement will indeed change the extent or, at least, the pattern of criminal activity, including abuses of power. The difficulties with such blueprints are twofold: first, the evidence supporting the allegations, particularly as they concern changing an existing society rather than examining a society that has changed itself, is far from persuasive; and second, there is a failure to consider the mat-ter of crime in a wide context. Crime, after all, is but one of the ills—and not always that—that besets the human condition: its control and the alteration of its nature must always be examined and weighed in regard to the character of the proposed arrangements which are alleged to produce its diminution.

More fundamentally, criminologists are not social philosophers, and by the nature of their calling and its recognition and reward system they find themselves compelled to confine their discourse to criminologically specific methods for the control of criminal activity, even though, in truth, such measures are very likely to be relatively insignificant and unresponsive to fundamental concerns. Criminologists feel pressed to write about what they know best, and in terms of knowledge they share with their colleagues, about things such as deterrence, penalty structures, and legal doctrines. We shall do so as well in the remainder of this paper, but we want to stress, as emphatically as possible, that the things we will talk about, though they may represent the most practical, immediate pathways for dealing with abuses of power, or even the most acceptable means for doing so, cannot be regarded as the most effective ways in the long run. The best method is to create a social ethos in which it does not occur to people that it is permissible to rape, to murder, to take property that reasonably can be said to belong to others, or to abuse power. That such events occur at very different rates in different societies—independent of legal arrangements or formal penalties—indicates beyond argument where ultimate solutions lie, though the information barely suggests how such solutions may be achieved by social planning.

Deterring the Abuse of Power

The major contemporary vehicle for deterring abuse of power has been the criminal law. Research on deterrence, most of which has been conducted within the past decade, indicates that some penalties deter some persons some of the time.[17] While this is a far from definitive statement (or one that is likely to be of much practical value), it supports with empirical evidence the idea that punishment and the threat of punishment *can* prevent crime. The key research question now is not: "Do penalties deter?", but rather: "Under what conditions do penalties deter?"

The presumed "rationality" of a criminal act is regarded as a key element in the likelihood that the behavior can effectively be deterred. One does not expect psychopathic murderers to be deterrable; nor is there an expectation that homicides that arise from emotional, unplanned circumstances can be controlled very effectively by changes in a penalty structure. To the extent that offenses result from seemingly freely made decisions and actions, deterrence becomes a significant possibility. There is very little direct research on the matter, though a recent investigation by Ezra Stotland and several collaborators indicates that stepped-up prosecution can inhibit home repair fraud.[18] The nature of the offenses and the attributes of the offenders are what make abuses of power appear notably susceptible to control measures.

The Offenses

Typically, abuses of power are the result of planning. Oftentimes, they involve coordination between and among individuals. Political corruption, for instance, often requires tacit or overt support and encouragement from both criminal and noncriminal groups in the community.[19] The offenses commonly are committed over a long period of time, whether they involve multiple violations, or are restricted to a particular kind of violation, such as a complex price-fixing conspiracy. There is no evidence that psychological pathology "compels" the commission of these kinds of crimes; and no evidence that they are spontaneous events. Nor is there reason to believe that legal sanctions are not rather carefully considered as a possible consequence of such acts, that is, as part of their likely "cost."

Abuse of power usually involves a conscious economic motive or a conscious political motive, such as the acquisition or maintenance of advantage over others. And it has been precisely in the economic research on deterrence that the strongest case for the effectiveness of legal sanctions has been made.[20]

The Offenders

White-collar offenders (and potential white-collar offenders) generally are persons who have a considerable stake in the community. The strongest restraining influence on their possible illegal behavior may be the likelihood of community stigma, a loss of their good reputation.[21] Such persons usually have devoted much of their adult lives to securing and maintaining their reputations, and apprehension and notoriety for the commission of crimes can jeopardize their social standing. As relatively powerful persons, such offenders seemingly have a greater degree of freedom of choice than those less well favored socially. While there may be particular pressures to commit the offense, either in the form of individual problems,[22] or in the form of normative expectations from others,[23] acts of illegal abuse of power seem to preclude a crude deterministic model of human conduct. A clear requirement for sanctions to deter is that the individual who is the target must be aware of the illegality of his or her act and the sanctions that might be imposed.[24] That abuse of power is the result of deliberate actions on the part of persons who choose their course has been indicated by studies of things such as home repair fraud,[25] computer crimes,[26] and collusive bidding.[27]

But, while research on deterrence suggests that legal sanctions will be an effective deterrent to crime only under certain circumstances,[28] and that persons who illegally abuse power appear to be ideal candidates for such deterrence, there are a number of aspects of the offenses and their perpetrators that make this expectation somewhat problematic.

First, in practice criminal sanctions are applied to only a small portion of crimes involving abuse of power, and, when applied to these, the sanctions are relatively lenient. There tends to be little threat of swift and certain detection and significant punishment. Where administrative rather than criminal sanctions are employed, the regulatory agencies usually suffer from inadequate resources and the sanctions available to them tend to be rather mild.

Second, the very rationality and preplanning involved in instances of abuse of power take into account the likelihood of punitive consequences.

Given actual conditions, then, the sanctions employed may decrease rather than increase deterrence. As one writer has noted:

> If the assumption that many white-collar criminals are sophisticated is accurate, then they have probably discerned that it is rare to serve much more than three years in prison, and virtually impossible to serve that much time if they plead guilty to the charges.[29]

Studies of persons who commit more traditional kinds of offenses, such as juvenile delinquents and adult property offenders, suggest that individuals who have had experience with the criminal justice system perceive much more accurately than others the nature of the risks they run.[30] It is precisely the rationality (in lieu of experience with the criminal justice system) of white-collar offenders that permits their accurate assessments of the likely response to their abuse of power.

Implementing Deterrence

Research findings on deterrence suggest that penalties for abuse of power should be increased. Specialized agencies geared to the detection of abuses of power could be formed and their work well publicized. Obviously, they require total independence, lest they be corrupted or controlled by those they seek to monitor. Criminal sanctions should become the likely consequence of conviction, when such sanctions are available. These measures could afford more protection to the community, lessen the apparent bias in the system favoring those in positions of power who violate the law, and increase the overall deterrence effect by raising the risk offenders run.

The blueprint is not quite so straightforward, however. Criminal justice operations involve an intricate network of institutions; a major change in policies toward persons who abuse power and commit white-collar offenses will seriously impinge upon other operations, often to the point that the blueprint cannot feasibly be translated into action. In addition, as with "ordinary crime," rearranging the response can probably advance the deterrent effect of the law only to a certain point.[31]

Consider what needs to be done in terms of what it is possible to do. Most crimes now are solved on the basis of information secured at the scene of the crime or from leads supplied to law enforcement agencies, not by means of prolonged investigations. Detection methods may be as advanced now as we know how to make them. For abuses of power, investigatory resources probably can be increased only so far, before the yield diminished so significantly that the expense would be highly disproportionate to the benefit. The number of prosecutors could be raised, as could the number of judges—though both of these tend to be costly enterprises. Correctional resources, however, can be altered only at a much slower pace. Policing effectiveness, therefore, if increased dramatically, would likely overload the other components of the system, and very likely lead to new compromises with the strict dictates of the deterrent blueprint. Some play in the system might be realized by decriminalizing some offenses, such as the so-called victimless crimes,[32] but the prospects for a large-scale reduction in the workload of the system are limited.

There remain notoriously complex legal problems that also inhibit the operation of effective deterrence models in regard to offenses involving abuse of power. Most of the behaviors are concealed in the fabric of normal business transactions. Further, until the element of intent can be established, under most legal systems there simply is no case to prosecute.[33] In the United States, for instance, it has been pointed out that antitrust law has proven unable to reach what are believed to be a very large array of instances of collusive pricing that do not generate detectable acts of communication among the colluding sellers.[34] Until or unless standards of strict liability are imposed, numerous known cases of abuses of power will not be amenable to prosecution. Strict liability standards, for their part, open the door for a different form of power abuse, that of prosecution based upon bias and conviction based upon less than satisfactory standards of guilt.[35]

Sanctions Other Than Criminal Penalties

While implementation of a sweeping program of criminal sanctions may prove impractical, at least in the short run, for dealing with abuse of power, there remain a number of other promising approaches to the same goal. There are, for instance, a wide range of *administrative* sanctions.

In spite of the frequency with which administrative sanctions are employed in regard to the abuse of power, virtually no study has been made of the preventive effects of such penalties. The general assumption is that consequences of law breaking, such as monetary fines, a common administrative recourse, are usually merely regarded as an expense of doing business, almost in the nature of a licensing fee. Quite often, it is assumed, the cost of the fine is passed along onto others, in business, for instance, in the form of higher prices to customers.[36] Research on deterrence, at the same time, has suggested that certainty rather than severity of sanctions is more important in achieving desired ends;[37] in this regard, *certain and severe fines* could prove more valuable than criminal penalties, presuming there was enough aversion on the part of the perpetrator to their imposition.

Adverse publicity could be used as a mechanism to discredit persons who are convicted of abuse of power. The taint of discrediting publicity appears to have an impact on the behavior of law violators in positions of power by changing their relationships with others, who may thereafter shun them.[38] It is through such notoriety that an offender's reputation is stigmatized. Labeling theorists in the United States and Britain have maintained that such labeling thrusts street offenders more deeply into violative behavior.[39] For offenses involving the abuse of power, the consequences of labeling may be otherwise. More conforming behavior may ensue in order to repudiate the unwanted stigma.

The Retributive Rationale

Deterrence is an admirable goal of criminal sanctions, but it is also one that may be realized only imperfectly, if at all, with criminal abuses of power. Another such objective is retribution. The idea of retribution, or *just deserts* as the concept is known in contemporary writings, can be employed to support a program aimed at dealing effectively with abuses of power. Punishment administered under the doctrine of just deserts is inflicted not because of a demonstration or even a belief that it will reduce crime, but because by his behavior the offender has come to deserve to be deprived of liberty or otherwise inconvenienced.

Four components of the just deserts view can be identified among recent statements of the position:

1. *The punishment is related to the crime, not to the criminal:* In this regard, the proper response to law-breaking is said to be a function of the quality of the interdicted behavior, having nothing to do with attributes of the perpetrator.
2. *Proportionality of sanction:* Specific crimes will have attached to them specific penalties, with little discretion allowed to administrators to vary the consequences for similar violations. The character of the sanction will be dependent upon the seriousness of the offense. Seriousness is, of course, a somewhat subjective valuation. It may be determined by legislative judgment, public opinion, or derived from studies of the "harm" involved in the outlawed behavior.
3. *Fairness:* The inflexibility of sanctions is said to produce fairness, in the sense that subjective judgments of legal or administrative officials are not allowed to enter into determinations of the boundaries of a sanction.
4. *A lack of concern for the consequences of the sanctioning process on the behavior of others or the future acts of the offender:* There is no interest in whether the penalty will deter, rehabilitate, incapacitate, or otherwise change either the offender or those who might duplicate his or her behavior.

The element of proportionality, perhaps the most central of retributionist principles, relies upon three determinations. First, a ranking of crimes according to their seriousness; second, a ranking of punishments along a dimension of severity; and third, a matching of the first two components so that equity is achieved.

How serious then are abuses of power so that we may establish a sanctioning system if we adopt the postulates of the just deserts approach to criminal justice? Many persons insist that there is a double standard in regard to ordinary kinds of crimes in contrast to crimes that involve abuse of power and are committed by persons who tend to be in the upper echelons of the social system. The typical critique is based upon an estimate of the amount of deprivation involved in seemingly corresponding kinds of activities. The person who robs a bank without a weapon, it will be pointed out, is apt to receive a lengthy prison term. The person who embezzles money from the same bank, it will be noted, will likely get a much milder penalty, even though the amount he may have stolen far exceeded that of the robber. The usual interpretation is that the robber was being punished for his *declassé* social position rather than in terms of the harm or threat that he represented. Additional inquiry might determine, however, that the differentiated punishments stemmed from an official belief, true or mistaken, that the embezzler was not likely to repeat his offense, regardless of the penalty, while the bank robber was prone to recidivism. There might well be further considerations: There is no likelihood that anybody will be physically hurt as a result of an embezzlement; bank robberies, on the contrary, have some likelihood of getting out of hand. Bystanders may panic and do something foolhardy, an escape car may injure a pedestrian in its haste to get away from the scene.

The issue that comes to the forefront, then, is whether abuse of power offenses are more serious than ordinary crimes that seem to involve the same degree of immediate harm to victims. There is also the question of whether in truth the criminal sanctions visited upon white-collar offenders are more lenient than those imposed upon traditional law violators, despite the seeming disparate outcomes. It is sometimes argued that white-collar offenders are inevitably more severely punished merely by the fact of their involvement in the criminal justice system and the consequent stigma of such involvement among their peers and colleagues. It may be true as well that ordinary criminals violate the law more often than those who abuse power before formal steps are taken to inflict sanctions. Finally, there is the question of whether the most appropriate step is to raise the penalties against persons who are convicted of abuse of power to the level of those for persons convicted of ordinary crimes, or whether to reduce the severity of sanctions of the ordinary criminals to where they are for persons involved in power abuse.

The Issue of Seriousness

Whether abuse of power is more serious than other kinds of crime depends in the final analysis upon the definition employed to determine seriousness. Few persons dispute that abuse of power accounts for more financial losses to society than ordinary crimes. On the other hand, there are those who maintain that what mostly is involved is a redistribution of resources: they argue, for instance, that lower-echelon civil servants take bribes from businessmen in order to supplement meager, otherwise inadequate salaries. Without the corruption much more widespread chaos would be the rule. An official position becomes, as Victor LeVine notes, a *situation acquisse.*[40] Arnold Heidenheimer distinguishes between what he calls the "toxic" and the "tonic" effects of corruption and suggests that "a smattering of corruption may help keep the masses satisfied; and may even aid in development efforts.[41] And the claim is sometimes made that corruption represents the assertion of personal relations against the impersonality of the bureaucratic machine, and that in this sense it is a more "authentic" response than conformity to abstract law; indeed, that it is a reinforcement of social solidarity against selfish individuals. We are in agreement with Shackleton on this matter when he maintains that such a view carries a heavy load of condescension, especially in regard to developing countries, and that analyses would indicate that corruption involves unacceptable social and political costs in all societies.[42]

Some criminologists downgrade the seriousness of power abuse on the ground that the basic criterion for judgment about such a matter is the degree of fear instilled in the public by the behavior.[43] The common assumption historically has been that citizens are very much more aggrieved by street crimes than by white-collar kinds of offenses, to some degree perhaps because such offenses are part and parcel of their own behavior. But there is considerable evidence emerging today[44] that criminologists have misinterpreted the evidence with respect to public perceptions of the seriousness of acts which abuse power. What may be a more prevalent attitude than suspected seems to rest upon two foundations. First is an existing or emergent awareness that there are fundamental and terrible dangers in a social system which permits unchecked abuses of power. As John Kleinig has put it: "The continued existence of a society of any worthwhile kind will depend on the general maintenance of a fair measure of *trust* between its members. Trust is perhaps the most important ingredient in social glue."[45] Second are considerations of equity. John Leonard states the matter thusly:

> Why doesn't it work both ways? . . . If, for instance, you hit your son on the head with a hammer and he dies, you will at least face jail. . . . If, on

the other hand, someone sells dirty milk or poisons fish and the infant death rate goes up, he is merely fined. And if the American medical profession fails to reduce our infant mortality rate to the level achieved by Oslo in 1931, nothing happens to anybody at all.[46]

The importance of the matter of *seriousness* in regard to control of abuses of power and white-collar crime cannot be overemphasized. Human life is riven with injustice and inequity, with differential access to resources and to life chances, with varying rules about what is permissible and what will not be allowed. Obviously, some persons have more to say about such matters than others (that is, to determine what shall be allowed and what forbidden, and what should be done about what is forbidden). This may be because they care more intensely about the issue or, more likely, because of the power they possess they are better able to translate their desires into official formulas. Some acts, obviously, are easier to denominate and to detect, which adds to the likelihood that reformative attention will be focused upon them. But it probably is not such logistic issues that most fundamentally fashion crime control priorities. It is rather the intensity and degree of perceptions of seriousness as these come to bear upon public debate and, ultimately, upon public policy.

It is for this reason that discussion of abuse of power at criminological congresses are preeminently necessary. The inclusion of the subject of abuse of power on our agenda documents the seriousness of the problem. There are, of course, numerous other methods for establishing seriousness, but as we shall see shortly, they have considerable methodological difficulties.

Measuring Seriousness

Seriousness, like power, is one of those terms that seems obvious enough, but that becomes quite slippery when an attempt is made to pin it down. In regard to crime, there appears to be no unambiguous method to determine the seriousness of particular acts. In the final analysis, influence groups, such as criminologists, make subjective judgments—fed by some data—on what they regard as meriting disprobation and reprobation.

Seriousness can be determined by allowing members of certain groups in a society, such as judges or legislators, to rank behaviors. But the selection of a group for the task is more or less arbitrary, and the results certainly reflect the values of members of the particular cadre. The sentiments of the chosen group may not correspond to those of the public at large. Perhaps the public should be sampled. Such a technique overcomes objections to special groups imposing their rankings on others, but it has its own troublesome features.

First, what if there is no public consensus in regard to specific offenses? There may be rather broad-based agreement that murder is more serious than petty theft, but there are a vast number of other behaviors in the area between these two about which there would likely be considerable disagreement. And undoubtedly religious fundamentalists would differ rather sharply from militant atheists about rankings for specific offenses. If, by chance, there were to be a high level of agreement—say 90 percent—there remains the problem that a majority, however high, may be tyranizing over a minority only on the basis of self-interest. And community surveys have the problem that they make everyone's opinion equally worthy, so that an institutionalized alcoholic is counted the same as an influential moral leader. This, of course, has elements of democracy at its best, but it also has distortive elements. After all, if the issue were to determine the distance from here to a place visible but distant, it seems much preferable to take the estimate of an experienced surveyor than to average the guesses of a representative sample of the population.

There also are problems in determining what constitutes seriousness that inhere in the manner in which the vignettes about which judgments are to be made are phrased, and how specific the details they include are. Persons may rank burglary of a church much differently than burglary of a commercial establishment or a tavern—and may rank these in a way other than they would burglary in general. Acts committed by juveniles may be seen in a different light than those carried out by adults; and the nature of victims—whether they are elderly or young, hitchhikers or pedestrians, out late having fun or on their way to work—may enter into decisions about seriousness. In the final analysis, seriousness issues may be informed by the opinions of the public or segments thereof, but to a large extent they will represent views which can be—and should be—considerably influenced by propaganda, in the same manner that interest groups, howsoever motivated, propagandize for tougher laws against drunken drivers, users of marijuana, and parents who abuse their children.

On the Matter of Penalties

Many of the same virtually irresolvable issues noted above arise in regard to assessment of proper penalties for abuse of power, plus a number of additional considerations. There is, for instance, no unambiguous judgment regarding what is a "more" or "less" serious penalty for a particular criminal act. Clearly, a $1,000 fine can impose intense hardship on a poor person, while representing no more than a minor inconvenience to a wealthy individual. Yet to punish on a subjective basis raises some enormously thorny issues. Years ago, de Beaumont and de Tocqueville noted that solitary confinement was a reasonable punishment for Americans, given their frontier taciturnity; but the penalty would be intolerable for Frenchmen, representing as it would an assault on their gregarious nature.[47] Should matters such as these be taken into account in passing sentences?

If we were to conduct a public opinion poll about the severity of penalties, some of the issues noted above again come into play. Moreover, there is a question of what penalties are to be ranked: legislatively set penalties, judicially imposed sentences, or categories based on the actual sanction, that is, the amount of time served in jail in contrast to the sentence imposed. Problems also arise in regard to the comparability of sentences. In a recent study in Arizona, persons were asked to rank order the severity of a variety of punishments. Using magnitude estimation measures, the investigators found that the following punishments all were ranked approximately equally: one year in jail, three months in prison, four years on probation, and a fine of $2,481.[48] Who decides which of these penalties to inflict? And on what basis?

Linking Penalties and Crimes

If the issue is not whether abuse of power ought to be handled under criminal statutes, then the question becomes the best way in which to go about carrying out enforcement. Two traditional legal reactions to offenses involving abuse of power—rehabilitation and incapacitation—are seldom seriously discussed with respect to such offenses. Few persons recommend that individuals convicted of abuse of power be punished to keep them from committing the same or similar offenses during a period of incarceration. Discussions of incapacitation traditionally take for granted that this objective is reserved for "dangerous" offenders.[49]

Rehabilitative efforts for their part revolve around efforts to change criminal motivation and attitudes. But it is difficult for persons working in criminal justice to conceive of persons who commit abuse of power offenses in rehabilitative terms. We do not think about such persons as being socialized into deviant norms or life styles, though pursuit of this line of inquiry might prove fruitful. Offenders in the white-collar classes are regarded as socializers rather than as the recipients of socialization efforts on the part of others. It is difficult to think of forms of treatment that would "rehabilitate" such persons in the correctional system. As Morris has noted:

> What would Jimmy Hoffa discuss with his caseworker, in or out of prison, relevant to Hoffa's psyche or the manipulation of power within a union? A discussion between Spiro Agnew and his probation officer, had any unfortunate been appointed to that task, is even more mind boggling.[50]

Conclusion

The idea of *socialization* suggests the possible utility of criminal sanctions in controlling abuses of power. Criminal sanctions express society's disapproval of conduct; that is, they represent to many persons an expression on the part of society's more legitimate normative framework of its condemnation. Abuses of power may not be controllable by means of deterrence, incapacitation, or rehabilitation, and there may be substantial problems involved with administering a system of punishment based on retributive principles. But most everyone endorses one point at least: these crimes should *not* be encouraged. Failure to bring to bear the criminal sanction can be interpreted as official indifference and can reinforce attitudes that permit or encourage abuses of power. On this ground, it may be argued—and it is so that we argue—that it is socially desirable to punish such offenses severely.

The consequences of legally stated and stringently enforced legal disapproval of abuse of power, which may represent the most important reformative tactic, are undoubtedly particularly difficult to assess. Jurisprudents insist that the law can operate in a subtle, indirect manner to condition behavior.[51] But there have been few attempts to determine empirically the role of the law as a socializing institution, and recent studies have posited the alternative interpretation that law may generate rather than resolve disputes and may produce divisiveness.[52] But there is evidence that persuades us that making conduct illegal and applying sanctions through justice processes against such conduct can influence individual attitudes against such conduct,[53] and can influence long-range behavior patterns.[54] In this sense, we have come full cycle to our early emphasis on the essential significance of altering an ethos, rather than trying to solve a significant cultural problem, such as abuse of power, by focusing on those who manifest the problem. Insofar as the deleterious consequences of abuse of power seem to rend the social fabric itself, it would appear to be a poor system of law and justice that did not proclaim in a stern manner its distaste for the behaviors and act in a tough way to make good on its statutory pronouncements. The policy need not be justified in terms of short-run benefit, such as the immediate reduction in the amount of the offense. The law can serve as a long-term symbolic socializer.

The failure to achieve significant incapacitative, rehabilitative, and deterrent effects with ordinary crimes is not seriously taken as an argument for the elimination of these offenses from the statute books. Decisions to punish can, and probably should, be based on other criteria as well, particularly criteria that take account of the wrongfulness of the conduct, and the need to express society's disapproval.

Processes of social control are not confined to direct influence (rehabilitation) or to intimidation (deterrence). Conformity to law is high where people desire to obey the law, or where they perceive the law as legitimate. This is the theme of discussions of social control that emphasize socialization,[55] the internalization of norms, [56] motivations aimed at pleasing others whose opinions we value,[57] and broader linkages between individual norms and values and institutional structures.[58] The most effective kind of social arrangement is precisely that kind that eliminates or precludes the need for punishment systems. The legal system can contribute to this process to the extent to which it pronounces conduct undesirable and to the extent to which persons view such pronouncements as legitimate.

Concretely, we advocate the following: (1) wherever possible, the criminal sanctions should be invoked against offenses involving abuse of power; (2) in those cases in which it is questionable whether a criminal conviction can be obtained, civil penalties should be employed; (3) those abuses of power offenses not presently governed by criminal law should be rendered illegal and designated as *criminal conduct*; and (4) sanctions should be employed even if there is no reason to believe that their use will yield immediate preventive results, because such sanctions are justified on the basis of their long-term educative effects, both on the offenders and on the public.

Notes

1. Philip Taubman, *New York Times* (April 4, 1980).

2. Joseph Jolz, *New York Daily News* (August 18, 1976).

3. *China News* (Hong Kong) (July 3, 1975).

4. Barry Newman, *Wall Street Journal* (December 8, 1977).

5. Richard F. Janssen, *Wall Street Journal* (August 24, 1976).

6. Guy Arnold, *Modern Nigeria* (London: Longman, 1977), p. 6.

7. Hans Konig, *A New Yorker in Egypt* (New York: Harcourt Brace Jovanovich, 1976), p. 84.

8. Stanislaus Andreski, *The African Predicament* (New York: Atherton, 1968). See generally O.P. Dwivedi *Public Service Ethics* (Guelph, Ontario: Department of Political Studies, University of Guelph, 1978).

9. William Endicott, *Los Angeles Times* (February 27, 1978).

10. Bertrand Russell, *Power: A New Social Analysis* (London: Allen and Unwin, 1938), p. 10.

11. Robert Bierstedt, "An Analysis of Social Power," *American Sociological Review*, 15 (December 1950), p. 730.

12. Edwin H. Sutherland, *White Collar Crime* (New York: Dryden Press, 1949); Edwin H. Sutherland, "White-Collar Criminality," *American Sociological Review*, 5 (February 1940), pp. 1-12.

13. Ronald Wraith and Edgar Simpkins, *Corruption in Developing Countries* (London: Allen and Unwin, 1963), p. 9.

14. Ibid., p. 166.

15. Herman and Julia Schwendinger, "Defenders of Order or Guardians of Human Rights?" *Issues in Criminology*, 5 (Summer 1970), pp. 123-157.

16. Dennis Wrong, *Power: Its Forms, Bases and Uses* (New York: Harper Colophon, 1980).

17. Jack P. Gibbs, *Crime, Punishment and Deterrence* (New York: Elsevier, 1975).

18. Ezra Stotland, Michael Britnall, Andrew L'Heureux, and Eva Ashmore, "Do Convictions Deter Home Repair Fraud?" in eds. Gilbert Geis and Ezra Stotland, *White-Collar Crime: Theory and Research* (Beverly Hills: Sage, 1980), pp. 252-265.

19. William J. Chambliss, *On the Take: From Petty Crooks to Presidents* (Bloomington: Indiana University Press, 1979).

20. Gordon Tullock, "Does Punishment Deter Crime?" *The Public Interest*, 36 (Summer 1974), pp. 103-111.

21. Ezra Stotland, "White Collar Criminals," *Journal of Social Issues*, 33 (1977), pp. 179-197.

22. Donald R. Cressey, *Other People's Money* (Glencoe, Ill.: Free Press, 1953).

23. Gilbert Geis, "The Heavy Electrical Equipment Antitrust Cases of 1961," in eds. Marshall Clinard and Richard Quinney, *Criminal Behavior Systems* (New York: Holt, Rinehart and Winston, 1967), pp. 139-150.

24. Gibbs, *Crime, Punishment, and Deterrence*, note 26.

25. Stotland et al., "White Collar Criminals," note 27.

26. Donn B. Parker, *Crime by Computer* (New York: Scribner's, 1976).

27. Michael D. Maltz and Stephen M. Pollock, "Analyzing Suspected Collusion Among Bidders," in Geis and Stotland, *White Collar Crime*, note 27 at pp. 174-198.

28. Johannes Andenaes, "General Prevention Revisited: Research and Policy Implications," *Journal of Criminal Law and Criminology*, 66 (September 1975), pp. 338-365.

29. Robert W. Ogren, "The Ineffectiveness of the Criminal Sanction in Fraud and Corruption Cases: Losing the Battle Against White-Collar Crime," *American Criminal Law Review*, 11 (Summer 1973), pp. 963-964.

30. Daniel S. Claster, "Comparison of Risk Perception between Delinquents and Nondelinquents," *Journal of Criminal Law, Criminology, and Police Science*, 58 (March 1967), pp. 80-86; Gary F. Jensen, "Crime Doesn't Pay: Correlates of Shared Misunderstandings," *Social Problems*, 17 (Fall 1969), pp. 189-201.

31. Robert F. Meier, "The Deterrence Doctrine and Public Policy: A Response to Utilitarians," in ed. James A. Cramer, *Preventing Crime* (Beverly Hills: Sage, 1978).

32. Gilbert Geis, *Not the Law's Business* (New York: Schocken, 1979).

33. Suzanne Weaver, *Decision to Prosecute: Organization and Public Policy in the Antitrust Division* (Cambridge, Mass: MIT Press, 1977).

34. Richard A. Posner, *Antitrust Law: An Economic Perspective* (Chicago: University of Chicago Press, 1976).

35. Hyman Gross, *A Theory of Criminal Justice* (New York: Oxford University Press, 1979).

36. William J. Chambliss, "Types of Deviance and Effectiveness of Legal Sanctions," *Wisconsin Law Review* (Summer 1967), pp. 703-719.

37. Gibbs, *Crime, Punishment, and Deterrence*, note 26; Andenaes, "General Prevention Revisited," note 37.

38. Brent Fisse, "The Use of Publicity as a Criminal Sanction Against Business Corporations," *Melbourne University Law Review*, 8 (June 1971), pp. 107-150.

39. Howard S. Becker, *Outsiders*, enlarged edition (New York: Free Press, 1973); Edwin H. Schur, *Interpreting Deviance* (New York: Harper and Row, 1979).

40. Victor T. LeVine, *Political Corruption: The Ghana Case* (Stanford: Hoover Institution Press, 1975), p. 97.

41. Arnold J. Heidenheimer, ed., *Political Corruption: Readings in Comparative Analysis* (New York: Holt, Rinehart and Winston, 1970), pp. 479-486. See also Joseph S. Nye, "Corruption and Political Development: A Cost-Benefit Analysis," *American Political Science Review*, 61 (June 1967), pp. 417-427.

42. R. Shackleton, "Corruption: An Essay in Economic Analysis," *Political Quarterly*, 49 (January-March 1978), pp. 25-37.

43. James Q. Wilson, *Thinking About Crime* (New York: Basic Books, 1975).

44. Robert F. Meier and James F. Short Jr., "Consequences of White-Collar and Corporate Crime," in ed. Herbert Edelhertz and Thomas D. Overcast, *White-Collar Crime* (Lexington, Mass.: Lexington Books, D.C. Heath and Company, 1981), pp. 81-102.

45. John Kleinig, "Crime and the Concept of Harm," *American Philosophical Quarterly*, 15 (January 1978), pp. 27-36.

46. John Leonard, *Private Lives in Imperial City* (New York: Knopf, 1979), pp. 49-50.

47. Gustave de Beaumont and Alexis de Tocqueville, *On The Penitentiary System in the United States and Its Application to France* (Carbondale: Southern Illinois University Press, 1964), p. 121.

48. Mark Warr, Robert F. Meier, and Maynard L. Erickson, "Normative Phenomena and Preferred Punishments for Crime," unpublished paper.

49. Theodore C. Chicaros and Gordon P. Waldo, "Punishment and Crime: An Examination of Some Empirical Evidence," *Social Problems*, 18 (Fall 1970), p. 200.

50. Norval Morris, *The Future of Imprisonment* (Chicago: University of Chicago Press, 1974), p. 20.

51. Gordon Hawkins, "Punishment and Deterrence: The Educative, Moralizing, and Habituative Effects," *Wisconsin Law Review* (1969), pp. 555-565.

52. William J. Chambliss and Robert D. Seidman, *Law, Order and Power* (Reading, Mass: Addison-Wesley, 1971); Lynn McDonald, *The Sociology of Law and Order* (London: Faber and Faber, 1976).

53. John Colombotos, "Physicians and Medicare: A Before-After Study of the Effects of Legislation and Attitudes," *American Sociological Review*, (June 1969), pp. 318-334.

54. Kai Erikson, *Wayward Puritans* (New York: Wiley, 1966).

55. Talcott Parsons, *The Social System* (New York: The Free Press, 1951).

56. John Finley Scott, *The Internalization of Norms* (Englewood Cliffs, N.J.: Prentice-Hall, 1971).

57. James Tedeschi, *The Social Influence Processes* (Chicago: Aldine, 1971).

58. Morris Janowitz, *The Last Half-Century* (Chicago: University of Chicago Press, 1978).

10 A Research and Action Agenda with Respect to White-Collar Crime

Unlike persons concerned with more traditional forms of crime, scholars and practitioners working on the problems of white-collar crime happily avoid at least one matter of moral perturbation: They do not need to deal with accusations that their work is but a thin camouflage of an unappetizing effort to keep the deprived in their downtrodden condition, or that it is part of a racist scheme to define as mere criminals persons who truly are political offenders. There is strong agreement in criminological circles—and perhaps this itself ought to arouse suspicion—that white-collar crime is bad, even evil, and that those seeking to understand and to combat it are enrolled in a worthy cause.

Beyond this, however, the subject matter itself is inordinately complex, its roots beyond altogether clear comprehension, its definition in great dispute. Indeed, efforts to pin down the issues associated with white-collar crime seem at times much like those of Stephen Leacock's fabled horseman who was seen riding off frantically toward all four points of the compass.

The Primary Postulation

In my opinion, one issue takes precedence above all others with respect to research and action bearing on white-collar crime. That issue, which will inform the largest part of this paper, has to do with the public definition of white-collar crime and the attitudes that are manifested toward the phenomena that constitute such crime. By this, I do not mean what the public thinks about diverse aspects of white-collar crime—that is, whether it regards offenses producing certain kinds of harms as seriously as it regards so-called street crimes that bring about equivalent degrees of injury. For me, the implicit policy question underlying such research holds the key ingredient for the direction of a consideration of white-collar crime. The issue, briefly put, is this: *How do we best produce a social and political atmosphere in which the matter of white-collar crime is regarded as of high importance, presuming, of course, that there is satisfactory evidence that it ought to be so regarded?*

From eds. Herbert Edelhertz and Thomas D. Overcast, *White-Collar Crime: An Agenda for Research.* (Lexington, Mass.: Lexington Books, D.C. Heath and Company, 1981), pp. 175-202.

Unless such a state of mind comes to prevail, white-collar crime is apt to be neglected as a matter of paramount concern, regardless of its inherent traits. On the other hand, if the public and the authorities come to see white-collar crime as a subject in urgent need of attention and remediation, then funds and personnel will be made available to carry out the kinds of work suggested in this conference. The issue is one that Becker has labeled *moral entrepreneurship.*[1] By this he means that situations are taken up by certain groups, which, on the basis of one or several of a very wide range of considerations, are able to convince others—particularly others who can exert social suasion—that what they are advocating is important.

At times, evils call attention to themselves spontaneously. This is particularly true if they come to be associated with a notorious incident, such as a coal-mine catastrophe; a Thalidomide scandal; a blatant and easily understood antitrust violation; or a situation involving infants, widows, or other stereotypically sympathy-arousing victims. But a more sensible path, and perhaps in the long run a more satisfactory one, is to have dedicated persons embark on an impassioned crusade in behalf of this or that reform. Such a crusade is most apt to encounter success, I believe, if it possesses intrinsic worth and is well fortified by impregnable persuasive evidence. It is toward the establishment of such conditions with respect to white-collar crime that the present blueprint is directed.

To carry the point a bit further, let us note that life is replete with indecencies and injustices. For diverse reasons, some are ignored and some downplayed, whereas others arouse enormous indignation and result in much enterprise being directed toward their amelioration. The concentration of resources and attention on high-lighted issues often serves to lessen the ills associated with them. In recent times, we have seen a federal focus on racial injustice, street crime, poverty, women's rights, and a number of other issues. But each of these problems had been around for a long time, and each was no worse (and in some respects was actually more benign) than it had been in earlier periods. None "cried out" for attention, despite the rhetoric commonly employed by those who demand that their concerns take precedence over matters others deem more important.

Most of the issues likely would not have come to the forefront if they did not contain some element of merit, some wrong needing redress—that is, if the fundamental logic of their appeal to the minds and hearts of the constituency they desired to create was not relatively persuasive. At the same time, it is obvious that they sought the advantage of one group at the expense of another, usually on the ground that such a rearrangement would more justly achieve fairness. On the other hand, numerous matters have come to command public attention that later judgment declared to be mindless or at least ill considered in terms of the achieved results. The prohibition of the sale of alcoholic beverages is a prime example.[2]

In this respect, it is of primary importance to document that proposed solutions to problems said to emerge from white-collar crime will leave things in a better state than they were earlier. This can raise arguable issues: There are, for instance, those who believe that the "harassing" of business operations by government regulations that carry heavy penalties produce, on balance, more undesirable than beneficial results.[3] They insist, for instance, that there should be incentives for things such as satisfactory occupational-safety records, rather than fines or prison sentences for violations. They argue that the cost of the marginal degree of protection that the regulations afford workers against such "iffy" things as workplace-"caused" cancer can prove so fiscally prohibitive that it will force plants to close and throw a large number of employees out of work.[4] Similar kinds of objections are raised against many other kinds of white-collar crime enforcement strategies.

Resolution of issues such as the foregoing should assume a very high priority on the agenda of research on white-collar crime. Part of the effort ought to include monitoring meticulously the consequences of attempts to control by law the abuses of power that are classed as white-collar crime. I believe that no legislated program ought to proceed without a sum of money being appropriated for an independent group that is given a long-term mandate to follow the career of the new program. The report of this group ought to go back to those who decided to try the new approach, so that its members may, if necessary, amend their original ideas, and so that they may learn in what ways their earlier views proved to be incorrect.

Documenting Developments

The fact that white-collar crime has, in the past five years, assumed considerable importance on the political and social scene in the United States should not be taken as a true testament to the growing seriousness of the problems the term embraces. Some things—such as crimes associated with the profusion of nuclear materials—could not have occurred earlier, since the technology was not at hand.[5] In this sense, the occurrence of more white-collar crime merely reflects additional technology and more-complicated life patterns. Indeed, it is not unlikely that there is less of the serious kinds of white-collar crime today than in earlier times—or, at least, less of the kinds of offenses that could have been committed both then and now, such as bribery and antitrust violations.

Nor is it likely that the emergent concern with white-collar crime is a function of the burgeoning social-science and legal research directed at the subject. The reverse is more likely to be true—that as the subject assumed public and political importance, scholars more often turned their attention to it. Why white-collar crime came forth as a major issue is a matter of considerable importance, because understanding the dynamics of the situation offers an opportunity to continue to fuel the flame—presuming, of course, that the question of white-collar crime is reasonably deemed to be one that needs and will benefit from increased attention.

It is, perhaps, worthwhile to pin down a few of the signposts that signify the recent movement of white-collar crime into the limelight as an issue of importance. This colloquium itself certainly is one item of evidence documenting the trend. No such meeting ever had been held until a few years ago, despite the introduction of the concept of white-collar crime into the social-scientific literature almost four decades ago. In the past eighteen months, there have been colloquia dedicated specifically to white-collar crime at the Temple Law School;[6] at the State University College of New York, Potsdam;[7] at the Battelle Human Affairs Research Center in Seattle, Washington;[8] and in Glen Cove, New York, under the sponsorship of Peat, Marwick, Mitchell, and Company.[9] Simultaneously, sessions on white-collar crime are now routinely incorporated into the programs of meetings of scholarly associations of sociologists, criminologists, and persons interested in issues of law and society. The 1980 national conferences of the Law and Society Association, held in Madison, Wisconsin; the American Sociological Association, in New York City; and the American Society of Criminology, in San Francisco, all included such panels. Two of the twelve sessions of the February 1981 meeting of the Western Society of Criminology in San Diego were devoted to white-collar crime, one under the heading of "Corporate Crime," and the other of "Government Crime." In 1980 at Caracas, Venezuela, white-collar crime, under the generic heading of *abuse of power,* was for the first time a major agenda item at a United Nations Congress on criminology. The subject also has come to the fore in the work of the Council of Europe, headquartered in Strasbourg, France.

In the U.S. Congress, hearings on white-collar crime currently are underway in the subcommittee on crime of the House Committee on the Judiciary.[10] At the same time, academic writing on the subject has grown almost geometrically.

Perhaps the surest sign of this development has been the decision by authorities at the Federal Bureau of Investigation to downgrade the bureau's efforts to solve offenses such as bank robbery, in order to concentrate more intensively on the spectrum of frauds, corruption, and violations of federal statutes that largely are designed to control the behavior of members of the more "respectable" elements of society. The enforcement priorities established by the Department of Justice now give preeminence to acts such as "crimes against the government by public officials, including federal, state, and local corruption" and "crimes against consumers, including defrauding of consumers, antitrust violations, energy pricing violations, and related illegalities."[11] In fiscal 1979, 21 percent of the FBI investigative resources was reported to have been allocated to efforts to combat white-collar crime or organized crime, compared with less than 10 percent each for crimes against the person and crimes against property.[12] Similarly, the Law Enforcement Assistance Administration has assiduously increased its attention to white-collar crime in terms of research and action grants.

Finally, the work of Ralph Nader and his colleagues merits special mention. It is likely that Nader's campaigns spearheaded priority reconsiderations with respect to white-collar crime. The fact that Nader, although he continues his muckraking with undiminished efficiency, appears to have less support today than in past years may be a reflection of a short public attention span and/or of a need for new heroes and new issues. If so, this too should be analyzed to derive lessons about the methods needed to avoid and overcome public cynicism with respect to efforts toward reform.

It is evident that white-collar crime has become defined in the United States—and, indeed, in most Western countries—as a matter of importance. How can that definition of the situation be solidified and turned to its most productive ends?

Programmatic Underpinnings

There are two basic dimensions involved in penetrating and holding fast public and political consciousness with respect to white-collar crime. Research and action programs ought to be directed to the enhancement of these dual conditions:

1. The first has to do with convincing persons that white-collar crime is a serious matter and that it is to their advantage to do something about it. This involves a joint appeal to conscience and to self-interest.
2. The second is related to the need to establish that there exist reasonable potentialities for resolution of problems of white-collar crime in a satisfying and satisfactory manner.

People have little patience with irresolvable issues. There is not much hope for sustaining interest very long if persons do not believe there is some hope for improvement, a hope best sustained by demonstrated evidence.

The issue of crime illustrates this point. Crime has always been with us, but only in 1964 in the United States did it surface as a paramount political issue. Both presidential candidates that year concentrated on convincing the electorate that they possessed the will and expertise to protect us from the outrages of street offenses. In 1966, President Johnson appointed a Commission on Law Enforcement and Administration of Justice to study the problem of crime and to formulate a national approach to the matter. Subsequent presidential elections saw opponents vying to convince the public that they would deal with matters of crime skillfully. In 1972, President Nixon stressed in his campaign that he now was winning the war against crime, noting that during the first six months of the year the crime rate *increase* was "only" one percent, lower than for any period during the previous decade.

Crime continues to be a matter of great public anxiety: In fact, it is likely that such anxiety is now greater than ever before in U.S. history. A September 1980 report, subtitled *America Afraid,* indicated that "fear of crime in the United States far outstrips the rising incidence of crime and is slowly paralyzing society."[13] But the issue was not mentioned by either major presidential nominee in his acceptance speech. Candidates were perfectly aware that federal policies at best could have only a marginal impact on the amount and kind of crime occurring. But such realities did not dissuade rhetoric. The abandonment of the issue probably is a function of the fact that it seems like a no-win situation, apt to haunt an incumbent in later years. It is noteworthy that the abandonment of crime as a national political issue has been accompanied by a severe reduction in the amount of federal funds allotted to research and action. The moral seems clear: Not only the significance of an issue, but also its potential resolution must inform research and policy devoted to it.

It follows from the foregoing observations that a step of overarching importance is to determine with respect to white-collar crime its biography both as a scholarly endeavor and as a matter of public concern. It was noted during this conference that the civil-rights movement, the unequal treatment of rich and poor, and the current economic malaise afloat in the United States (the last carrying with it a need for scapegoats) may lie at the core of the increase in attention to white-collar crime. I can offer no better explanatory roster, but I suspect that the matter is a good deal more complicated, particularly if it is examined historically and cross-culturally. It might be worthwhile to try to pinpoint both social conditions and personal attitudes as they relate to views—and to the intensity of such views—with respect to different forms of white-collar crime. Are feelings about the need for economic equality related closely to indignation about illegal forms of exploitation of others? Or are general economic conditions better bases for predicting the level of concern about this or that kind of white-collar crime? Who believes what about the subject, and what do people do, and what do they say they are willing to do about white-collar crime? A clearer mapping of the nature and behavior of the constituency is needed.

It would, of course, be particularly valuable to be able to document longitudinally the drift of public opinion on a wide spectrum of issues, and to relate these views and their alteration to changes in attitudes about white-collar crimes. It would have been useful to have followed carefully developments in the Watergate scandal in order to determine how these bore on attitudes about upper-class illegalities in general and how they related to the level of confidence in politics and business throughout the nation. Was it those who were most loyal to the president who later became the most cynical? Or did these people—and, if so, which of them?—take refuge in explanations and rationalizations of the kind that protect all of us from some of the discomfiting aspects of life?

Documenting the ebb and flow of public opinion on white-collar crime has two particularly important policy ingredients. First, it allows a determination of how people's feelings about different aspects of the situation are related to their own situation and to external events. Second, the tapping and circulation of such views tends to legitimize and strengthen them. The indignation of many people about street crime led others, who had not given the problem much thought, to become indignant themselves when the problem was effectively called to their attention. It may be that, in truth, people have trouble summoning up much indignation about most aspects of white-collar crime. If so, this is worth knowing. It does not follow—even, or especially, in a democracy—that the prevailing positions should determine policy. The results only indicate (presuming that those who form policy themselves believe white-collar crime to be a serious problem) that ways must be found to persuade others of the accuracy of views contrary to their own. It is always easier to do this if the nature of public opinion is thoroughly known and appreciated.

I particularly favor institutionalizing the monitoring of sentiments over a continuing period of time. Short-term surveys tend to have only a short-lived impact, and this transience defeats the purpose of keeping the subject and the temperature of feelings about it continuously in the limelight. The census bureau or a Gallup-type organization with an ongoing mandate would be particularly valuable in carrying out work that spotlights attitudes and the conditions that affect such attitudes with respect to white-collar crime.

The Definitional Dilemma

In this section I will consider the much-addressed matter of settling on a "proper" definition of the bounds of the realm of white-collar crime. This matter has preoccupied many persons since the birth of the concept. Some argue that without precision of definition, generalizations float and lack adequate anchorage. Others insist that some common-sense guidelines ought to suffice until more information is at hand to allow sophisticated distinctions to be drawn between the diverse kinds of behavior that are being studied as part of the work on white-collar crime. These persons believe that there is a general understanding of what kinds of acts clearly constitute white-collar crime, with some acceptable fuzziness at the interstices. Things such as antitrust violations and Medicaid fraud by physicians would be well within the ambit of white-collar crime. Some other illegalities can only arguably be regarded as falling within the definitional confines of the category—for example, organized schemes to cheat home owners by pretending to do roof repairs after the customers have been gulled into believing that their homes require such work. Cheating on applications for food stamps or welfare payments by persons in the lower socioeconomic strata also is not a clear contender for classification as white-collar crime. Why such acts should (or should not) be regarded as white-collar crime is debatable, and the decision will go to whoever makes the most persuasive case in terms of the utility of one or another classificatory scheme for the purpose of insight and action.

The task of defining white-collar crime is in many ways wearisome, perhaps best left to those with a predilection for medieval theological debates. What is required for the moment is taxonomy, based on:

1. Existing law (note, for instance, the U.S. Department of Justice's precise listing of each of the statutes it enforces that it considers as falling within the category of white-collar crime).[14]
2. Determinations of forms of harm.
3. Categorization of the traits of offenders, especially their position in the occupational structure, as such position bears on their illegal behavior.
4. Modus operandi.
5. Types of victims of the offenses, whether customers, competitors, the general public, or the offender's own organization, among others.

Each of these delineations would have its particular value, depending on the task it is called on to perform; each could form the basis for additional discussion and refinement.

There remains also the possibility of discarding the term *white-collar crime* on the ground that it is too imprecise—even, perhaps, too inflammatory. There is a tendency, particularly outside the United States, to employ terms such as *economic crime* and *occupational crime* for the kinds of acts regarded here as white-collar crime. I would resist such a temptation, despite its greater intellectual purity, on the basis of the argument that pervades this chapter—that it is essential for satisfactory resolution of problems associated with white-collar crime for a forceful constituency to dedicate itself to this end. However metaphorical and imprecise, the term *white-collar crime* conjures up a real set of ills, and is particularly satisfactory in solidifying an emotional and intellectual concern about such ills. I take seriously David Gordon's speculation that it is not that the police and the public show greater concern about working-class crime because greater interpersonal violence is involved, but, rather, that working-class crime is seen to involve greater interpersonal violence because the police show greater concern about it.[15]

The Sense of Seriousness

It is argued that the idea of *harm* remains the "most underdeveloped concept in our criminal law."[16] The concept of harm is by no means a simple one. An elaborate philosophical discussion by John Kleinig of the ramifications of harm argues that "there is not much mileage to be gained by explicating harm in terms of loss, damage, or injury," because these are nothing but synonyms for most crime; therefore, they lack analytical power. Kleinig advocates as more promising the characterization of harm as "interference with or invasions of a person's interests;" but he grants that the idea of *interests,* if it is to be the basis of testable propositions, poses some heady definitional problems.[17]

Nonetheless, the need to establish with some precision the parameters of real and perceived harm from a variety of forms of white-collar crime seems to me to carry a very high research priority. Recently, many white-collar-crime research veterans have been put in our place by a number of writers who regard as inaccurate our conclusions about what we consider a mood of public indifference toward most varieties of white-collar offenses.[18] The conclusion of recent work is that if harms resulting from white-collar offenses are congruent with those resulting from street crimes, then the public will regard such offenses as equivalently serious and dangerous, and will call for equally stern, if not sterner, punitive measures against the perpetrators of such offenses. This conclusion stems largely from a reworking of data gathered by Rossi and his colleagues as part of a general sampling of public opinion about a variety of criminal activities.[19]

This is an extraordinarily important line of research. It demands further exploration and fine tuning. It is important because, if true, it provides a firmer basis for more effective action against white-collar crime. Of course, there is also a subtler agenda that lies behind such work. By establishing a priori the idea that measurement of stipulated harms is an important area to be examined, such equivalence then assumes that very importance. It thereafter becomes difficult to argue that a victim is less dead if killed by pollution than if killed by an intrafamily homicide. But the equivalence of the deaths—in a society attuned to cause and effect and to locating blame—must be documented and highlighted if the comparison is to be manifest and effective.

Obviously, there is a vital need for a study that moves beyond obtaining simple public responses to questionnaire items in which the rich details of the various white-collar offenses are presented in shorthand as truncated, brief items. Although similarly truncated queries are used as interview items for both traditional street offenses and white-collar crimes, the former has a much broader repertoire of affect. Mention a mugger, and a whole barrage of stereotypes that excuse and/or aggravate the offense comes into play. The fact is that the behaviors about which the questions are asked represent much more complicated matters than the item the respondent is presented with. For the white-collar crime, we have not only the objective harm that finds its way into the questionnaire inquiry but, among other things, often a defendant of good manners and amiable mien, who has purchased a lawyer who can, articulately and persuasively, put the very best light on sometimes fuzzy and arguable factual situations. Indeed, as the Ford Pinto case so well illustrated, the fundamental issue of the defendant's criminal responsibility for the harm—assumed out-of-hand in the questionnaire studies—often is much more problematic in white-collar crime cases than in the usual street offenses. (That is, there has been a death; a gunshot caused it; did the defendant or did someone else produce that death by firing the gun? Contrast this with: There has been a death caused by cancer; was the cancer, which did not show up until years later, induced by the asbestos dust that the worker inhaled? Was the defendant responsible for the site conditions that produced the asbestos-fiber-level violations? Did he know that he was acting in a criminally negligent manner?)

On these lines, I would advocate strong support of extensive research seeking to plumb the range of public attitudes toward white-collar offenses and offenders, and the nuances of such attitudes. A variety of videotaped trials, with their components varied along important dimensions, could be employed as stimuli. Respondents should not only be members of the general public and specialized publics (such as prosecutors and corporate officials), but also persons gathered into jury-like groups.

There is also much to be learned from follow-up inquiries with members of juries who sat through trials of persons prosecuted for white-collar crimes. There is a growing literature suggesting that most lay persons do not readily comprehend the often complicated and abstruse evidence that such trials may entail.[20] They are said to reach their verdicts in terms of spurious consideration, often in a so-called mumpsimus manner.[21] There is a belief that such juries, failing to appreciate the state's evidence, are apt to decide, more readily than they should, that there is a benefit of a doubt working for the white-collar-crime offender. Other commentators, on the contrary, believe that regular jury members are best suited for *all* kinds of criminal trials, because the integrity of the jury system guarantees things that would be lost under a system of blue-ribbon juries made up of persons particularly competent to weigh white-collar-crime evidentiary matters. This is a testable proposition, and it ought to be tested.

The aim of the suggested public-opinion and jury probes should be to determine and to circulate widely the state of responsiveness to diverse aspects of white-collar crime. In the course of such statements, it would not be remiss to point out discrepancies that come to be perceived between different forms of death-dealing behavior, and to suggest reasons for this situation, if it proves to be so. It should also prove valuable if we were able to secure satisfactory evidence of the relationship between white-collar crime and other forms of criminal behavior. It is believed by many persons that the existence of upper-class lawbreaking impels other kinds of violations— that is, those within their domain—by persons with less power and fewer resources.

Additional Activist Inquiries

Statistics

There exists a pressing need for a continuing statistical series that addresses the extent of white-collar crime. Most authorities concede that, for starters, it would be necessary to confine the reporting system to offenses that come under the jurisdiction of the federal regulatory agencies and the U.S. Department of Justice. There now exists an outstanding review of possible data sources on white-collar crime and a sophisticated critique of their shortcomings and potentialities if certain reforms were introduced.[22]

I would take a first step toward further research and action in this realm by inaugurating as quickly as possible, either within the Department of Justice or externally, what for now would have to be a primitive centralized reporting procedure. It would rely on information supplied by the agencies that enforce white-collar-crime laws. Such agencies would be given guidelines for reporting, but it would be appreciated that by and large the information they would provide would not be comparable from one agency to another in any serious way. Comparison would require an array of interpretative aids and suitable reservations about what the reports mean.

The annual document that would emerge from this operation would serve as a research-action-propaganda mechanism. For one thing, it would draw the attention of the public to the work in the criminal arena of the federal agencies, and to some of the results of that work. In so doing, it would reinforce incentives of the agencies to do this part of their job particularly effectively. Like the Uniform Crime Reports, the document would provide a source for continuing public enlightenment and agitation.

Presumably, in the long run the proposed project, by its very existence, would exert continuing leverage on the agencies for more equivalent kinds of reporting, and for a better rationalization of their procedures, where such reforms are appropriate. It would force the agencies to explain publicly any striking changes either in their activities or in their reporting systems from one year to the next by putting their crime-related work under closer scrutiny. And it would provide research workers with a readily available source of information for use in hypothesis testing and other kinds of research work for which some statistical baseline is essential.

Costs

The statistical inventory just proposed could provide a basis for some tentative attempt to gather cost figures for white-collar crime. No person who has dealt with the subject of white-collar crime is immune to the recurring question from media and political sources: Just how much does white-collar crime cost the public? Some of the less gun shy, or more reckless, in the field have attempted to attach numerical quantities that they maintain reflect the cost of white-collar crime. Such persons in general are not notably careful to employ any precision in designating exactly what the figures cover. Indeed, once a set of numbers receives prominent display, future commentators are apt to seize on it, perhaps add an inflation factor to bring it up to date, and carry on from there.

Obviously, cost figures are believed to be an important element of the study of white-collar crime. It probably is not much use to take the high-minded position that the numbers now in circulation are totally meaningless, except as part of a scare tactic or part of an effort to call attention, somewhat raucously, to the significance of white-collar crime as a national issue. I have no objection to tactics of spotlighting. But it seems both important and responsible to base the attention on information that has true meaning, and on results that can be obtained—or rebutted—by others who follow the same data-gathering processes. At the moment, the situation with respect to cost estimates for white-collar crime meets neither of these criteria.

The cost issue, then, deserves some research priority, but probably only to the extent that probes are directed scrupulously to carefully specified kinds of issues. This work should not be done by other than highly skilled economists, preferably persons with considerable training in the matter of placing financial consequences of particular behaviors within relevant categories.

Media

The media represent the catalyst by means of which attitudes toward white-collar crime and white-collar criminals are crystallized. I believe there is no arguing that the media in the United States have not, to date, been notably attentive to matters of white-collar crime, except when they involve notoriously "newsworthy" figures or dramatic illegal actions. At the same time, it was observed during our colloquium that the *Wall Street Journal*, the voice of the business community, abounds with reports of frauds, extortions, violations, and sundry other white-collar crimes. The amount of space devoted by that newspaper of the corporate world to law violations within the ranks of its major subscribers seems a bit surprising to a constant reader. This may offer a clue to the fact that an untapped source of important information and action about white-collar crime lies within the business world itself. If businessmen could be convinced that rectitude pays—both in terms of public relations and by eliminating corrupt competitors—the fight against white-collar crime would have enrolled some powerful allies. The domain of business attitudes toward white-collar crime, then, needs thorough exploration.

There never has been a good counting of what the media say and how much they report about white-collar crime. Content analyses and line counts comparing papers such as the *Wall Street Journal* with other dailies, with the weekly news magazines, and with the television networks and local stations could provide valuable information. The items that appear in these outlets could be compared with the news releases from regulatory agencies and from the prosecutorial offices from which a large part of such information is gleaned. In addition, it would be interesting to relate public opinion about white-collar crime to particular news stories about its occurrence. There now exist excellent mass-communication techniques that could be employed to determine the things that newspaper readers see and how much and what they retain—or distort. These techniques should be brought into play for research on white-collar crime.

There is a further need to compare the perceptions of the parties involved in news stories with the facts that are transmitted to the public. It is commonplace among virtually all persons who receive media attention that what they say and do is distorted, or at least is placed in an inaccurate, or perhaps an unflattering, light. Do white-collar offenders feel that they get a fair deal when their cases are covered? Do prosecutors? What distortions do they believe are inserted into the reports of their activities? How do they handle the press and the television crews? And what implications does all of this have for basic issues in white-collar crime: its detection, the framing of public opinion about it, and its control?

The best-known commentary on this issue of media handling of white-collar crime is the examination of media response to the General Electric antitrust conspiracy in 1961, which concluded that because of the "negative and emasculated reporting of this issue by the bulk of the nation's press [the] reaction of the American public to the largest antitrust suit in our history has generally been that of mute acquiescence."[23] Harris Steinberg, an attorney who defends white-collar persons accused of crimes, disagrees, maintaining that trials of white-collar offenders are subject to extensive reports in the media and that they produce acute discomfort among defendants because they influence their standing with colleagues whose good opinion they value.[24] Note, however, the following courtroom interchange:

> Federal District Judge Barrington D. Parker told Mr. Helms [the former director of the CIA, accused of lying under oath about the agency's contributions to undermine the Allende government in Chile] before sentencing: "You dishonored your oath and now you stand before this court in disgrace and shame."
>
> "I don't feel disgraced at all," Mr. Helms later told reporters outside the courtroom after sentencing.[25]

It may be noted that Helms's attorney, Edward Bennett Williams, had told the judge in the courtroom that Helms would "bear the scar of a conviction for the rest of his life." Following the trial, Williams told newspaper reporters that his client would "wear his conviction like a badge of honor."[26]

Another particularly fine source on the subject of white-collar crime involves the trade publications of the business community. These outlets often express much more frankly and openly—since they are oriented toward the in-group—the opinions that permeate the industries that are served by the publications.

Case Studies

Differences continue to exist among persons working in the area of white-collar crime about the need to accumulate, to a much greater extent than we have to date, elaborate case studies of individual offenses. A contrary view is that a more pressing task is to take what we now have and attempt to generalize about it. There are also those who believe that there has been too much free-floating investigation of white-collar crime, and that the basic requirement now is to have such work guided by theoretical notions of some sophistication.

The simplest answer—and, I believe the truest one at this time—is that all these kinds of work require attention and resources. There is no need to exhort persons to concentrate on theory—it has deep disciplinary support—but I think that a strong case should be made for the continuing accumulation of detailed examinations of individual cases of white-collar offending, particularly those employing the corporate form to carry out the lawbreaking. Such studies should fuel grander theoretical explorations and, in particular, can provide sparks of insight that otherwise would be overlooked by persons who started with predetermined questions that exclusively occupied their attention.

It is correctly maintained that case-study work has a tendency toward the journalistic. But journalism itself is not an unencumbered exercise; it too is directed by a set of postulates that determine what a reporter will or will not see, and what he or she will report. In that sense, case studies of white-collar crime conducted by trained criminal-justice research workers inevitably will be responsive to the kinds of issues that are stressed in the education that the research workers have received, an education most usually in sociology, economics, criminal justice, or law. It usually is a good idea to have as large as possible an accumulation of factual information before venturing too far theoretically. It is the little facts, the elder Huxley once remarked, that break the back of the grand theories (Huxley also cynically noted that, though moribund, such grand theories have a tendency to carry on as if they were viable).

Case studies, with their particularity and their drama, make interesting and appropriate targets of inquiry. Throughout this colloquium there has been constant reference to this or that case in order to support a more general position. We heard both informally and in the prepared papers about the Ford Pinto case, the Lockheed overseas bribes, and the Firestone 500 scandal, among many others. Detailed examination of episodes such as these refines, expands, or contradicts our current beliefs, and points to new areas in which productive insights might lie.

Again, longitudinal probes tying the cases to public attitudes might well prove valuable. How did people view the culpability of the Ford Company in the Pinto case? What did they think of the Indiana statute? Did their views change as the evidence in the trial unfolded? Did they agree with the verdict, and did it produce any alteration of their original position? How did Ford personnel see the prosecution, and what, if any, behavior and attitudinal changes did it introduce into their ranks and those of their competitors?

A research approach in this vein that I have always favored—although it has its problems—involves the monitoring on diverse sites of essentially similar kinds of cases. How is Medicaid fraud handled in California, New York, North Dakota, and Georgia? The work of different researchers at different sites often can produce complementary materials that illuminate an issue much more brightly than do uncoordinated kinds of examinations.

Organizational Studies

Undoubtedly, the most important recent surge in white-collar crime work has been the movement toward a focus on organizational function and structure as these bear on the amount and types of violations.[27] Most fundamentally, this work replaces emphasis on the individuals involved in the offenses with a focus on the organizational climate. It considers matters such as the interaction of executives, the ethos of the bureaucratic structure, the play of the market, business demands, and ethical codes as forming the roots of white-collar crime. A particular advantage of such work is that it brings to bear concepts that have been tested and refined in a well-established field of inquiry on an area of work where they largely have been overlooked. The title of an article by Edward Gross quintessentially delineates the nature of this newer work; it is called "Organizations as Criminal Actors."[28]

In this article, Gross demonstrates how an organizational focus can prove fruitful for pinpointing imperatives pressing toward illegal behavior when he notes a study that examined data on violations of antitrust laws and FTC rules by private firms and found an inverse relationship between the "munificence" of an organization's environment and the likelihood of its being cited for unfair market practices and restraint of trade.[29] This conclusion duplicates an earlier result obtained by Lane, and is in line with some of the findings of Clinard's updating and refinement of the pioneering study of corporate crime by Sutherland.[30] Further pursuit of organizational analysis in the area of white-collar crime should enjoy a high research priority. Also, the vast accumulation of materials by Clinard offers a corpus of data for reanalysis in terms of a number of particularistic hypotheses that are implicit or suggested in the more general study. Finally, there is a need to integrate the large body of literature on the delinquent activities of juvenile gangs with the study of white-collar crime. Theoretical and empirical work on gangs stands out as probably the best large and cumulative collection of materials in criminology, and it has a direct bearing on how groups organize in terms of their behavior vis-à-vis the law.[31]

What I particularly would like to see in organizational studies of white-collar crime would be on-site investigation—that is, participant-observer work carried out by persons who obtain employment within the corporate world and report on the basis of ethnographic field study about the day-to-day job climate and activities, and the manner in which these bear on attitudes and behaviors with respect to the laws regulating the company's activities.

Various speakers also have discussed the possible value of ethical codes in containing business behavior that otherwise might violate the criminal law. Generally, outsiders are skeptical about the utility of such codes, suggesting that they look good on paper but are by and large ineffective. They are often seen as placating exercises designed to quiet external criticisms of a business or trade. But the matter seems worth more detailed scrutiny. How are such codes generated, what do they say (and not say), and how seriously are they taken by those who promulgate them and those to whom they are directed—indeed, how well are their contents known to the relevant parties?

More generally, the absorption of behavior standards with respect to the law, as these standards penetrate an organizational structure, demands close investigation. Again, longitudinal study appears likely to produce particularly worthwhile information, especially continuing study of a panel of junior executives from the time they enroll in business school through the period when they move up (if they do so) into the ranks of management. Howard S. Becker and his associates have provided a model in his study of the socialization of medical students into the role of practicing doctor, but we lack a good study that duplicates this kind of investigation for the business schools, and beyond their doors.[32] At what point does the young career person begin to identify with goals that involve violation of the law, and in what manner does he come to this position? And how about the whistleblowers? What takes place within themselves or in their corporate experience that pushes them to inform on their employer?

Similarly, we ought to know more precisely the nature of the rationalizations that permit violators in the world of white-collar crime to carry out their illegal acts. We suspect that virtually all offenders against the criminal law incorporate a set of "explanations" of their behavior that redefines it in a light that they find comfortable to live with. "The law was inexact," they might say. Or, "We never knew we were violating any law." "We did what we did for the best interest of our employees." Or, "Nobody lost anything through our actions." These are among the innumerable responses of accused white-collar law violators. The nature of such responses, their distribution by offense and offender, is worth examination. It has been suggested in one investigation that the most effective manner for dealing with "respectable" lawbreakers—shoplifters, in this instance—is to penetrate the shell of their structure of rationalizations and force them to redefine their behavior in more meretricious terms.[33] It would seem especially important to compare offenders with nonoffenders with respect to a large number of factors that must illuminate the distinction between law-abiding and lawbreaking acts.

Miscellaneous Matters

A number of other matters merit passing attention as promising research realms. Interviews with incarcerated white-collar offenders could yield material parallel to that which we have derived from studies of other kinds of inmates: The offenders could reflect on their past behavior, inform us about their presumed future, and give us ideas about their perception of the suitability of sentence. More than most personnel involved in white-collar crime, these people represent an available study population, literally one with time on its hands, and probably one that would prove reasonably cooperative. Similarly, retired business executives with no existing stake in their careers probably could provide valuable ideas about the acts and attitudes of the workplace while they were involved in it that could bear on our understanding of white-collar crime. Courtrooms also offer outstanding research sites, since the Sixth Amendment allows untrammeled access to their environs; an astute observer, watching a series of white-collar-crime trials, could add greatly to our knowledge of their dynamics. Similarly, the Freedom of Information Act offers an unequaled opportunity to obtain data that long has been denied researchers and that could prove invaluable for more informed studies of white-collar crime.[34] Finally, there is a need to launch and evaluate programs designed to incorporate awareness of white-collar crime in students at the secondary level, in colleges and universities, and in professional schools.

Controlling White-Collar Crime

The ultimate goal of concomitantly increasing concern and encouraging research about white-collar crime is to enhance the quality of life for the general public and for those who currently are harmed by such behaviors. There is a need in this context to determine the effectiveness of existing and proposed methods for dealing with white-collar crime and those who perpetrate it.

As in most aspects of criminological work, the issue of *deterrence* is a crucial issue with respect to white-collar crime. Considerable controversy exists about the fairness and efficacy of a panoply of punishments that are suggested for white-collar-crime offenders. The penal sanction is sometimes said to be notably useful in deterrence terms because white-collar criminals in general are believed to be rational planners and persons particularly responsive to the shame and degradation of incarceration. Other writers feel that the focus on criminal enforcement and penal sanctions so emasculates efficiency—largely because of the complex nature of the cases—that it is counterproductive.[35] There also is a strong belief that penal sanctions usually are much too harsh for white-collar crime, and that there are other enforcement consequences that would prove more effective in terms of both specific and general deterrence.

Equal-protection laws seem to inhibit any truly experimental designs that might definitively test some of the basic propositions surrounding these disparate viewpoints. But there are naturalistic conditions that can be scrutinized closely; that is, we can concentrate on monitoring carefully the apparent consequences of one or another method that is employed for dealing with specific instances of white-collar crime. In terms of consent decrees, for instance—a subject that has aroused some controversy—it would appear worthwhile to determine how businesses feel about the severity of such decrees, and how their future behavior appears to be influenced by the entering of a consent decree against them. Certainly, the effectiveness of the sanction of publicity, strongly recommended in some well-argued papers by Fisse, should be looked at along a variety of exploratory dimensions.[36]

It needs to be considered also that some punishments can result in behaviors worse than those they were designed to alleviate. An illustration is provided in the area of sex offenses by Graham:

> In Scotland, even more feared than the pillory was the punishment of having to appear in church every Sunday for a given number of weeks . . . to be harangued for half an hour in front of the congregation by the minister—for which, in some churches, offenders were fastened to the wall in iron collars, or jougs. This was the penalty for adulterers and fornicators of both sexes, and was greatly feared. So much so, that it caused a sharp rise in the infanticide rate, for women who had illegitimately become pregnant preferred to risk the capital penalty for infanticide rather than admit the facts and suffer such extreme humiliation.[37]

The range of penalties proposed for white-collar crime involving corporations has included suspension of corporate managers and board members, temporary bans on corporate advertising because of deceptive practices, required publication of violations to inform consumers, and imposition of corporate bankruptcy.[38] Determining the comparative utility of such sanctions is not a simple matter, but it is one that requires considerable attention. In the area of probation, too, the idea that a white-collar offender, as a condition of his probation, must submit to a reasonable audit of his financial dealings and must provide periodic statements of his income and expenses, is another innovative measure—among many others proposed—that ought to be given a trial and subjected to evaluation.[39]

A detailed analysis of the role of statutory requirements as they bear on the effective delineation and control of white-collar crime also must receive a high priority on any research agenda. The Library of Congress recently completed a review of laws dealing with the liability of corporate officials for the negligence of persons who are supposed to be under their supervision.[40] We could use further inventories of laws and their implications for dealing with white-collar offenses and offenders. August Bequai, for example, records what he regards as the archaic nature of the legal and administrative arrangements in the federal government today for dealing with complex white-collar crimes. First, he refers to consumer-fraud cases:

Prosecuting consumer fraud cases, as with other white-collar crimes, is seriously hampered by various drawbacks. It is difficult, for example, to prove that, in fact, the outcome has been the product of a willful intent to defraud the public rather than an error in business judgement. In addition, the felons in these cases argue that their agents, and not they, were behind the scheme. Proving that both agent and principal acted jointly is rarely an easy task. Felons also argue, in defense, that it is merely salesmanship, that in every business there concededly is an element of "puffing." Liability is difficult to attach to the actual manipulators, and as a consequence, prosecution usually takes the form of an injunction or consent agreement. Criminal actions are rare and hampered by a judiciary that metes out lenient sentences against those convicted of frauds.[41]

There recently have been some fine detailed studies of the sentencing practices and dynamics behind them in white-collar-crime cases.[42] As the implications of this work are absorbed, they undoubtedly will suggest fruitful follow-up investigations. But how do we deal with Bequai's sweeping allegation that:

In large part, white-collar crime prosecutions have been hampered by bureaucratic redtape, absence of a firm commitment, the politicized nature of the present U.S. Attorney's Offices, and a hesitancy to shift prosecutorial strategies. The entire federal prosecutorial apparatus is in need of review and revision.[43]

This appears rather broad, but it does suggest that we could probably benefit from an organizational study of the prosecution of white-collar crime on both federal and state levels. In fact, the determination of the proper roles of state as compared with federal authorities in the field requires closer attention. My initial recommendation would be for the identification of particularly effective organizational arrangements, which then will be regarded as model programs, and for the subsequent reporting and dissemination of information about the arrangements and tactics that appear to be the foundation of their achievements.

With respect to prosecutorial tactics, the matter of whether white-collar-crime cases are pursued as civil suits or moved against under criminal law is another issue worthy of study. Instances that appear to me to merit criminal prosecution may well not be so treated because the persons involved, whatever desire for "revenge" or "justice" they may hold against the depredators, harbor an even greater desire to get a money settlement or reward. They would rather sue than see a crime prosecuted. State and federal attorneys are apt either to be overloaded with work or moved by a spirit that dictates that they will not do anything more than they absolutely must. There was a common-law doctrine, since fallen into disuse, that might well be reexamined as part of a general research probe into the whole issue of sanctions against white-collar crime. It required that:

> Where injuries are inflicted on an individual under circumstances which constitute a felony, that felony could not be made the foundation of a civil action at the suit of the person injured against the person who inflicted the injuries until the latter had been prosecuted or a reasonable excuse shown for his non-prosecution.[44]

There remains a dearth of useful information from other societies with respect to the enforcement procedures and sanctions that they employ for white-collar-crime violations. Such materials might well suggest more effective ways we could marshal our resources for the same purposes. Chambliss has argued that, overall, socialist societies manifest less crime than capitalist societies. He believes that the seemingly striking variations in crime rates between places such as China and the Soviet Union are primarily a function of their degrees of commitment to the "true" principles of Marxist doctrine.[45] Criminologists working in communist societies like to point out that they have no corporate crime; but this is a bit of semantic sleight-of-hand, since they have no corporations. There is ample evidence that violations of the laws regulating their employment behavior by managers and employees of communist collectives are not at all uncommon,[46] and it may be that the extent of such crime provides support for Smigel's thesis that people find it easier to steal from impersonal organizations than they do from individuals or from small, more intimate business enterprises.[47]

The vast array of cross-cultural information on white-collar crime that barely has been tapped to date might inform us about why some societies seem to produce a cadre of relatively honest and trustworthy political officeholders, whereas others are plagued by dishonesty among their officials.[48] In Japan, theorists speculate that custom and structural variables insist that officeholders often engage in illegal practices, largely as a function of fiscal demands placed on them by their constituents.[49] We might well learn more about our own society by distancing ourselves a bit to look at what happens elsewhere.

A Concluding Caveat

To take on the task of establishing some research and action priorities, in the manner that has been attempted here, itself implies an understanding of the elements of the process that will prove most effective in reaching preordained goals. That we possess such an understanding is, of course, arguable. We do not truly know whether the most effective approach to stipulated success is to make available "suitable" sums of research money and to allow the imaginations and interest of those seeking such funds to dictate what they propose to accomplish, or whether the outcome is likely to be more satisfactory if preestablished, detailed blueprints are drawn up and workers forced to toil only within these set boundaries. There are strong arguments on both sides. Note, for instance, Cottrell's conclusion about the same problem and its consequences for the quality of the wall paintings and artifacts that are found in the tombs of early Egyptian pharaohs:

> In art the freedom of the craftsman was restrained by a rigid religious convention, but within the limits set by this convention, perhaps because of them, the Old Kingdom sculptors produced work of an austere beauty and majesty; work which . . . was never equalled by Egyptian craftsmen of later centuries.[50]

Cottrell's thesis regarding the enabling aspects of set boundaries finds support in Proust's remark that the "tyranny of rhyme" often forces poets "into the discovery of their finest lines."[51] These arguments for rigid structure and explicit guidelines, so that the worker does not flounder because of an overly amorphous assignment, are seconded by Riesman with respect to matters closer to our work here. Riesman suggests that superior results often are achieved in response to a mundane pragmatic issue, compared with the work done when grander concerns underlie the effort:

> [W]hen I examine the work done by scholars in universities in comparison with the applied work done in answer to some client's need, I cannot argue that the track of the discipline produces in general more seminal research than the quest of an answer to an extra-academic problem. Only a very rare person will be an intellectual self-starter.[52]

On the other side, the unbridled play of curiosity, the freedom to think in an unrestricted manner, is believed by some to be likely to yield the highest dividends. Indeed, arguments might be set forth that the basic thrust of our work here is counterproductive, since it formalizes too much, and in a collaborative manner, things that best should be individual enterprises. Let it be remembered that, in large measure, we all are present today because Edwin H. Sutherland, a lone scholar, working by himself with only library resources, came (by means of an obscure process that he called *differential association*) to produce the classic work on a topic virtually ignored theretofore, a topic that he labeled *white-collar crime*. I have recently, with a colleague, traced in some detail the personal and intellectual sources that constituted Sutherland's patrimony; it seems that he chose his subject largely because it was one that interested him, and one about which he had strong feelings.[53] Most assuredly, the roots of his concern did not emerge from a preconstituted agenda. In short, like our subject, our purpose too contains many contentious components. At the very least, its efficacy should not be taken for granted. Indeed, even the commitment to a more decent world, the commitment that I suggested lies behind work on white-collar crime, does not go unchallenged. Note the observation made by a character in a novel written by a law professor at the University of Michigan: "One receives only imperfect justice in this world; only fools, children, left-wing Democrats, social scientists, and a few demented judges expect anything better."[54] If so, our work here enlists us as part of a motley group, indeed.

Notes

1. Howard S. Becker, *Outsiders* (New York: Free Press, 1963), pp. 147-163.

2. Joseph R. Gusfield, *Symbolic Crusade* (Urbana: University of Illinois Press, 1966).

3. James Q. Wilson, *The Politics of Regulation* (New York: Basic Books, 1980); James Greene, *Regulatory Problems and Regulatory Reform: The Perceptions of Business* (New York: Conference Board, 1980).

4. Compare Seymour Martin Lipset and William Schneider, "The Public View of Regulation," *Public Opinion*, 2 (January-February 1979), pp. 6-13.

5. Herbert Edelhertz and Marilyn Walsh, *The White-Collar Challenge to Nuclear Safeguards* (Lexington, Mass.: Lexington Books, D.C. Heath and Company, 1978).

6. "Symposium on White-Collar Crime," *Temple Law Quarterly*, 53, no. 4, 1980, pp. 975-1146.

7. Eds. Peter Wickman and Timothy Dailey, *White-Collar and Economic Crime: Multidisciplinary and Cross-National Perspectives* (Lexington, Mass.: Lexington Books, D.C. Heath and Company, 1981).

8. Eds. Herbert Edelhertz and Charles Rogovin, *A Strategy for Containing White-Collar Crime* (Lexington, Mass.: Lexington Books, D.C. Heath and Company, 1980).

9. See Robert K. Elliott and John J. Willingham, *Management Fraud: Detection and Deterrence* (New York: Petrocelli, 1980).

10. See. U.S. Congress, House of Representatives, Committee on the Judiciary, Subcommittee on Crime (95th Congress, 2nd Session), *White-Collar Crime* (Washington, D.C.: U.S. Government Printing Office, 1979); Ibid. (96th Congress, 2nd Session), *Corporate Crime* (Washington, D.C.: U.S. Government Printing Office, 1980).

11. U.S. Attorney General, *National Priorities for the Investigation and Prosecution of White Collar Crime: Report of the Attorney General* (Washington, D.C.: U.S. Government Printing Office, 1980).

12. Ibid.

13. A-T-O Inc., *Figgie Report on Fear of Crime: America Afraid* (New York: Ruder and Rinn, 1980). See *Los Angeles Times* (19 September 1980).

14. U.S. Attorney General, *National Priorities for the Investigation and Prosecution of White Collar Crime* (Washington, D.C.: U.S. Government Printing Office, 1980).

15. David M. Gordon, "Capitalism, Class, and Crime in America," *Crime and Delinquency*, 19 (April 1973), pp. 163-186.

16. G.O.W. Mueller, "Criminal Theory: An Appraisal of Jerome Hall's Studies in Jurisprudence and Criminal Theory," *Indiana Law Journal*, 34 (Winter 1959), p. 220.

17. John Kleinig, "Crime and the Concept of Harm," *American Philosophical Quarterly*, 15 (January 1978), pp. 27-36.

18. Laura Schill Schrager and James F. Short, Jr., "How Serious a Crime? Perceptions of Organizational and Common Crimes," pp. 14-31 in ed. Gilbert Geis and Ezra Stotland, *White-Collar Crime: Theory and Research* (Beverly Hills: Sage, 1980); Marilyn E. Walsh and Donna D. Schram, "The Victim of White-Collar Crime: Accuser or Accused," in *ibid.*, pp. 32-51.

19. Peter H. Rossi, Emily Waite, Christine E. Bose, and Richard E. Berk, "The Seriousness of Crime: Normative Structure and Individual Differences," *American Sociological Review*, 39 (April 1974), pp. 224-237.

20. See, for example, "Now Juries Are on Trial: 'Big Cases' Call Into Question Their Ability to Do Justice," *Time*, (3 September 1979). A few federal judges have refused to allow jury trials in such cases, relying on a footnote in a 1970 Supreme Court decision that suggests that the Seventh Amendment right to a jury may be limited by "the practical abilities and limitations" of jurors.

21. In dictionary definition, *mumpsimus* refers to "an error or prejudice obstinately clung to; the term is supposedly taken from the story of an illiterate priest who, in his devotions, had for thirty years used *mumpsimus* for the proper Latin word *sumpsimus*, and who, on his mistake being pointed out to him, replied, 'I will not change my *mumpsimus* for your new *sumpsimus*. . . . .' "

22. Albert J. Reiss, Jr., and Albert Biderman, *Data Sources on White-Collar Law-Breaking* (Washington, D.C.: U.S. Government Printing Office, 1980).

23. *New Republic* (20 February 1961), p. 7.

24. Harris B. Steinberg, "The Defense of the White-Collar Accused," *American Criminal Law Quarterly*, 3 (Spring 1965), pp. 129-138.

25. Quoted in Joseph Heller, *Good as Gold* (New York: Pocket Books, 1980), p. 357.

26. Ibid.

27. A key article is M. David Ermann and Richard J. Lundman, "Deviant Acts by Complex Organizations: Deviance and Social Control at the Organizational Level of Analysis," *Sociological Quarterly*, 19 (Winter 1978), pp. 55-67.

28. Edward Gross, "Organizations as Criminal Actors," in eds. Paul R. Wilson and John Braithwaite, *Two Faces of Deviance* (St. Lucia: University of Queensland Press, 1978), pp. 199-213.

29. Barry M. Staw and Eugene Szwajkowski, "The Scarcity-Munificence Component of Organizational Environments and the Commission of Illegal Acts," *Administrative Science Quarterly*, 20 (September 1975), pp. 345-354.

30. Robert E. Lane, "Why Businessmen Violate the Law," *Journal of Criminal Law, Criminology, and Police Science*, 44 (July 1953), pp. 151-165; Marshall B. Clinard, *Illegal Corporate Behavior* (Washington, D.C.: U.S. Government Printing Office, 1979).

31. Among the best known works are Albert K. Cohen, *Delinquent Boys* (New York: Free Press, 1955); Richard A. Cloward and Lloyd Ohlin, *Delinquency and Opportunity* (New York: Free Press, 1960); James F. Short, Jr., and Fred L. Strodtbeck, *Group Process and Gang Delinquency* (Chicago: University of Chicago Press, 1965); and Walter B. Miller, "Lower Class Culture as a Generating Milieu of Gang Delinquency," *Journal of Social Issues*, 14 (April 1958), pp. 5-19.

32. Howard S. Becker, Blanche Geer, Everett C. Hughes, and Anselm L. Strauss, *Boys in White: Student Culture in Medical School* (Chicago: University of Chicago Press, 1961).

33. Mary Owen Cameron, *The Booster and the Snitch* (New York: Free Press, 1964).

34. Susan Long, *The Internal Revenue Service: Measuring Tax Offenses and Enforcement Response* (Washington, D.C.: U.S. Government Printing Office, 1980).

35. Christopher D. Stone, *Where the Law Ends* (New York: Harper and Row, 1975).

36. See, for example, Brent Fisse, "The Use of Publicity as a Criminal Sanction Against Business Corporations," *Melbourne University Law Review*, 8 (June 1971), pp. 107-150.

37. Henry G. Graham, *The Social Life of Scotland in the Eighteenth Century* (London: A & C Black, 1899), p. 43.

38. Morton Mintz and Jerry S. Cohen, *America, Inc.* (New York: Dial, 1971).

39. Elsie L. Reid, "Looking at the Law," *Federal Probation*, 41 (June 1977), p. 50.

40. See U.S. House of Representatives, *Corporate Crime*.

41. August Bequai, *White-Collar Crime: A Twentieth-Century Crisis* (Lexington, Mass.: Lexington Books, D.C. Heath and Company, 1978), p. 53.

42. See Kenneth Mann, Stanton Wheeler, and Austin Sarat, "Sentencing the White-Collar Criminal," *American Criminal Law Review*, 17 (Spring 1980), pp. 479-500; Ilene Nagel Bernstein, John L. Hagan, and Celestia

Albonetti, "Differential Sentencing of White-Collar Offenders in Ten Federal Courts," *American Sociological Review*, 45 (1980), pp. 802-820.

43. Bequai, *White-Collar Crime*, p. 151. See also Suzanne Weaver, *The Decision to Prosecute* (Cambridge, Mass.: MIT Press, 1977).

44. *Smith v. Selwyn*, 3 K.B. 98 (1914).

45. William Chambliss, Paper presented at Conference on Crime in Developing Countries, Ibadan, Nigeria, July 1980.

46. Walter D. Connor, *Deviance in Soviet Society* (New York: Columbia University Press, 1972).

47. Erwin O. Smigel, "Public Attitudes Toward 'Chiseling' With Reference to Unemployment Compensation," *American Sociological Review*, 18 (February 1953), pp. 59-67.

48. Ronald Wraith and Edgar Simpkins, *Corruption in Developing Countries* (London: Allen, 1963).

49. Mamoru Iga and Morton Auerback, "Political Corruption and Social Structure in Japan," *Asian Survey*, 17 (June 1977), pp. 556-564.

50. Leonard Cottrell, *The Last Pharaohs* (London: Pan, 1977), p. 21.

51. Marcel Proust, *Swann's Way*, trans. C.K. Scott Moncrieft (New York: Modern Library, n.d.), p. 28.

52. David Riesman, "Law and Sociology," in ed. William Evan, *Law and Sociology* (New York: Free Press), p. 41.

53. Gilbert Geis and Colin Goff, "Edwin H. Sutherland: A Biographical and Analytical Commentary," Paper presented at Conference on White Collar and Economic Crime, Postdam College of Arts and Sciences, Potsdam, New York, February 1980.

54. Walter F. Murphy, *The Vicar of Christ* (New York: Macmillan, 1979), p. 93.

11 Edwin H. Sutherland: A Biographical and Analytical Commentary

Gilbert Geis and *Colin Goff*

The thirty-fourth annual meeting of the American Sociological Society (ASS)—convened in Philadelphia in 1939 during the academic recess between Christmas and the New Year—was held jointly with the fifty-second gathering of the American Economic Association (AEA). On 27 December, Jacob Viner of the University of Chicago delivered his presidential address to the AEA. According to the program, his topic was to have been "Does Gold Have a Future?" But Viner's thoughts on this matter must remain uncertain. By the time of the session, he had abandoned his announced subject. The presidential address now bore the title "The Short View and the Long in Economic Policy," and had nothing to say about the prospects for gold.[1]

The joint meeting of the AEA and the ASS was held at the Benjamin Franklin Hotel, which still stands at Ninth and Chestnut Streets in downtown Philadelphia. Room rates ranged from $3.50 to $6.00.[2] Newspapers of the day were reporting that the Archbishop of Canterbury had suggested prayers in support of Finland's resistance to a Russian invasion; that the British were instituting sugar and meat rationing; and that Mussolini had paid a visit to the Pope. At home, it was noted mournfully that Roosevelt's fiscal proposals included the seventh unbalanced federal budget in a row. Elsewhere, Al Capone had been admitted to a Baltimore hospital with an undisclosed ailment, and probes by Martin Dies's House Committee on un-American Activities were said to have bared a "Red drive" on the West Coast.

Viner's presidential address was at eight o'clock on the evening of 27 December. He was followed to the podium in the hotel's Crystal Room by Edwin H. Sutherland of Indiana University, president of the sociological society, whose title was "The White Collar Criminal." Sutherland's address altered the field of criminology in fundamental ways throughout the world, although it would take all of the more than forty years since that night for the impact of the address to be appreciated fully and reflected in the mainstream of criminological work. Sutherland was fifty-six years old at the time of his presidential address. Little in his earlier work would have prepared

Gilbert Geis and Colin Goff in eds. Peter Wickman and Thomas Dailey, *White-Collar and Economic Crime: Multidisciplinary and Cross-National Perspectives.* (Lexington, Mass.: Lexington Books, D.C. Heath and Company, 1981), pp. 3-31.

the audience for his fiery indictment of persons who ever after would be known by the label that Sutherland put on them that night: *white-collar criminals.*

In addition to its scholarly component, Sutherland's material clearly represented a strong personal and political testament. His work on white-collar crime abounds with expressions of indignation, anger, and vituperation. Note as but one example (though one of the most inflammatory) the following from *White Collar Crime*, the monograph Sutherland wrote in 1949:

> . . . the utility corporations for two generations or more have engaged in organized propaganda to develop favorable sentiments. They devoted much attention to the public schools in an effort to mold the opinion of children. Perhaps no groups except the Nazis have paid so much attention to indoctrinating the youth of the land with ideas favorable to a special interest, and it is doubtful whether even the Nazis were less bound by considerations of honesty in their propaganda.[3]

This seems a surprising outburst from a person who uniformly is described by those who knew him well as "imbued with sincerity and objectivity," "soft-spoken," a man of "paternal wisdom" who "never taught in terms of sarcasm, ridicule, or abuse."[4] His colleague at Indiana University, Jerome Hall, observed that Sutherland was "distinguished by an attitude of extraordinary objectivity and thorough inquiry maintained on a high level" and was an individual who "knew how to keep his feelings and personality from intruding into the discussion."[5] What clues might we find in Sutherland's heritage that would help account for his eruption on white-collar crime, which contrasts so markedly with his much more meticulous, even rather pedantic, earlier work in criminology?

Fortunately, details of Sutherland's family background are readily recaptured. In 1935 his father, a Baptist educator and minister, then eighty-seven years old, finished three book-length manuscripts, one of them an account of his own life. The typescripts, which were desposited by their author in the library of the American Baptist Historical Society in Rochester, New York, provide considerable insight into the milieu and the ideological atmosphere that constituted Sutherland's early environment.

These manuscripts set forth some of the principles held by Edwin Sutherland's father that undoubtedly served to fashion the son's character. Both father and son were critical, tough on others,[6] and unstintingly self-critical.[7] They shared also a traditional dedication to service, to doing good, to making the world a better place, and to taking the side of the underprivileged and downtrodden. Most notably, there is a religious commitment that, at its best, demands that the ethics of Christianity be attained in the marketplace. At times, the tone of Sutherland's work on white-collar crime is reminiscent of the preaching of outraged biblical prophets. There is a theological insistence that something other than strict legal denotation demark the realm of acceptable behavior, a matter that would involve Sutherland in considerable debate with those who adhered more firmly to law-book codes as the only criteria by which criminological judgments should be made.[8] Snodgrass has pointed out that Sutherland grew up to love bridge, golf, cigarettes, magazines, movies and jigsaw puzzles, and that he was not particularly religious as an adult. Nonetheless Snodgrass noted, he remained a man of compulsive virtue and integrity, a man who may have given up the orthodoxy of his Baptist upbringing, but never lost its scruples.[9]

Sutherland certainly was tougher on entrenched interests than was his father. In one segment of the elder Sutherland's *History of Nebraska Baptists*, he praises the railroads for providing free passes to itinerant religious preachers. This policy, George Sutherland suggests, arose from the railroads' awareness that ministers brought stability and prosperity to an area, thus ultimately benefiting the railroads.[10] This puts the self-interest of both preachers and the railroads in a benevolent light. The son was less benign; indeed, railroads take some of the heaviest blows in his work on white-collar crime.[11]

The independence of the frontiersman constituted an essential aspect of Sutherland's patrimony. In his study of homeless men in Chicago, Sutherland points out how migration from the protective rural countryside into the jungle of the city had been disconcerting for so many shelter residents.[12] So it must have been for Sutherland as well. The ruses and rudeness, the predation and pitilessness—all must have been unnerving for the Baptist minister's son from Nebraska when he first came to Chicago.

Sutherland's mixture of rural integrity and self-reliance, his combined fear and scorn of city-bred sophistication, and his religious zeal for social reform also marked the characters of a large number of the early leaders of American sociology.[13] In time, Sutherland was indoctrinated by the prevailing imperatives of his sociological trade into the ethos of "scientific" objectivity. Especially in his textbook, he was unsparing in his exposure of the false syllogism, the sloppy logic, the unsupported inference, and the generalization rooted in fancy rather than fact. But behind all this lay his Nebraska Baptist heritage, a heritage that would break through—for better and for worse—when Sutherland in his later years came to study and write about white-collar crime.

Sutherland's Forebears

Edwin Sutherland's great-grandparents migrated to Canada from Scotland and ultimately settled in the fishing and lumbering village of St. George, New Brunswick, where George Sutherland, Edwin's father, was born in 1848. In the 1850s depressed economic conditions drove the Sutherlands to

Wisconsin. The family settled in Eau Claire, where George was graduated from high school. The Sutherlands supported themselves by farming; almost eighty years later, George Sutherland would recall that an unfair share of the chores fell to him. "My father," he wrote critically, "was not interested in farming. He would rather visit his neighbors than plow a furrow or hoe a row of potatoes." From his mother George acquired a strong religious sense, from his father a fervid antagonism toward liquor, "the great corrupter of mankind."[14] George's earliest experiences with organized religion are recounted in the independent, self-deprecatory tone that so permeates his description of his life:

> Soon after my uniting with the church I was made a clerk. . . . I do not think that I made a particularly brilliant clerk, but I attended the church meetings and took down what was done. I was criticized because I did not speak loud enough and did not read loud enough. It was said that my reports could not be heard. They could have remedied that, since my resignation was always before the Church.[15]

After finishing high school, George Sutherland taught locally. In 1872, when he was first old enough to vote, he marked his ballot for the candidate of the Prohibition party. He reveals a great deal about himself and about attitudes that must have been transmitted to his children when he recounts the nature of his affiliation with the Prohibition party:

> I was not very active. . . . I met with them a few times. I was on one occasion president of the state nominating convention in Nebraska, but the people who composed the party seemed to me to be angular, stiff, non-conciliatory, refusing to go out of their way a tittle of a hair's breadth to win an adherent.[16]

In 1876 Sutherland was ordained a Baptist minister, an event that led him to observe, more than fifty years later, "I was a good deal more orthodox on that day than I am at the present time."[17] He received a divinity degree from the Baptist Union Theological Seminary of the University of Chicago the following year. In 1881 he was appointed to teach Greek and bookkeeping at the Nebraska Baptist Seminary in Gibbon, which was then in its second year of operation. Gibbon, named after a Civil War general, lies almost adjacent to the Platte River in the southeastern part of the state. It was a frontier town, founded ten years earlier by the Soldier's Free Homestead Colony, a group of sixty families brought together in the East by a speculator desiring to settle lands ceded to the Union Pacific Railroad to encourage roadbed construction.[18]

Edwin H. Sutherland was born in Gibbon on 13 August 1883. Less than a year later, the family relocated in Kansas, where for the next nine years

George Sutherland served as head of the history department at Ottawa College. "It is my judgment," he would later write, "that for the man who
likes books and young people, teaching in a college is the height of human
bliss."[19] The father's point was not lost on some of the Sutherland children.
Edwin's brother became an educational psychologist, teaching for a while
at the University of Illinois, at Yale, and later at Louisiana College, a Baptist school in Pineville;[20] the youngest child, George, became a pediatrician
on the faculty of Rush Medical College in Philadelphia.

When the Nebraska Baptist Seminary, in dire financial straits, moved
thirty miles east to become Grand Island College, George Sutherland was
recruited for the presidency. He remained in that office for eighteen years,
from 1893 to 1911. During this period the college was in incessant financial
difficulty, a predicament that it managed to overcome, according to the
school's historian, only because of the extraordinary energy and personality
of its president.[21]

After leaving the presidency of Grand Island College in 1911, Sutherland accepted a position in St. Louis with the Society for the Friendless, a
group dedicated to aiding former prison inmates. Sutherland reports going
to the public library to read up on criminology, since "I knew little about
the business in which I was engaged."[22] While he was at work, his overcoat
was stolen. He was neither amused nor sympathetic:

> While I had been industriously gathering information on behalf of those in
> prison or who ought to be there, some of these people were showing their
> customary gratitude to one who was trying to do them good. I had the dis-
> comfort of going home through rain and storm, cold and shivering. That
> criminal was not unlike others for whom good men had labored and made
> sacrifices.[23]

Sutherland soon found that despite his considerable labors he was raising hardly more than enough money to pay his own salary, with little left to
help former inmates. His employers seemed satisfied, but Sutherland, believing that under the circumstances his solicitations were unethical, quit.
He dabbled for a while in real estate,[24] and he did some teaching at Grand
Island College. ("I was asked to withdraw from the teaching force of the
college," he writes, "for the reason that my personality was so striking and
impressive that no president could stand up against me."[25]) After that, he
preached and did pastoral work at neighboring churches on a contract
basis. In 1929, when be was eighty-one, Sutherland again was named president of Grand Island College. He held that position for the next two years,
until during the Depression Grand Island College was absorbed by Sioux
Falls College in South Dakota.

Sutherland barely mentions his family in his 181 pages of autobiograph-
ical memoir. He states that he married Lizzie T. Pickett in 1877 and that she

was from Connecticut (they had met in Chicago), "active in Christian service," "a good Sunday school teacher," and "one who led the singing and prayer meetings."[26] That is all that we will learn from her husband about Lizzie Pickett. The Sutherland children, too, are discussed in only a single paragraph, but affectionately:

> I had three children when I went to Ottawa. Arthur, born in Minock [Illinois]; Nellie, born in Chicago, and Edwin, born in Gibbon. During our nine years sojourn in Ottawa there came to us four more, Bertha, Lillian, Stanley, and Fred. Seven is a large number to those who have none. Some seemed to think that it was too large a number for respectable people to have. On the meager salary I received, we found it hard to feed and clothe them. But when they had grown up, when they were occupying important places in the world of service, when at times they gathered together in the old homestead, it looked then as though there were none too many, that without them, the world would be much poorer.[27]

The final line of Sutherland's reminiscences reads, "Perhaps my executors will complete this autobiography by writing here an account of my decease."[28] No one did. George Sutherland died at the age of ninety-five, on 11 December 1943, four years after his son's presidential address to the American Sociological Society.

Sutherland's Career

Almost all of Edwin Sutherland's earlier years, up to the age of twenty-one, were spent in Grand Island, Nebraska. This city, which had a population of about six thousand in Sutherland's time, owed its early growth to a favorable position as a railroad distribution point. It is located almost in the center of the United States, and was founded in 1866 (less than two decades before the Sutherlands arrived), partly in the quixotic belief that its location would persuade the federal government to place the national capital in Grand Island.[29]

Sutherland received the A.B. degree from Grand Island College, where his father was president, in 1904. He was one of seventy students to complete a baccalaureate degree during his father's eighteen-year tenure at the college. Most of those enrolled at Grand Island did academic work that today would be equivalent to the level of the later years of high school. Sutherland immediately went to teach Greek and Latin at Sioux Falls College in South Dakota, Grand Island's sister Baptist institution. While he was in Sioux Falls, from 1904 to 1906, Sutherland enrolled in a correspondence course in sociology offered by the University of Chicago. The course, a prerequisite for graduate study in history (the field that Sutherland intended to pursue) used a textbook by Charles R. Henderson, a Baptist minister turned sociologist. Henderson, a man much in the spirit of Sutherland's father, was once described by a journalist who watched him preside over an international penology conference as "giving fire, dignity, and spiritual earnestness to the gathering."[30] It is particularly noteworthy that the edition of Henderson's textbook that Sutherland used contains a number of statements that Sutherland himself would echo more than thirty years later in setting forth his ideas about white-collar crime. Note, for instance, this pronouncement by Henderson:

> The social classes of the highest culture furnish few convicts, yet there are educated criminals. Advanced culture modifies the form of crime; tends to make it less coarse and violent, but more cunning; restricts it to quasi-legal forms. But education also opens up the way to new and colossal kinds of crime, as debauching of conventions, councils, legislatures, and bribery of the press and public officials. The egoistic impulses are masked and disguised in this way, the devil wearing the livery of heavenly charity for a cloak of wrong. Many of the "Napoleons" of trade are well named, for they are cold-blooded robbers and murderers, utterly indifferent to the inevitable misery which they must know will follow their contrivances and deals. Occasionally eminent legal ability is employed to plan raids upon the public in ways which will evade the penalties of the criminal code, and many a representative of financial power grazes the prison walls on his way to "success."[31]

The correspondence course led Sutherland to change his graduate concentration to sociology when he attended the University of Chicago from 1906 to 1908. He also worked during part of this period with the Juvenile Protective Association in the city. A significant portion of his academic work was with W.I. Thomas, an iconoclast who may well have been influential in moderating the hold of religious orthodoxy on Sutherland's mind. From 1909 to 1911, Sutherland returned to Grand Island as a faculty member. In 1911 he went back to the university, where two years later he received the Ph.D degree. His dissertation, done in conjunction with the work of the Chicago Commission on Unemployment, was titled, "Unemployment and Public Employment Agencies."

Sutherland then took a teaching position in the sociology department at William Jewell College in Liberty, Missouri, another Baptist institution, where he spent the six years between 1913 and 1919. At William Jewell, where he occupied the John E. Franklin chair of sociology, his teaching assignments included classes in Trade Unionism, Social Problems in Rural Life, Socialism, Charities and Corrections, and Social Politics. In 1918 Sutherland married Myrtle Crews, his landlady's daughter. They would have one child, a daughter.

After leaving William Jewell, Sutherland engaged in something of a Cook's tour of the Big Ten universities. He taught at the University of Illinois for seven years (1919-1926); went to the University of Minnesota for three (1926-1929); and then to the University of Chicago for five years (1930-1935). Failing to secure a tenure guarantee at Chicago, he departed for Indiana University and remained there for the next fifteen years, until his death in 1950. He made brief excursions for visiting appointments at the University of Kansas (1918); Northwestern University (1922); the University of Washington in St. Louis (1942); and San Diego State College during the summer before he died. There was also a year, 1929, with the Bureau of Social Hygiene in New York City, a period that included a brief trip to England to examine the prison system.

What can be said about Sutherland's career pattern? Certainly, there is some indication of a parochial tendency in that Sutherland never ventured very far for very long from the social milieus that he understood and with which he was probably particularly comfortable. In other words, he was exposed to little that might directly challenge his midwestern upbringing, although his years in Chicago must have broadened considerably his understanding of crime and criminals. By the time he came to write on the subject of white-collar crime, Sutherland had spent virtually all of his life very far indeed from the center of political and economic power in the United States. In this country, cities such as Washington and New York are where things happen, where wealth and power (and white-collar crime) are concentrated, where meaningful field work can be undertaken at the source rather than with second-hand reports in the library. Sutherland could not draw on friendship networks, personal discussions, or similar sources for information and viewpoints about white-collar crime. The national and international corporate and political world was for him an almost entirely alien environment. This may explain why, in trying to document white-collar crime by means of case histories, Sutherland resorts to a pedestrian recital of the small-time shenanigans of a college student who worked on weekends as a shoe salesman[32]—a story, according to Donald Cressey, based on Sutherland's personal experiences.

White-collar-crime studies, in fact, have suffered continuously from the age-old tradition of locating major centers of learning in geographically remote and bucolic settings, presumably so that contemplation is not disturbed by mundane affairs. It is noteworthy that scholars based in New York, including Paul Tappan, Richard Quinney, and Erwin Smigel at New York University, make up a sizable percentage of the limited cadre of persons who have contributed significant material on white-collar crime. Washington, D.C., unfortunately, has no preeminent university within the city, although several institutions are now striving for such distinction. Clinard did his work on the black market as a form of white-collar crime following a wartime assignment with the Office of Price Administration in Washington;[33] and much of the recent white-collar-crime scholarship of a team at Yale University, under the direction of Stanton Wheeler, has been based on the assignment of researchers to federal regulatory agencies in Washington. Sutherland's own work on white-collar crime clearly reflects his upbringing and the pattern of his academic career, and can be much better understood and interpreted when it is examined in this light.

The Presidential Address

At least two dozen persons who participated in the American Sociological Society meetings of 1939 are alive today. Not surprisingly, given the time interval and the generally untheatrical nature of such academic events, none of the handful to whom we have talked recalls Sutherland's address. Thorsten Sellin of the University of Pennsylvania, a member of the program committee in 1939 and now living in retirement in New Hampshire, says that he no longer "can remember a thing" from that night. Sellin had known Sutherland for some time, however. In 1927, on a visit to his parents' home in Minneapolis, Sellin paid a special call at the University of Minnesota, where Sutherland was teaching, in order to become acquainted. The two maintained close ties through the years. Sutherland, Sellin observes, was "a very, very retiring person. Modest. Chary of hullabaloo. Very quiet."[34]

As noted, Sutherland's earlier work gave virtually no indication that he suddenly would turn his attention to white-collar crime. His criminology textbook, in its tenth edition in 1978—the revisions having been undertaken by Donald Cressey after Sutherland's death—and perhaps the longest survisor in the realm of social science texts, had paid hardly any attention to the kinds of criminal activity that formed the focus of the Philadelphia talk.

Later, in a speech before the Toynbee Club of DePauw University in Indiana, Sutherland would say that he had been collecting material on white-collar crime since 1928, more than a decade before his ground breaking presidential address.[35] We have found only one published clue to this work: a passing observation in a 1932 article that advocates the use of the concept of *culture* for understanding the crime patterns of immigrants to America. Sutherland notes of his idea: "It is not suggested as a total explanation of delinquency even in the delinquency area, and it certainly does not explain the financial crimes of the white-collar classes."[36] Further, in a 1936 book, written with Harvey J. Locke (one of Sutherland's very few collaborators), the authors employ the term *white collar worker* as a classificatory category to distinguish the 7 percent of the people living during the Depression in Chicago's shelters for unemployed men who had been "professional men, business men, clerks, salesmen, accountants, and men who previously held minor political positions."[37] Obviously, the terms *crime* and *white collar* were prominent in Sutherland's professional vocabulary; given his subject matter, their denotive linkage was almost inevitable.

Sutherland's presidential address, some five-thousand words in length, merits close analysis. The *Philadelphia Inquirer*, in a prominently placed news story the following day, took note of Sutherland's address in terms which suggested that it had pointed to a radical departure from accepted approaches to criminal-behavior theories. The report was headlined "Poverty Belittled as Crime Factor," with the subhead "Sociologist Cites Fraud in Business." Sutherland's audience of economists and sociologists was said to have been "astonished" by the presentation. Certainly the reporter was taken with Sutherland's speech, which he suggested in a figurative sense "threw scores of sociological textbooks into a wastebasket."[38] The *Inquirer* writer's observation would prove to have been more hopeful than prescient.

The *New York Times* also gave Sutherland favorable, albeit more restrained, coverage. Its news report suggested that Sutherland launched a pointed attack against white-collar criminality.[39] This is the first, though hardly the last, commentary that refused to take seriously Sutherland's patently disingenuous disclaimer at the end of the first paragraph of his paper. Sutherland made a comparison between crime in the upper class and crime in the lower class which he contended was "for the purpose of developing theories of criminal behavior, not for the purpose of muckraking or the reform of anything except criminology."[40] The *New York Times* story indicated that the reporter knew better: he could recognize a muckrake when he saw one.

Perhaps fearing to seem defensive, both the *Inquirer* and the *Times* in their stories gave prominent mention to Sutherland's implied criticism of the press. "In many periods," Sutherland said, "more important crime news can be found on the financial pages than on the front pages" of the nation's dailies. The papers also noted Sutherland's scarcely profound observation that white-collar crime of his day was more suave and deceptive than such crime had been in the time of the robber barons. They also found newsworthy the observation that much of white-collar crime was like "stealing candy from a baby;" that is, that the matchup between offender and victim was highly uneven.

White-Collar Criminality

Given the joint nature of the professional meeting at which he was speaking, Sutherland at the outset tried to draw the scholarly community of economists into a concern with white-collar crime, a mission that had little success then or any more since. For economists, white-collar criminal acts are usually viewed as one among many calculated business risks; apprehension by the authorities means only that a cost is added to the loss side of the ledger. There is in economics virtually no material examining the efficacy of variant penalty structures on business behavior, or relating organizational structure and function to law violation. The farthest economists (as well as political scientists) are apt to venture into the study of white-collar crime is to address questions about whether corruption in developing countries is functional or dysfunctional.[41] That economists lately have come to regard traditional forms of crime and penalties, such as capital punishment, as matters worthy of attention may indicate that with time they will begin to focus on white-collar crime, on offenses that one might have thought, given their expertise, would have captured their disciplinary fancy earlier.

Sutherland's presidential address gropes ponderously toward a definition for white-collar crime, an issue that has preoccupied many scholars since his time. Sutherland's definition is placed in a footnote, presumably indicating that he found the matter of little importance. Elsewhere, one of the present writers has suggested that the footnoted statement seems like "a parody of pedantic obscurantism,"[42] and many readings thereafter have offered no reason to alter this judgment.

In his 1949 monograph Sutherland would note, also in a footnote, that he meant to employ the term *white collar* in the sense that Alfred A. Sloan, Jr. did; that is "principally" to refer to business managers and executives.[43] It is an eccentric reference. Sloan, who had become the president of General Motors, made a fortune during the halcyon days of the automobile industry. Certainly Sutherland did not mean to restrict his inquiries to men of Sloan's enormous wealth and power. Sloan and Sparkes contains neither any references nor anything of particular relevance to social or business stratification, the matters of importance to Sutherland.[44] A biographical sketch of Sloan notes that he characteristically wore collars "of an arresting height and as stiff as a Buick mudguard."[45] Perhaps, if he knew of this, Sutherland was impressed enough with its symbolism to have Sloan represent the class whose crimes form Sutherland's research topic. Oddly, Sutherland, who was a meticulous person in such respects, incorrectly cites the title of Sloan's book, which was actually *Adventures of a White-Collar Man*, not *An Autobiography of a White Collar Worker*.

There are a number of themes set forth in Sutherland's presidential address that should have (but as yet have not) been addressed by later scholars. Many of the ideas are repeated; few are investigated. Sutherland maintains, for instance, that white-collar crime is more deleterious to a community's morale than is street crime:

> White-collar crimes violate trust and therefore create distrust, which lowers social morale and produces social disorganization on a large scale. . . . Other crimes have relatively little effect on social institutions or social organizations.[46]

Many of us may agree, but the issues require restatement in a testable form — and testing. Sutherland insists that white-collar criminals tend to be relatively protected from the harsher consequences of lawbreaking, in part because of a class congruence between them and those responsible for writing and enforcing laws and exacting penalties. Again, the thesis needs to be broken down into operationally defined variables and empirically verifiable hypotheses.

Taking only Sutherland's presidential address, the following items are among those propositions advanced that ought to be examined more closely:

1. "White-collar criminality is found in every occupation, as can be discovered readily in casual conversation with a representative of an occupation by asking him what crooked practices are . . . in his occupation" (p. 1).
2. The practice of politics is more honest than the conduct of business (p. 3).
3. "Political graft almost always involves collusion between politicians and businessmen, but prosecutions are generally limited to the politicians" (p. 4).
4. White-collar criminals are not regarded as really criminals by themselves, the general public,[47] or by criminologists (p. 7).
5. Differences in the implementation of the criminal law are due chiefly to the disparity in the social positions of white-collar and lower-class offenders (p. 7), and not, for instance, to the complexity of proof for one as against the other type of behavior.
6. Because of their social status, upper-class persons, potential white-collar offenders themselves, have a "loud voice" in determining what goes into the statutes and how the criminal law affecting them is implemented and administered (p. 6).[48]
7. "Even if poverty is extended to include the economic stresses which afflict business in the period of depression, it is not closely correlated with white-collar criminality" (p. 9).

A major problem with Sutherland's work on white-collar crime and, arguably, a significant reason for the relative dearth of work on the topic during the past four decades, seems to us to lie in his ineffectual and almost pretentious effort to force the review of white-collar crime into a grand theory of criminal behavior. Sutherland may have sensed the difficulty himself; in many instances he was his own sharpest critic. "I believe the concept of white-collar crime is questionable in certain respects and I hope to elaborate on these in a later publication," Sutherland wrote to Paul Tappan on the last day of 1946.[49] That further statement was never forthcoming; perhaps, had it been, white-collar crime would have grown more successfully as a subject of research and theory. Absent clarification by Sutherland, however, his dicta became dogma.

Sutherland implacably insisted that a single theory be made to explain the entire range of criminal behavior, and he placed that burden on a rather simple collection of statements about human learning that he called *differential association*.[50] "Favorable" or "unfavorable" learning with respect to the imperatives of the criminal law was seen by Sutherland as the process distinguishing noncriminal from criminal behavior. Differential association was derived in part from Lindesmith's analytical induction,[51] which, like differential association, seems beyond scientific demonstration, though—as Cressey has observed—the theory has considerable pedagogical utility, if one's aim is to stimulate critical thinking about the importance of values and culture in shaping the form and the extent of criminal behavior.[52]

The difficulty is that white-collar offenses, however they come to be defined, are extremely heterogeneous acts and are not susceptible of decent understanding by means of a rudimentary learning theory. Antitrust violations may resemble, say, Medicare fraud in that the perpetrators have more education than do persons who commit muggings. But the fraud and the restraint of trade cannot satisfactorily be explained by differential association. Emphasis on differential association, in fact, deflects attention from significant ideological matters such as power relationships and other social-structural issues.

White-collar crime is a political designation, rendered, like crime itself, by those who want to label, study, or call particular attention to certain kinds of social and political harm, real or imagined. The harms and their perpetrators designated by criminal law tend to have a very loose connective character: To provide some of them with a common name, such as white-collar crime or white-collar criminals, allows attention to be focused in a shorthand manner. Wrangling, both sophisticated and sophistical, over the "proper" definition of white-collar crime will never be satisfactorily resolved unless the overt and covert purposes, both political and scientific, underlying the search for definition, are clearly indicated. But fruitful approaches to the examination of behaviors that common sense indicts to be white-collar crime can be launched without resolution of the term's definition.

In his presentation, Sutherland might have focused on the issue that Cressey later raised: why white-collar crime had for so long been neglected as an object of study, an issue that could yield fruitful theoretical insights.[53] Perhaps, had Sutherland taken this or other alternative paths toward his professional goal of making his material "scientific," the result would have been both more evocative and more provocative of subsequent, cumulative, paradigmatic work on white-collar crime. As it was, the spate of studies that immediately followed Sutherland's efforts all felt compelled to look at their data in relation to the applicability of differential association theory. For none did the theory quite fit;[54] but, once the task had been set, the job became to refine differential association analysis rather than to look too far afield for other kinds of explanatory mechanisms and models.

The scholarly career of the concept of white-collar crime is captured effectively by a recent review of criminological literature. A survey of one hundred leading (that is, most cited) scholars in the field found that they regarded Sutherland's work on white-collar crime as the fourth most important contribution ever made on the subject. But Sutherland was virtually neglected in terms of a concomitant count of citations. Becker's *The Outsiders* and Glueck and Glueck's *Unraveling Juvenile Delinquency* were found to have been cited 648 times each. Cloward and Ohlin's *Delinquency and Opportunity* had 535 citations. Sutherland's work on white-collar crime had a mere 44 citations.[55] The discrepancy between the scholars' ratings on importance, on the one hand, and the actual number of citations to the work on white-collar crime, on the other, attests to a condition of benign neglect. Undoubtedly, the "importance" rating would have risen had more later work on white-collar crime been conducted.

In addition, Wolfgang and his colleagues found that out of nearly 3,700 books and articles they reviewed, only 92, or approximately 2.5 percent, dealt with white-collar or corporate criminality, even when studies on organized crime were included in the tabulations. If the organized-crime studies were removed from the category, no more than 1.2 percent of all writings in criminology dealt with subjects such as corporate crime, fraud, embezzlement, corruption, and bribery.

A study conducted with respect to material included in *Sociological Abstracts* from 1945 to 1972 yielded the same result. In most of the years, there was no more than one article devoted to white-collar crime. The most in any single twelve-month period was nine, in 1964, and most of these were on the subject of organized crime.[56]

This situation is puzzling in light of the common belief that many persons are drawn to criminal-justice research and teaching careers out of reformist zeal. Schuessler has suggested that the affluence of U.S. society during recent decades undermined concern with white-collar crime, a hypothesis that deserves scrutiny.[57] The political atmosphere during the McCarthy era of the 1950s probably muted criticism by academics and other persons of establishment figures and organizations. Perhaps, having lain dormant, the subject of white-collar crime needed especially favorable conditions for the kind of renaissance that it is now experiencing. The increased personnel in criminology also may be related to renewed interest in white-collar crime, as scholars seek to cultivate intellectual fields that have not yet been adequately harvested. The prod of Marxist criminology assuredly has also given credence and impetus to a critical posture toward persons in powerful positions in the society and toward the arrangements that got and keep them there. The work of Ralph Nader also has demonstrated the feasibility of gathering meaningful information about white-collar crimes.

For Sutherland, these developments would have been a matter of some personal pride. Our review of Sutherland's background and career, as well as the panegyrics of his colleagues and many of his former students, stress his dedication to a search for truth and describe a personality marked by decency, integrity, and compassion. Sutherland fundamentally was a populist, agrarian liberal. He had no interest in the overthrow of capitalism, although he certainly leaned toward socialism as the preferable economic system. On the podium in Philadelphia in 1939, what Sutherland really said, once the camouflage is removed, is that white-collar crime is wrong—indeed, that often it is despicable—and that sociologists and economists ought to pay close attention to such matters and join with him in a crusade to do something about them.

Sutherland's work on white-collar crime has been subject, perhaps, to overly vigorous strictures in this paper. It will receive much harder blows as the pace and the depth of study of white-collar crime increases. It must be recognized, however tough the critiques, that they are the kinds of backhanded accolades that mark significant scholarly work. That he must be attended to is the glory of Sutherland's contributions. He himself seemed, at least in print, amiable about this process of scientific maturation.

Sutherland's work on white-collar crime—his very invention of the term —is deeply and strongly rooted in our intellectual and public soil. We could cover page after page with illustrations of the manner in which Sutherland's pioneering contributions have influenced public policy and common understanding. That at this conference, almost a hundred years after Sutherland's birth in a frontier village on the Nebraska plains, we attend to his singlehanded creation of a realm of preeminent intellectual and policy importance is the most significant tribute that he could have desired.

Notes

1. Jacob Viner, "The Short View and the Long in Economic Policy," *American Economic Review*, 30 (March 1940), pp. 1-15.

2. We want to thank Russell Dynes of the American Sociological Society for providing a copy of the 1939 meeting program.

3. Edwin H. Sutherland, *White Collar Crime* (New York: Dryden Press, 1949), p. 210.

4. Howard W. Odum, "Edwin H. Sutherland, 1883-1950," *Social Forces*, 29 (March 1951), p. 802.

5. Jerome Hall, "Edwin H. Sutherland, 1883-1950," *Journal of Criminal Law and Criminology*, 41 (November-December 1950), p. 394.

6. Edwin H. Sutherland, "Critique of Sheldon's *Varieties of Delinquent Youth*," *American Sociological Review*, 16 (February 1951), pp. 10-13.

7. Edwin H. Sutherland, "Critique of the Theory," in eds. Albert Cohen, Alfred Lindesmith, and Karl Schuessler, *The Sutherland Papers* (Bloomington: Indiana University Press, 1956), pp. 30-41.

8. Paul W. Tappan, "Who Is the Criminal?" *American Sociological Review*, 12 (February 1947), pp. 96-102.

9. Jon Snodgrass, "The Gentle and Devout Iconoclast," in Snodgrass, "The American Criminological Tradition: Portraits of Men and Ideology in a Discipline," Ph.D. dissertation, University of Pennsylvania, 1972, pp. 217-308.

10. George Sutherland, "History of Nebraska Baptists," unpublished manuscript (Rochester, N.Y.: American Baptist Historical Society, 1935), p. 25.

11. E. Sutherland, *White Collar Crime*, pp. 89-94.

12. Edwin H. Sutherland and Harvey J. Locke, *Twenty Thousand Homeless Men: A Study of Unemployed Men in Chicago Shelters* (Philadelphia: Lippincott, 1936).

13. Gilbert Geis, "Sociology and Sociological Jurisprudence," *Kentucky Law Journal*, 52 (Winter 1964), pp. 267-293.

14. George Sutherland, "Autobiography," unpublished typescript in manuscript collections of the American Baptist Historical Society, Rochester, N.Y., 1935, p. 155. All quotes reprinted with permission.

15. Ibid., p. 27.

16. Ibid., p. 35.

17. Ibid., p. 94.

18. Mabel Vohland, *Trail Dust to Star Dust* (Kearney, Neb.: Zimmerman Printing and Lithographers, 1971).

19. G. Sutherland, "Autobiography," p. 144.

20. We have not yet resolved a contradiction in our sources on this matter. Snodgrass (*Gentle Iconoclast*, p. 219) places Arthur at Louisiana College, but the director of the Norton Memorial Library at the college reports that a survey of the catalogues for the 1930s and 1940s had not turned up a Sutherland on the faculty. An inquiry was also made of persons on the campus who might have had personal knowledge, but this too proved fruitless.

21. Herbert E. Hinton, *A Brief History of Grand Island College* (Rochester, N.Y.: American Baptist Historical Society, 1970).

22. G. Sutherland, "Autobiography," p. 162.

23. Ibid., pp. 162-163.

24. An inferential bit of evidence with respect to the influence of father on son comes in an article by Edwin Sutherland in which, among other things, he discusses "professions in which the problem is to control human

behavior" and free associates in his designation of such professions to the four occupations his father had followed: "salesmanship, teaching, preaching, and social work." (Sutherland, "Crime and the Conflict Process," *Journal of Juvenile Research*, 13 (January 1929), p. 46.)

25. G. Sutherland, "Autobiography," p. 177.

26. Ibid., p. 100.

27. Ibid., p. 149.

28. Ibid., p. 181.

29. Works Progress Administration, *Nebraska: A Guide to the Cornhusker State* (Lincoln: Nebraska State Historical Society, 1939).

30. Gilbert Geis, Introduction, in Eugene Smith, *Criminal Law in the United States* (Dubuque, Iowa: Brown Reprints, 1971), p. iv.

31. Charles R. Henderson, *Introduction to the Study of the Dependent, Defective, and Delinquent Classes*, 2nd edition (Boston: D.C. Heath, 1901), p. 250.

32. Sutherland, *White Collar Crime*, pp. 226-228.

33. Marshall B. Clinard, *The Black Market: A Study of White-Collar Crime* (New York: Holt), 1952.

34. Thorsten Sellin, Telephone conversation with Gilbert Geis, 12 January 1980. Printed with permission.

35. Edwin H. Sutherland, "Crimes of Corporations," in *The Sutherland Papers*, pp. 78-96.

36. Edwin H. Sutherland, "Social Process in Behavior Problems," *Publications of the American Sociological Society*, 26 (August 1932), pp. 59-60.

37. Sutherland and Locke, p. 62.

38. "Poverty Belittled as Crime Factor," *Philadelphia Inquirer* (December 28, 1939), p. 17.

39. "Hits Criminality in White Collars," *New York Times* (December 28, 1939), p. 12.

40. Edwin H. Sutherland, "White-Collar Criminality," *American Sociological Review*, 5 (February 1940), p. 1. All quotes reprinted with permission.

41. For general reviews see Naomi Caiden, "Shortchanging the Public," *Public Administration Review*, 39 (May-June 1979), pp. 294-298; ed. Arnold J. Heidenheimer, *Political Corruption: Readings in Comparative Analysis* (New York: Holt, Rinehart and Winston, 1970).

42. Gilbert Geis, "Avocational Crime," in ed. Daniel Glaser, *Handbook of Criminology* (Chicago: Rand-McNally, 1974), p. 284.

43. Sutherland, *White Collar Crime*, p. 9.

44. Alfred P. Sloane, Jr. and Boyden Sparkes, *Adventures of a White-Collar Man* (New York: Doubleday Doran, 1941).

45. "Sloane, Alfred Pritchard, Jr.," *Current Biography 1940*, p. 472.

46. Sutherland, "White-Collar Criminality," p. 5.

47. See Laura Shill Schrager and James F. Short, Jr., *How Serious a Crime? Perception of Organizational and Common Crime*, in ed. Gilbert Geis and Ezra Stotland, *White-Collar Crime* (Beverly Hills: Sage, 1980), pp. 14-31.

48. Neal Shover, "The Criminalization of Corporate Behavior: Federal Surface Coal Mining," in Geis and Stotland, pp. 98-125.

49. Ed. Karl Schuessler, *Edwin H. Sutherland on Analyzing Crime* (Chicago: University of Chicago Press, 1973), p. xxi.

50. Edwin H. Sutherland, *Principles of Criminology*, 4th edition (Philadelphia: Lippincott, 1947), pp. 5-9.

51. Alfred R. Lindesmith, "Edwin H. Sutherland's Contributions to Criminology," *Sociology and Social Research*, 35 (March-April 1951), pp. 343-349.

52. Donald R. Cressey, Foreword, in Edwin H. Sutherland, *White Collar Crime* (New York: Holt, 1961), pp. iii-xiii.

53. Ibid.

54. Clinard, *The Black Market*; Donald R. Cressey, *Other People's Money: The Social Psychology of Embezzlement* (New York: Free Press, 1953).

55. Marvin E. Wolfgang, Robert M. Figlio, and Terence P. Thornberry, *Evaluating Criminology* (New York: Elsevier, 1978).

56. Stanton Wheeler, "Trends and Problems in the Sociological Study of Crime," *Social Problems*, 83 (June 1976), pp. 526-534.

57. Schuessler, *Sutherland on Crime*.

12 On Theory and Action for Corporate Crime Control

John Braithwaite and
Gilbert Geis

A historic date in the saga of corporate crime is February 7, 1961. On that day, a gaggle of senior executives from major corporations, including vice-presidents of General Electric and Westinghouse, were sent to prison for price fixing. The event moved a man who said his contract with General Electric called for personal appearance tours to write a letter to the editor of the *Los Angeles Times*.[1] The correspondent asserted that GE operated according to the highest of principles—"higher I might add than some elements of government which are so bent on destroying business."

At the time of another white-collar crime watershed, the writer of the earlier letter—Ronald Reagan of Pacific Palisades—was Governor of California. His reaction to Watergate also is preserved in the *Los Angeles Times*:

> Gov. Reagan said Tuesday the Watergate spies should not be considered criminals because they "are not criminals at heart." . . . Reagan conceded that the bugging of the democratic headquarters was illegal but called "criminal" too harsh a term. . . . "I think the tragedy of this is that men who are not criminals at heart and certainly not engaged in criminal activities committed a criminal or illegal act and now must bear the consequences," he said. . . . "There are men," Reagan said, "whose lives are being very much changed by this. I doubt if any of them would even intentionally double park."[2]

Within weeks of Reagan's election as President, his advisors were signaling a soft line on white-collar crime. Evelle J. Younger, chair of Reagan's advisory group on criminal justice, made the following observation:

> The emphasis on white-collar crime will continue, but most of us on the task force will want to focus attention on violent crime, crime in the street," in order to "make the nation safer for the law-abiding citizen."[3]

Besides its seeming pro forma reference to white-collar crime, the statement is notable for its failure to appreciate that enforcement of laws against white-collar crime also protects the general populace, not only financially,

John Braithwaite and Gilbert Geis, in *Crime and Delinquency*, 28 (April 1982), 292-314. Reprinted with permission.

but also from the physical harm associated with matters such as unnecessary surgery, pollution, dangerous drugs, unsafe vehicles and carcinogenic conditions in the workplace.

More pointed were the comments of Donald E. Santarelli, a former Justice Department official who was advising the Reagan transition team. Santarelli criticized what he called the Justice Department's "preoccupation with white-collar crime" under Jimmy Carter. He too recommended renewed emphasis on "the type of crime that the public lives in fear of, which is violent street crime, not economic crime." Criminal statutes, in Santarelli's view, should only be applied to business activity where the conduct was "clearly willful, egregious, and malevolent."[4] It might have been thought that a better standard of enforcement would be one that sought to prosecute acts in terms of whether they violated the law.

The post-Watergate era had witnessed a modest redeployment of prosecutorial resources from crime in the streets to crime in the suites.[5] Reversing this nascent trend will cost the American people dearly in loss of life and monetary victimization.[6] Criminal justice interventions to reduce street crime, whether mediated by principles of deterrence, rehabilitation, or incapacitation, can at best have only modest effects on the rate of offending. In contrast, it will be argued in this paper that deterrence, rehabilitation, and incapacitation are viable strategies for fighting crime in the suites. This argument will be advanced in the context of a more general set of propositions asserting that the conventional wisdom of criminology with respect to traditional crime should be inverted with corporate crime.

There also is a broader purpose in our presenting the six propositions which follow. We seek to establish that corporate crime is a conceptually different phenomenon from traditional crime. Corporate crime is defined as conduct of a corporation, or of individuals acting on behalf of a corporation, that is proscribed and punishable by law.[7] As we will see later, reforms to make the law an effective weapon against corporate crime are being demolished on the strength of caveats carried over from jurisprudence pertaining to crime in the streets. The propositions that follow specify reasons why principles developed in relation to traditional crime should not be assumed to apply to corporate offenses. Once the domains are accepted as conceptually separate, the burden of proof shifts; the opponent of legislation to control corporate crime must show why caveats from traditional criminal law should be regarded as relevant to the control of corporate crime.

Six Basic Propositions

Proposition 1: With most traditional crimes, the fact that an offense has occurred is readily apparent; with most corporate crimes the effect is not readily apparent.

When one person murders another, the corpse is there for people to see; or at least the fact that a person has disappeared is readily apparent. When, on the other hand, a miner dies from a lung disease people may never appreciate that he has died because his employer violated mine safety regulations. Inevitably, most such violations are undetected.[8] People who pay more to go to a movie because of price fixing among theater owners will not be aware that they have been victims of a crime. When taxes go up because Defense Department officials have accepted bribes to purchase more expensive ships or missiles than the country needs, no one knows that a crime has occurred and that we have all been its victims.

Such is the limited power of individuals for ill that when they perpetrate a traditional crime there is usually only one victim (or, at most, only a few victims) for each offense. These individual victims become acutely aware of the fact that another person has dealt them a blow. The structural reality of much corporate crime, in contrast, is one of diffuse effects. A million one-dollar victimizations will not generate the kind of public visibility that a single million-dollar victimization will.

Even when the effects of corporate crime are concentrated rather than diffuse, victim awareness is often not there. If a consumer pays an extra thousand dollars for a used car that has had its odometer turned back, he or she will almost never be aware of the fraud.[9] Consumers might think that they have been sold a lemon, but not that they have been victims of business crime. Similarly, when patients die from using a dangerous drug that was approved by health authorities on the strength of a bribe from a pharmaceutical company, a practice common in many countries,[10] the crime is not apparent. Low visibility also follows from the fact that often the only witnesses to a crime are themselves implicated in the offense.[11]

This first proposition has important implications for the difference between how law enforcers must go about controlling corporate versus traditional crime. Traditional crime control is reactive. The police normally do not investigate until a citizen reports a victimization.[12] For corporate crimes, whose visibility is almost invariably masked through being embedded in an ongoing transaction, the reactive model must be discarded for a proactive enforcement stance.[13]

Proposition 2: Once an offense becomes apparent, apprehending a suspect can be difficult with traditional crime, but is almost always easy with corporate crime.

When a house is robbed, or when a car is reported as missing, it is often a difficult job for the police to find the burglar or the car thief. Great public expense is incurred to achieve unremarkable clearance rates for these types of offenses.[14] In contrast, in the unlikely event that a sick worker discovers his illness is the result of an industrial health violation at work, almost by definition the law enforcement agency can identify a corporate suspect—the worker's employer. There was no need for the police to print "Wanted" posters or to set up roadblocks to find the corporate suspect when it was discovered that bribes were accepted in many countries throughout the world to secure sales of Lockheed aircraft.

This second proposition more than counterbalances the first in its implications for the potential effectiveness of corporate crime control. Corporate crime investigators cannot enjoy the luxury of sitting back in their offices waiting for the telephone to ring to notify them of the offense, but they are saved the tribulations of identikit photos, fingerprinting, and all the other paraphernalia that burden police in pursuit of traditional types of suspects.

Our first two propositions together may constitute an argument for tactics that might involve or border on entrapment.[15] It is an argument that demands consideration in corporate crime cases. Under the reactive enforcement model for traditional crimes, entrapment is hardly necessary. Law enforcement agencies have quite enough offenses reported to them and need not create more. Should they decide that they do want to create more offenses, given how little the police know about who is committing most of them, deciding whom to entrap would be difficult.

In contrast, if one accepts the inevitability of a proactive enforcement model for white-collar crime, investigators may have little choice but to create their own offenses. For some types of white-collar crimes entrapment may be one of the few ways of doing this. The present authors differ with respect to the FBI's tactics in the Abscam case; but consider the options available for the conviction of political bribe-takers. The FBI does not have citizens calling the agency claiming to be victims of political bribes, yet it does have intelligence on who the corrupt politicians are. Such intelligence rarely is sufficient to sustain criminal charges. The use of entrapment ruses for corrupt politicians may be more necessary and less indiscriminate than is the entrapment of, say, drug users by offering them a deal. It can also be argued that holders of public office and the primary beneficiaries of the economic system have a special obligation to obey the law and to resist temptation.

Readers may conclude that entrapment is unacceptable with respect to either white-collar or traditional crime. However, the balance of considerations which lead to this conclusion under the proactive model of white-collar crime enforcement should be very different than the factors weighed for the types of offenses that can be handled under the reactive model.

Proposition 3: Once a suspect has been apprehended, proving guilt is usually easy with traditional crime, but almost always difficult with corporate crime.

Especially for less serious traditional crimes, the authorities have little difficulty in obtaining a conviction, particularly when they are willing to plea bargain.[16] When enforcement officers decide that a corporation probably is guilty of an offense and deserves to go to court, a conviction is usually *not* the result. Indeed, it does not normally eventuate that the matter *will* go to court.[17] The costs of corporate prosecutions are both financial (legal fees) and political (votes, campaign contributions), which may produce understandable caution among conservative bureaucrats in dealing with powerful actors.

Even where these costs are deemed to be bearable, the government will often lose in court because the complexity of the law[18] or the complexity of the company's books[19] makes it impossible to prove their case beyond reasonable doubt. There is a considerable difference, for instance, between convicting a corporation which takes money by fraud and convicting an individual who takes it at the point of a gun: "Criminal intent is not as easily inferred from a taking executed through a market transaction, as it is from a taking by force."[20] Corporations, unlike individuals, have the resources to employ the legal talent to exploit this inherent complexity. Good lawyers who use complexity to cast "reasonable doubt" on the applicability of existing statutes to the behavior of their client also use complexity to protract proceedings and thereby push up the cost disincentives for the prosecution to continue with formal proceedings.[21]

There also is the complexity of the organizational reality of corporate action. Every individual in a large organization can present a different version of what company policy was, and individual corporate actors can blame others for their own actions (x says he was following y's instructions, y says that x misunderstood instructions she had passed down from z, ad infinitum). So how can either company policy or any individual company employee be guilty?[22] Even if this is not what actually happened,[23] it is difficult for the prosecution to prove otherwise.

There is, in addition, the complexity of science. Pollution, product safety, and occupational safety and health prosecutions typically turn on causal attribution to a corporation of the harm alleged. In cases that involve scientific dispute, proof "beyond reasonable doubt" is rarely, if ever, possible. Science deals with probabilities, not certainties. The superstructure of science is erected on a foundation of mathematical statistics which estimate a probability that inferences are true or false. Logically, proof beyond reasonable doubt that A "causes" B is impossible. It is always possible that an observed correlation between A and B is explained by an unknown third variable, C. The scientist can never eliminate all the possible third variables. Hence, to require proof beyond reasonable doubt that a violation of the Food, Drug and Cosmetic Act caused an observed level of drug impurity, which in turn caused 50 deaths, is to require the impossible.

The problem is illustrated by the Federal OSHA statute. It requires proof that the violation was willful and caused death before a criminal conviction can stand. OSHA counsel explained to one of the authors that when 51 Research-Cottrell workers were killed by the collapse of scaffolding for a water tower, the fact that OSHA regulations had been violated was clear, the fact that workers died was clear, but proving beyond reasonable doubt that it was the violations (rather than other factors) that caused the scaffolding to collapse was another matter. The complexity of the forces that caused the scaffolding to collapse was such that it was represented by a computer simulation. OSHA counsel decided, undoubtedly correctly, that a computer simulation was more complexity than any jury could stand.

That the complexity of corporate crime and the power and legal resources of defendants make convictions much more difficult than with traditional crime hardly needs to be labored.[24] This difficulty rather than the low visibility of offenses (Proposition 1) is the real stumbling block to effective corporate crime control. Consequently, it will be the barriers to conviction rather than those to discovery and apprehension that will be the focus of reforms considered in the final part of the paper.

Proposition 4: Once an offender has been convicted, deterrence is doubtful with traditional crime, but may well be strong with corporate crime.

Specific must be distinguished from general deterrence. The former refers to the deterrence of the offender who is actually convicted. The case for specific deterrence is weak with traditional crime. Offenders who are incarcerated may be more embittered than deterred by the experience. They appear less likely to learn the error of their ways in prison than to learn better ways of committing crime.[25] This is not likely to be true of persons convicted of a corporate crime. A feature that distinguishes traditional from corporate crime is that the illegitimate skills (for example, safecracking) involved in the former are learned in criminal settings (for example, prison), while the illegitimate skills (for example, concealing transactions) of the corporate criminal are learned in legitimate noncriminal settings. While the illegitimate skills of burglars may be developed while they are incarcerated, those of crooked accountants will simply become increasingly out of date as they languish in prison.

A major risk in apprehending the traditional criminal is that the stigmatizing process will push him further and further into a criminal self-concept. This is the contention of labelling theory.[26] West and Farrington note about their findings on juvenile delinquents:

Court appearances may aggravate already tense family situations, alienate youths still further from their teachers and employers, and discourage their more respectable companions of either sex from continuing to associate with them. The sanctions imposed by the courts in the shape of fines are likely to increase the delinquent's debts, thereby increasing the temptation to dishonesty, while doing nothing to teach him to manage his finances better. Even supervision by a probation officer can be a mixed blessing, if it helps to confirm the youngster's self-identification with delinquent groups.[27]

These labelling arguments cannot readily be applied to corporate offenders. They are likely to regard themselves as unfairly maligned pillars of respectability, and no amount of stigmatization is apt to convince them otherwise. One does meet people who have a mental image of themselves as a thief, a safecracker, a prostitute, a pimp, a drug runner, and even a hit man but how often does one meet a person who sees himself as a corporate criminal? The young black offender can often enhance his status back on the street by having done some time, but the reaction of the corporate criminal to incarceration is shame and humiliation.[28]

Such an observation has important implications. Although the labelling hypothesis makes it unwise to use publicity as a tool to punish juvenile delinquents, it is sound deterrence to broadcast widely the names of corporate offenders. Corporations and their officers are genuinely afraid of bad publicity arising from their illegitimate activities.[29] They respond to it with moral indignation and denials, not with assertions that "if you think I'm bad, I'll really show you how bad I can be," as juvenile delinquents sometimes do.

Chambliss argues that white-collar criminals are among the most deterrable types of offenders because they satisfy two conditions: they do not have a commitment to crime as a way of life and their offenses are instrumental rather than expressive.[30] Corporate crimes are almost never crimes of passion; they are not spontaneous or emotional, but calculated risks taken by rational actors. As such they should be more amenable to control by policies based on the utilitarian assumptions of the deterrence doctrine.[31]

Individual corporate criminals are also more deterrable because they have more of those valued possessions that can be lost through a criminal conviction—status, respectability, money, job, a comfortable home and family life. As Geerken and Gove hypothesize: "the effectiveness of [a] deterrence system will increase as the individual's investment in and rewards from the social system increase."[32]

In general, the arguments about the deterrability of individuals convicted of corporate crimes are equally applicable to the corporations themselves. Corporations are future oriented, concerned about their reputation and quintessentially rational. Although most individuals do not possess the information necessary to calculate rationally the probability of detection and punishment,[33] corporations have information-gathering systems designed precisely for this purpose. Hence, conclude Ermann and Lundman: "[B]usiness concerns have regularly engaged in price fixing . . . under the correct assumption that the benefits outweigh the costs."[34]

The specific deterrent value of fines can be questioned for both traditional[35] and corporate[36] offenders. A large fine imposed upon a poor property offender might leave him little option but to steal again so as to be able to pay the fine. With corporations the problem is to be able to set a fine large enough to have a deterrent effect.

> The $7 million fine which was levied against the Ford Motor Company for environmental violations was certainly more than a slap on the wrist, but it rather pales beside the estimated $250 million loss which the company sustained on the Edsel. Both represent environmental contingencies which managers are paid high salaries to handle. We know they handled the latter—the first seven years of the Mustang more than offset the Edsel losses. One can only infer that they worked out ways to handle the fine too.[37]

Although the fine itself may be an ineffective deterrent when used against the corporate criminal, other sanctions associated with the prosecution—unfavorable publicity, the harrowing experience for the senior executive of days under cross-examination,[38] the dislocation of top management from their normal duties so that they can defend the corporation against public attacks—can be important specific deterrents.

General deterrence is an effect more difficult to establish empirically. General deterrence refers to the consequences of a conviction for those who are not caught, but who through observing the penalties imposed on others decide not to violate the law. The state of the evidence on general deterrence for common crime, and how scholars interpret that evidence, is in turmoil.[39] It seems fair to say, however, that there has been a growing disillusionment with how much crime prevention can be achieved through deterrence, particularly of the lower-class offender.

The evidence on the deterrent effects of sanctions against corporate crime is not nearly so voluminous, but the consensus among scholars is overwhelmingly optimistic concerning general deterrence.[40] This may in part reflect an uncritical acceptance of the empirically untested assumption that because corporate crime is a notably rational economic activity, it must be more subject to general deterrence.

However, the faith in the efficacy of general deterrence for corporate crime is not totally blind. If surveys in which business executives are asked whether the pending introduction of a piece of legislation affected their behavior mean anything, then the Australian Trade Practices Act of 1974 would seem to have had an impact.[41] Survey respondents claimed that the introduction of the act, with its relatively severe penalties, caused them to abandon certain price-fixing agreements with competitors and introduce antitrust "compliance programs." A more sophisticated study by Block et al.

found that U.S. Justice Department antitrust prosecutions in the bread industry had significant and notable specific and general deterrent effects on price fixing. The degree of deterrence was surprising, given that bread price fixers have never been sent to jail and that fines average only 0.3 percent of the annual sales of the colluding firms. The Block et al. data suggest that deterrence mainly is mediated by civil treble damage suits that follow in the wake of criminal convictions.[42]

The most impressive evidence is from Lewis-Beck and Alford's study of U.S. coal mine safety enforcement. Using a multiple interrupted time-series analysis, these authors were able to show that the considerable increases in enforcement expenditure which followed the toughening of the mine safety legislation in 1941 and 1969 were both associated with dramatic reductions in coal mine fatality rates. The cosmetic 1952 Federal Coal Mine Safety Act, which actually arrested the rate of increase in Bureau of Mines enforcement expenditures, had no effect on fatality rates. Controls introduced into the regression models refute an interpretation that the historical trends are the result of technological advances in mining, changes in mine size, or variations in the types of mining operations. The most parsimonious interpretation of the data is that the coal mine accident death rate is less than a quarter of its level prior to the 1941 legislation because of the deterrent effects of law enforcement.[43]

Proposition 5: Although incapacitation is not apt to be very effective or acceptable for controlling traditional crime in a humane society, it can be a highly successful strategy in the control of corporate crime.

Traditional criminals can be incapacitated if the society is willing to countenance severe solutions. If we execute murderers, they will never murder again; or we can lock them up and never let them out. Pickpockets can be incapacitated by our cutting off their hands. Most contemporary societies are not prepared to resort to such barbaric methods. Instead, the widely used punishment is imprisonment for periods of months or years. Only partial incapacitation is in effect while the offender is incarcerated. Offenders continue to murder, to rape, and to commit a multitude of less serious offenses while they are in prison. Indeed, chances of being a victim of homicide in the United States are five times as high for white males inside prison than for those outside.[44] The partial incapacitation of prison lasts only as long as the sentence.

The limits of incapacitation as a policy become more apparent when we ask who is to be incapacitated? A substantial body of evidence shows that no matter how we attempt to predict dangerousness, the success rate is very low.[45] Any policy of selective incarceration to "protect society" will result in prisons full of "false positives."

The most sophisticated study of the reduction in crime which might be achieved by incapacitation is by Van Dine et al. For their Ohio cohort, a severe sentencing policy of a flat five-year term for any adult or juvenile convicted of a felony would have prevented only 7.3 percent of the reported crimes of the cohort. Such estimates are of limited value, of course, because there is no way of knowing how many unreported crimes might also have been prevented. Nevertheless, even under generous assumptions about the prevention of unreported crime, Van Dine et al. conclude that incapacitation can never be a cost-effective rationale for a tough sentencing policy. Notwithstanding this conclusion, Van Dine and his colleagues fail to take account of a variety of homeostatic forces more recently considered by Reiss[47] which further weaken incapacitative effects. For example, to what extent do criminal groups recruit new members to replace those who are incarcerated, or increase their own rate of offending to make up for the shortfall in criminal production arising from the absence of one member from the group? More fundamentally, studies such as that of Van Dine et al. make the false assumption that if a thousand offenses were committed by offenders during a period of freedom, then a thousand crimes would have been prevented if those people had been in prison for that period. The assumption is false because most offenses are not committed by lone offenders.[48] If the man who drove the getaway car in a robbery had been in prison, the robbery may still have gone ahead without him. For these additional reasons, we are even more strongly inclined to agree with the conclusion of Van Dine et al. that "we do not know how to bound a whole class of wicked people, and the evidence of this research suggests that we never will."[49]

Incapacitation is more workable with corporate criminals because their kind of criminal activity is dependent on their being able to maintain legitimacy in formalized roles in the economy. We do not have to cut off the hands of surgeons who increase their income by having patients undergo unnecessary surgery. All we need do is deregister them. Similarly, we can prevent people from acting in such formal roles as company directors, product safety managers, environmental engineers, lawyers, and accountants swiftly and without barbarism. Should we want only short-term incapacitation, we can, as Stone advocates, prohibit a person "for a period of three years from serving as officer, director, or consultant of any corporation. . . ."[50] Moreover, an incapacitative court order could be even more finely tuned—the prohibition could be against the person serving in any position entailing decision making that might influence the quality of the environment. Corporate crime's total dependence on incumbency in roles in the economy renders possible this tailor-made incapacitation. It makes the shotgun approach to incapacitation for common crimes look very crude indeed. However, the substitution problems that plague traditional incapacitative models are also a major constraint on the efficacy of incapacitating individuals who have been responsible for corporate crime. If the corporation is committed to cutting corners on environmental emissions, it can replace one irresponsible environmental engineer with another who is equally willing to violate the law.

This is where court orders to incapacitate the whole organization become necessary. Capital punishment for the corporation is one possibility: the charter of a corporation can be revoked, the corporation can be put in the hands of a receiver, or it can be nationalized. Although corporate capital punishment is not as barbaric as individual capital punishment, it is an extreme measure which courts undoubtedly would be loath to adopt, especially considering the unemployment caused by terminating an enterprise (though this does not apply to nationalizing it). Even though court-ordered corporate death sentences may be politically unrealistic, there are cases where regulatory agencies through their harassment of criminal corporations have bankrupted fairly large concerns.[51]

A less draconian remedy is to limit the charter of a company to prevent it from continuing trading in an area of its operations where it has flagrantly failed to respect the law. Alternatively, as part of a consent decree, a corporation could be forced to sell that part of its business which has been the locus of continued law violation. The regulatory agency should participate in the negotiations to ensure that the sale is to a new parent with an exemplary record of compliance.[52] This kind of remedy becomes increasingly useful in an era when the diversified conglomerate is the modal form of industrial organization. Forcing a conglomerate to sell one of its divisions would, in addition to having incapacitative effects, be a strong deterrent in cases where the division made sound profits. Deterrence and incapacitation can be achieved without harm to the economy or to innocent employees.

Effective incapacitative strategies for corporate crime are, therefore, possible. All that is required is for legislatures, courts, and regulatory agencies to apply them creatively, to overcome the conservatism which leaves them clinging to the failed remedies carried over from traditional crime. The goal of incapacitation illustrates better than any other how the effective and just means for achieving criminal justice goals cannot be the same with corporate crime as with traditional crime. Consider, for example, the application to the Olin Mathieson Chemical Corporation of a law that forbids offenders convicted of a felony from carrying guns. Mintz has described what happened after Olin Mathieson was convicted of conspiracy concerning bribes to get foreign aid contracts in Cambodia and Vietnam:

> It happened that there was a law which said in essence that a person who had been convicted of a felony could not transport a weapon in interstate commerce. This created a legal problem for Olin, because it had been convicted of a felony, was in the eyes of the law a person and had a division

that made weapons for use by the armed forces. Congress resolved the dilemma by enacting a law that, in effect, got Olin off the hook.[53]

Here we are struck by the absurdity of automatically applying to corporations an incapacitative policy designed for individuals. It will be argued later that this absurdity of applying law governing the behavior of individuals to the crimes of collectivities is the fundamental impediment to effective corporate crime control.

Proposition 6: Even though rehabilitation has failed as a doctrine for the control of traditional crime, it can succeed with corporate crime.

The disenchantment of criminologists in the past two decades with rehabilitation as a response to traditional crime has been even more profound than has the disillusionment with deterrence. The high tide of this change was the publication of the massive and detailed review of the effectiveness of correctional rehabilitation programs by Lipton, Martinson, and Wilks.[54] Even though Martinson stated at a later time that their review should not be used to justify a wholesale rejection of rehabilitation as a goal for the criminal justice system, the raw data which aroused the mood of pessimism are still there for all to see, and since the publication of the review there has hardly been a flood of studies showing that rehabilitative programs really do reduce crime.

There is little reason to suspect that individuals responsible for corporate crime, or white-collar crime generally, should be any more amenable to rehabilitation than are traditional offenders. Although rehabilitating individuals would seem as unpromising with corporate as with traditional offenders, rehabilitating the corporation itself is a different matter. Many corporate crimes arise from defective control systems, insufficient checks and balances within the organization to ensure the law is complied with, poor communication, and inadequate standard operating procedures which fail to incorporate safeguards against reckless behavior. Sometimes these organizational defects are intentional, manifesting a conscious decision by the corporate hierarchy to turn a blind eye to corner cutting in order to get results.[55] Sometimes the defects reflect sloppiness or managerial negligence. The chief executive of a pharmaceutical company, for example, might consciously ignore a situation in which his quality control director was overruled by the production manager when a batch of drugs is rejected for want of purity. If the organzation were reformed so that the person responsible for achieving production targets was no longer able to overrule quality control, and if only the chief executive officer could reverse a quality control finding, and then only in writing, the chief executive could no longer avoid the situation.

Regulatory agencies have an arsenal of weapons with which to force corporations to correct criminogenic policies and practices. They can insist upon things such as abolition of off-the-books accounts, multiple approvals for specified actions, routine reporting of certain matters to committees of outside directors, and internal compliance groups who report directly to the board with recommendations for sanctioning individuals who fail to abide by corporate policies. Rehabilitation is a more workable strategy with corporate crime than with traditional crime because criminogenic organizational structures are more malleable than criminogenic human personalities. A new internal compliance group can be put in place much more readily than can a new superego. Moreover, state-imposed reorganization of the structure of a publicly traded company is not so unconscionable an encroachment on individual freedom as is state-imposed rearrangement of a psyche.[56]

Andrew Hopkins, in the only systematic published study of the rehabilitation of corporate offenders, concluded that most companies prosecuted under the consumer protection provisions of the Australian Trade Practices Act introduced at least some measures to assure that the offense did not recur.[57] Case studies based on interviews by Brent Fisse and one of the present authors with executives involved in major American corporate crimes confirm Hopkins' finding. In the aftermath of a scandal that involved them, many, though not all, corporations changed internal policies and procedures in ways that would reduce the probability of reoffending. Much of this corporate rehabilitation undoubtedly took place because of prodding by regulatory agencies. Large corporations tend to be responsive to the demands of regulators in making internal reform following the unveiling of a corporate crime in part because they want to get the regulators out of their hair.[58]

A number of formal mechanisms can be used to bring about corporate rehabilitation: consent decrees negotiated with regulatory agencies,[59] probation orders placing the corporation under the supervision of an auditor, environmental expert or other authority who would ensure that an order to restructure compliance systems was carried out,[60] or by courts withholding sentence of convicted corporations until they produce a report on the weaknesses of their old compliance systems and implement new ones.[61]

Discussion

It has been argued that the largely discredited doctrines of crime control by public disgrace, deterrence, incapacitation, and rehabilitation could become highly successful when applied to corporate crime. More generally, it has been argued that when the accumulated insight of criminology tells us that something is true of traditional crime in many respects we can expect the opposite to be true of corporate crime.

Hence, there is a reason for optimism that where we have failed with street crime, we might succeed with suite crime. There is justification for regarding President Reagan's signaling of a return to pre-Watergate criminal justice priorities as contrary to the public interest. Because corporate crime is more preventable than other types of crime, the persons and property of citizens can be better protected, and restitution is also a more viable goal for corporate criminal law. Convicted corporations generally have a better capacity than do individuals to compensate the victims of their crimes.

Even though corporate crime is potentially more preventable and its victims are more readily compensated, there is no guarantee that either prevention or restitution will happen under traditional legal systems. This is because of our third proposition: convictions are extremely difficult in complex cases involving powerful corporations. There are at least two ways of dealing with this problem. One is for regulatory agencies to achieve the goals of deterrence, incapacitation, and rehabilitation by non-prosecutorial means. They readily can do this if they have sufficient bargaining power. Consider the tactics of the SEC in the foreign bribery scandals of the latter half of the 1970s. In many cases the agency may have effected significant deterrence through the adverse publicity that followed public disclosure of the largest scandals,[62] a modicum of incapacitation in cases where corporations forced responsible senior executives into early retirement,[63] and a considerable amount of rehabilitation through consent orders that mandated audit committees of outside directors, outlawed off-the-books accounts, and other reforms. While far from eliminating the prospect of bribery, these responses certainly made it much riskier and therefore less rational business practice.[64]

In an illuminating article detailing why law enforcers so often opt for informal enforcement, Philip Schrag discusses why he abandoned the prosecutor's stance that he brought to his position as head of the enforcement division of the New York City Department of Consumer Affairs. A variety of frustrations, especially the use of delaying tactics by company lawyers, led to a *direct action* model being substituted for the *judicial* model. Nonlitigious methods which were increasingly used included threats and use of adverse publicity, revocation of licenses, writing directly to consumers to warn them of company practices, and exerting pressure on reputable financial institutions and suppliers to withdraw support of the targeted company. As Schrag pointed out, the dilemma of the direct action model is that it gets results without any regard to the due process rights of targeted "offenders."[65]

An alternative to substituting the direct action for the judicial model is to reform the law so that the conviction of guilty corporations is made easier.[66] The precise nature of such reform is beyond the scope of the present paper. What we have attempted is to establish a case for the premise to undergird such a program of law reform: *the fact that a principle has been found to be justified in dealing with traditional crime is not a satisfactory rationale for its application to corporate crime.* If valid, the six propositions in this paper force the conclusion that corporate crime is a conceptually quite different domain from traditional crime. Consequently, we should never reject a strategy for controlling corporate crime merely because that strategy has been found wanting, either on justice or efficacy grounds, with traditional crime.

Consider, for example, the right to trial by jury in criminal cases. In some Anglo-Saxon jurisdictions there have been debates regarding abolition of the right to trial by jury for a variety of corporate and other white-collar crimes. The rationale for such a move has been expressed in the following terms: "It has been said that if the jury cannot understand the issues, the right to a jury may conflict with something more basic, the right to a fair trial."[67] Nicholas de B. Katzenbach, former U.S. Attorney-General and now IBM general counsel, once said: "The better your case, the better off you are with a judge. The weaker your case, the better off you are with the jury."[68]

In New South Wales, Australia, when such a measure was considered, the reaction from the financial establishment was vociferous. The influential *Australian Financial Review* argued: "In moving away from trial by jury as a right on charges which can lead to imprisonment, NSW appears to be going out on a limb from the trunk of English law."[69] A counter-proposition could be that we should dynamite the "trunk of English law" and plant a new tree better suited to the climate of corporate offenses. Where, then, should the burden of proof lie—with the reform proposal to control corporate crime or with the tried and true forest of traditional laws? If corporate crime and traditional crime are accepted as conceptually different domains, we would suggest that it is the opponent of legislation to control corporate crime who should show why caveats from the traditional criminal area should be regarded as relevant to the control of corporate crime.

Unfortunately, as new reforms emerge that are designed with traditional individual offenses in mind, not only is the burden of proof with those who would oppose the automatic imposition of the reforms on corporate offenses, but moreover, questions about the reforms' effect on white-collar and corporate crime are rarely asked. The U.S. Supreme Court has denied corporations the privilege against self-incrimination, while individuals still enjoy that privilege.[70] And the Court has accepted that publicly traded companies "can claim no equality with individuals in the enjoyment of a right to privacy."[71] So why could we not also see a dismantling of many of the protections designed to safeguard the powerless individual from abusive use of the superior power of the state when it is powerful corporations that are being protected?[72] When a corporation is on trial in a case in which no individuals can lose their liberty as a result of the verdict, for example, why could not proof "on the balance of probabilities" be substituted for proof "beyond reasonable doubt?"[73]

Corporations will fight vigorously attempts to deny them any due process protections that are available to individuals. Yet the law of individualism can never be effective against the crimes of collectivities. As Fisse has observed: "[I]ndividualistic strength is not enough to match collectivist might without undermining the very traditions of justice for which individualism stands."[74] Unless we can accept corporate crime as a conceptually separate problem from traditional crime, the powerful will continue to ensure that "collectivist might" prevails in courts of law. This will be achieved by appeal to "the very traditions of justice for which individualism stands."

Notes

1. *Los Angeles Times* (October 31, 1961).
2. *Los Angeles Times* (May 2, 1973).
3. *New York Times* (November 14, 1980). Reprinted with permission.
4. Ibid.
5. Jack Katz, "The Social Movement Against White-Collar Crime," in eds. Egon Bittner and Sheldon L. Messinger, *Criminology Review Yearbook, Volume 2* (Beverly Hills: Sage, 1980), pp. 161-184.
6. For a discussion of various estimates of the cost of white-collar crime, see Miriam S. Saxon, *White-Collar Crime: The Problem and the Federal Response* (Washington, D.C.: Congressional Research Service, Library of Congress, April 14, 1980). When product safety, environmental and occupational safety, and health offenses are considered, it is easy to establish a case that injury to persons as well as property is greater for white-collar crimes.
7. Following Sutherland, we take the view that to exclude civil violations from a consideration of corporate crime is an aribtrary obfuscation because of the frequent provision in law for both civil and criminal prosecution of the same corporate conduct. (Edwin H. Sutherland, *White Collar Crime* (New York: Dryden Press, 1949).) Conduct subject only to damages awards without any additional punishment (for example, fine, punitive damages) is, however, not within the definition of corporate crime adopted here.
8. Joel Swartz, "Silent Killers at Work," *Crime and Social Justice*, 3 (1975), pp. 15-20; W.G. Carson, "White-Collar Crime and the Enforce-

ment of Factory Legislation," *British Journal of Criminology*, 10 (1970), pp. 383-398.

9. John Braithwaite, "An Exploratory Study of Used Car Fraud," in eds. Paul R. Wilson and John Braithwaite, *Two Faces of Deviance* (Brisbane: University of Queensland Press, 1978), pp. 101-122.

10. John Braithwaite, *Corporate Crime in the Pharmaceutical Industry* (London: Routledge and Kegan Paul, 1981), ch. 2.

11. John Hagan, Ilene H. Nagel (Bernstein), and Celesta Albonetti, "Differential Sentencing of White-Collar Offenders," *American Sociological Review*, 45 (1980), pp. 802-820.

12. Albert J. Reiss, Jr., *The Police and the Public* (New Haven: Yale University Press, 1971), ch. 2.

13. Carson ("White-Collar Crime," p. 390) found that only 5 percent of Factories Act violations in Britain were reported to, as opposed to discovered by, the Factories Inspectorate. Even with consumer affairs offenses in which there are victims who become aware of their victimization, a proactive approach is typically required to stop the offense before the bird has flown and aggrieved consumers begin to trickle into the agency (see Philip G. Schrag, "On Her Majesty's Secret Service: Protecting the Consumer in New York City," *Yale Law Journal*, 80 (1971), p. 1586). On proactive enforcement tactics generally, see Herbert Edelhertz, *The Investigation of White-Collar Crime: A Manual for Law Enforcement Agencies* (Washington, D.C.: Law Enforcement Assistance Administration, 1977).

14. In 1976 in the United States, only 14.4 percent of motor vehicle thefts were cleared by arrest. For property crimes generally the clearup rate was 18 percent and for violent offenses, 45.5 percent. *Sourcebook of Criminal Justice Statistics—1978* (Washington, D.C.: Law Enforcement Assistance Administration, June, 1979), p. 502.

15. See generally *Sorrells v. United States*, 287 U.S. 435 (1932).

16. Only 2.8 percent of defendants in cases terminated before U.S. District Courts in 1977 were found not guilty. *Sourcebook of Criminal Justice Statistics—1979* (Washington, D.C.: Law Enforcement Assistance Administration, 1980), p. 555.

17. Marshall Clinard, Peter C. Yeager, Jeanne Brissette, David Petrashak, and Elizabeth Harris, *Illegal Corporate Behavior* (Washington, D.C.: U.S. Department of Justice, 1979), p. 291; Ross Cranston, *Regulating Business: Law and Consumer Agencies* (London: Macmillan, 1979).

18. Adam Sutton and Ron Wild, "Corporate Crime and Social Structure," in Wilson and Braithwaite, *Two Faces of Deviance*, pp. 177-198; John Braithwaite, "Inegalitarian Consequences of Egalitarian Reforms to Control Corporate Crime," *Temple Law Quarterly*, 53, no. 4 (1981), pp. 1127-1146.

19. Adam Sutton and Ron Wild, "Companies, the Law and the Professions: A Sociological View of Australian Companies Legislation," in ed.

Roman Tomasic, *Legislation and Society in Australia* (Sydney: Allen and Unwin, 1979); Abraham J. Briloff, *Unaccountable Accounting* (New York: Harper and Row, 1972).

20. Gilbert Geis and Herbert Edelhertz, "Criminal Law and Consumer Fraud: A Sociolegal View," *American Criminal Law Review*, 11 (1973), p. 1006. See *Holland v. United States*, 348 U.S. 121, 139-140 (1954); *United States v. Woodner*, 317 F.2d 649, 651 (2d Cir., 1963).

21. For various examples, see Mark J. Green, *The Other Government: The Unseen Power of Washington Lawyers*, rev. edition (New York: Norton, 1978).

22. It may be that individual corporate actors are following standard operating procedures which were written by a committee, many of the members of which are now retired, deceased, or working elsewhere. Consider Simeon M. Kriesberg, "Decisionmaking Models and the Control of Corporate Crime," *Yale Law Journal*, 85 (1976), pp. 1091-1129.

23. In *Corporate Crime in the Pharmaceutical Industry*, Braithwaite concludes that many corporations present to the outside world a picture of diffused accountability for law observance, while ensuring that lines of accountability are in fact clearly defined for internal compliance purposes.

24. Cf. Herbert Edelhertz, *The Nature, Impact and Prosecution of White-Collar Crime* (Washington, D.C.: National Institute of Law Enforcement and Criminal Justice, 1970); Christopher Stone, *Where the Law Ends: The Social Control of Corporate Behavior* (New York: Harper and Row, 1975). In the civil area, note also Wanner's evidence that corporate plaintiffs, in a sample of 7,900 cases, win more, settle less, and lose less than individual plaintiffs. Craig Wanner, "The Public Ordering of Private Relations: Part I: Initiating Civil Cases in Urban Trial Courts," *Law and Society Review*, 8 (1974), p. 421; Craig Wanner, "The Public Ordering of Private Relations: Part II: Winning Civil Cases in Urban Trial Courts," *Law and Society Review*, 9 (1974), pp. 293-306.

25. Peter Letkemann, *Crime as Work* (Englewood Cliffs, N.J.: Prentice-Hall, 1973).

26. Edwin Lemert, *Social Pathology* (New York: McGraw-Hill, 1951); Howard S. Becker, *Outsiders: Studies in the Sociology of Deviance* (Glencoe, Ill.: Free Press, 1963).

27. Donald J. West and David P. Farrington, *The Delinquent Way of Life* (London: Heinemann, 1977), p. 162.

28. Marshall Clinard, *The Black Market: A Study of White-Collar Crime* (New York: Holt, 1952); Gilbert Geis, "The Heavy Electrical Equipment Antitrust Cases of 1961," in eds. Marshall Clinard and Richard Quinney, *Criminal Behavior Systems* (New York: Holt, Rinehart and Winston, 1967); Kenneth Mann, Stanton Wheeler, and Austin Sarat, "Sentencing the White-Collar Offender," *American Criminal Law Review*, 17 (1980), pp. 479-550.

29. W.B. Fisse, "The Use of Publicity as a Criminal Sanction Against Business Corporations," *Melbourne University Law Review*, 8 (1971), pp. 250-279.

30. William J. Chambliss, "Types of Deviance and the Effectiveness of Legal Sanctions," *Wisconsin Law Review* (Summer 1967), pp. 703-719.

31. See "Corporate Crime: Regulating Corporate Behavior Through Criminal Sanctions," *Harvard Law Review*, 92 (1979), pp. 1235-1236.

32. Michael R. Geerken and Walter R. Gove, "Deterrence: Some Theoretical Considerations," *Law and Society Review*, 9 (1975), p. 509.

33. Dorothy Miller, Ann Rosenthal, Don Miller, and Sheryl Ruzek, "Public Knowledge of Criminal Penalties: A Research Report," in ed. Stanley Grupp, *Theories of Punishment* (Bloomington: Indiana University Press, 1971), pp. 205-206.

34. M. David Ermann and Richard J. Lundman, "Deviant Acts by Complex Organizations: Deviance and Social Control at the Organizational Level of Analysis," *Sociological Quarterly*, 19 (1978), p. 64.

35. Jocelynne A. Scutt, "The Fine as a Penal Measure in the United States of America, Canada and Australia," in eds. Hans-Henrich Jescheck and Gerhardt Grebing, *Die Geldstrafe im Duetschen un Auslandischen Recht* (Baden-Baden: Nomos Verlagsgesellschaft, 1978), pp. 1062-1181.

36. Trevor Nagel, *The Fine As A Sanction Against Corporations*, Honours dissertation, University of Adelaide Law School, 1979; Laura Shill Schrager and James F. Short, "Toward a Sociology of Organizational Crime," *Social Problems*, 25 (1978), pp. 407-419.

37. Edward Gross, "Organizations as Criminal Actors," in Wilson and Braithwaite, *Two Faces of Deviance*, p. 203.

38. See the Abbott case study in Braithwaite, *Corporate Crime in the Pharmaceutical Industry*, ch. 4. One informant said of his fellow executives who were acquitted in this case: "The guys who were defendants in that case, some of them are basket cases today. They've never been the same since."

39. Eds. Alfred Blumstein, Jacqueline Cohen, and Daniel Nagin, *Deterrence and Incapacitation: Estimating the Effects of Criminal Sanctions on Crime Rates* (Washington, D.C.: National Academy of Sciences, 1978); Jack Gibbs, *Crime, Punishment and Deterrence* (New York: Elsevier, 1975). For an innovative perspective on the practical constraints of system capacity in making deterrence work in practice, see Henry N. Pontell, "Deterrence: Theory Versus Practice," *Criminology*,, 16 (1978), pp. 3-46.

40. Marshall B. Clinard and Peter C. Yeager, *Corporate Crime* (New York: Free Press, 1980); Saxon, *White-Collar Crime*; Richard A. Posner, *Antitrust Law: An Economic Perspective* (Chicago: University of Chicago

Press, 1976); Kenneth Elzinga and William Breit, *The Antitrust Penalties: A Study in Law and Economics* (New Haven: Yale University Press, 1976); Stephen A. Yoder, "Criminal Sanctions for Corporate Illegality," *Journal of Criminal Law and Criminology*, 69 (1978), pp. 40-58.

41. G. deQ. Walker, "The Trade Practices Act at Work," in ed. John P. Nieuwenhuysen, *Australian Trade Practices* (London: Croom Helm, 1976), pp. 146-147. Walker refers to an unpublished survey by the Macquarie University School of Economic and Financial Studies.

42. Michael K. Block, Frederick C. Nold, and Joseph G. Sidak, "The Deterrent Effect of Antitrust Enforcement," *Journal of Political Economy*, 89 (June 1981), pp. 429-445.

43. Michael D. Lewis-Beck and John R. Alford, "Can Government Regulate Safety: The Coal Mine Example," *American Political Science Review*, 74 (1980), pp. 745-756.

44. Marvin Wolfgang provided this figure during a discussion.

45. See, for example, Ernest A. Wenk, J.O. Robison, and G.W. Smith, "Can Violence Be Predicted?", *Crime and Delinquency*, 18 (1972), pp. 393-402; eds. John P. Conrad and Simon Dinitz, *In Fear of Each Other: Studies of Dangerousness in America* (Lexington, Mass.: Lexington Books, 1977).

46. Stephen Van Dine, John P. Conrad, and Simon Dinitz, *Restraining the Wicked* (Lexington, Mass.: Lexington Books, 1979), pp. 17-34.

47. Albert J. Reiss Jr., "Understanding Changes in Crime Rates," in eds. Stephen E. Fienberg and Albert J. Reiss, *Indicators of Crime and Criminal Justice: Quantitative Studies* (Washington, D.C.: U.S. Government Printing Office, 1980).

48. Reiss (*ibid.*) points out that National Crime Survey data indicate that only 30 percent of offenders in victim-reported crime incidents were lone offenders.

49. Van Dine et al., *Restraining the Wicked*, p. 125.

50. Stone, *Where the Law Ends*, p. 148-149.

51. Schrag ("Her Majesty's Service") recounts how Detective, a publicly traded company which was defrauding consumers, was bankrupted in the aftermath of a direct action campaign by the New York City Department of Consumer Affairs.

52. The coal industry is a classic illustration of how some corporations are well known to have a superior compliance performance compared to others. Generally, it is the mines owned by the large steel corporations, with the safety compliance systems they bring from their parent industry, which have superior safety performance. In 1978-1979 Westmorland Coal Company had an injury incidence rate seven times as high as the mines owned by U.S. Steel. Ben A. Franklin, "New Effort to Make Mines Safer," *New York Times* (November 22, 1980), pp. L29, L32.

53. Morton Mintz, *By Prescription Only* (Boston: Houghton Mifflin, 1967), p. 383.

54. Douglas Lipton, Robert Martinson, and Judith Wilks, *The Effectiveness of Correctional Treatment: A Survey of Evaluation Studies* (New York: Praeger, 1975).

55. Stone, *Where the Law Ends*, pp. 199-216.

56. For a critique of the rehabilitative model in these terms for individual deviance, see Phillip Bean, *Rehabilitation and Deviance* (London: Routledge and Kegan Paul, 1976).

57. Andrew Hopkins, "Anatomy of Corporate Crime," in *Two Forms of Deviance*, Wilson and Braithwaite, eds., pp. 214-231.

58. As Galbraith points out, "In the American business code nothing is so iniquitous as government interference in the *internal* affairs of the corporation." John Kenneth Galbraith, *The New Industrial State*, 3rd. edition (Harmondsworth: Penguin, 1978), p. 81.

59. This technique has been particularly popular with the U.S. Securities and Exchange Commission. For a more refined version of this general approach, see Fisse's development of the idea of court-imposed "preventive orders." W.B. Fisse, "Responsibility, Prevention and Corporate Crime," *New Zealand Universities Law Review*, 5 (1973), pp. 250-279.

60. "Structural Crime and Institutional Rehabilitation: A New Approach to Corporate Sentencing," *Yale Law Journal*, 89 (1979), pp. 561-585; John C. Coffee Jr., "Corporate Crime and Punishment: A Non-Chicago View of the Economics of Criminal Sanctions," *American Criminal Law Review*, 17 (1980), pp. 419-478.

61. Fisse notes the use of adjournment of sentence as a "back-door to enter the internal affairs of an offender" by reference to *Trade Practices Commission v. Pye Industries Sales Pty. Ltd.*, A.T.P.R. 40-089 (1978). W.B. Fisse, "Criminal Law and Consumer Protection," in eds. A.J. Duggan and L.W. Darvall, *Consumer Protection Law and Theory* (Sydney: Law Book Company, 1980).

62. While this adverse publicity may have had impacts on company morale, such effects in most cases did not filter through to significantly depress stock prices. The stock market impacts were somewhat more notable, however, with the companies named early in the foreign bribery campaign. Paul A. Griffin, *Sensitive Foreign Payment Disclosures: The Securities Market Impact* (Stanford University. Graduate School of Business, June 1977, mimeographed).

63. These included chief executive officers in the case of some corporations (for example, Lockheed, Northrop, Gulf). The new chief executives in some cases really seemed to act as if they were the new broom attempting to sweep things clean.

64. Edward D. Herlihy and Theodore A. Levine, "Corporate Crisis: The Overseas Payment Problem," *Law and Policy in International Business*, 8 (1976), pp. 547-629. Note also Arthur F. Mathews, "Recent Trends in SEC Requested Ancillary Relief in SEC Level Injunctive Actions," *Business Lawyer*, 31 (1976), pp. 1323-1352.

65. Schrag, "Her Majesty's Service."

66. It is interesting to juxtapose this alternative against the direct action approach with respect to the due process protections available to targets of government sanction. Perhaps if corporations are not stripped of some due process protections so that convictions become more possible, governments will increasingly be forced to take the direct action route with its total absence of due process.

67. *Time* (December 3, 1979), p. 61.

68. *Wall Street Journal* (June 9, 1980), p. 1.

69. *Australian Financial Review* (March 22, 1979).

70. *Hale v. Henkel*, 201 U.S. 43, 75 (1906); Note, "The Constitutional Rights of Associations to Assert the Privilege Against Self-Incrimination," *University of Pennsylvania Law Review*, 112 (1964), p. 394.

71. *United States v. Morton Salt Co.*, 338 U.S. 632 (1950); quoted with approval in *California Bankers Association v. Schultz*, 416 U.S. 21, 65-66 (1974).

72. See Friedman's discussion of the questionable rationales for applying a variety of due process protections to corporations. Howard M. Friedman, "Some Reflections on the Corporation as Criminal Defendant," *Notre Dame Lawyer*, 55 (1979), pp. 173-202.

73. Herbert L. Packer, *The Limits of the Criminal Sanction* (Palo Alto: Stanford University Press, 1968, p. 131) sets loss of liberty apart as the sanction which demands the full panoply of due process protections whenever there is any risk of its application.

74. W.B. Fisse, *Corporate Criminal Responsibility and Alternative Means of Preventing Corporate Crime* (1979), p. 31. On file at the Australian Institute of Criminology.

Index

About the Author

Gilbert Geis is professor, Program in Social Ecology, University of California, Irvine. He received the Ph.D. from the University of Wisconsin in 1953. In 1982, he was named by U.C.I. as the Distinguished Faculty Lecturer on the basis of "significant contributions to knowledge through distinguished research." In 1969, he was named the Outstanding Professor in the California State Universities and Colleges system. In 1979, he received the Paul Tappan Award from the Western Society of Criminology for research contributions to the field, and in 1980 was given the Stephen Schafer award by the National Organization for Victim Assistance for "outstanding achievements in victim-witness research."

Professor Geis is a former president of the American Society of Criminology and has held visiting appointments at the Institute of Criminology and at Wolfson College, Cambridge University; the Faculty of Law, Sydney University; Harvard Law School; the School of Criminal Justice, State University of New York; and the College of Human Development, Pennsylvania State University. He has written extensively about a wide variety of criminological and legal issues.